YEAR OF THE RAT

YEAR OF THE RAT

*How Bill Clinton and Al Gore
Compromised U.S. Security
for Chinese Cash*

EDWARD TIMPERLAKE
AND
WILLIAM C. TRIPLETT II

Since 1947
REGNERY
PUBLISHING, INC.
An Eagle Publishing Company • Washington, DC

Library of Congress Cataloging-in-Publication Data

Timperlake, Edward.
Year of the rat: how Bill Clinton and Al Gore compromised U.S.
security for Chinese cash / Edward Timperlake and William C. Triplett II.

p.   cm.
Includes index.
ISBN 0-89526-249-5 (alk. paper)
1. Political corruption—United States. 2. Campaign funds—Corrupt practices—United States. 3. United States—Politics and government—1993–
4. United States—Foreign relations—China. 5. China—Foreign relations—
United States. I. Triplett, William C. II. Title.
JK2249.T56 1998
324.7'8'097309049—dc21   98-42168
                                                                 CIP

Published in the United States by
Regnery Publishing, Inc.
An Eagle Publishing Company
One Massachusetts Avenue, NW
Washington, DC 20001

Distributed to the trade by
National Book Network
4720-A Boston Way
Lanham, MD 20706

Printed on acid-free paper
Manufactured in the United States of America

10 9 8 7 6 5 4 3 2 1

Books are available in quantity for promotional or premium use.
Write to Director of Special Sales, Regnery Publishing, Inc.,
One Massachusetts Avenue, NW, Washington, DC 20001,
for information on discounts and terms or call (202) 216-0600.

TABLE OF CONTENTS

PREFACE TO THE PAPERBACK EDITION   ix

CHAPTER ONE   The Faustian Bargain   1

PART ONE: LIPPO LIES

CHAPTER TWO   Lippo and the Riadys   7

CHAPTER THREE   John Huang the Magician   23

CHAPTER FOUR   The Week That Was (I)   33

CHAPTER FIVE   "My Man in the American Government"   43

CHAPTER SIX   The Week That Was (II)   61

CHAPTER SEVEN   Women of the China Connection   71

PART TWO: TRIADS AND OTHER CROOKS

CHAPTER EIGHT   A Tale of Three Cities   87

CHAPTER NINE   Charlie Trie   107

PART THREE: CHINA'S CONTINUING THREATS

CHAPTER TEN   Penetrating the System   123

CHAPTER ELEVEN   Appeasement at Any Cost   135

CHAPTER TWELVE   Milspace   159

CHAPTER THIRTEEN   Red China, Blue Waters   187

CHAPTER FOURTEEN   The Communists Go Capitalist   205

CHAPTER FIFTEEN   Conclusion   215

PART FOUR: UPDATE

NEW! CHAPTER SIXTEEN   Where Are They Now?   231

NEW! CHAPTER SEVENTEEN   Obstruction of Justice   247

NEW! CHAPTER EIGHTEEN   Paying the Price for Bill and Al   263

NOTES   269

INDEX   303

*1996, the year Bill Clinton
and Al Gore were reelected,
was the Chinese Year of the Rat.*

PREFACE TO THE PAPERBACK EDITION

The President, Vice President, *and all civil Officers of the United States, shall be removed from office on impeachment for, and conviction of, treason,* bribery, *or other high crimes and misdemeanors [emphasis added].*

—CONSTITUTION OF THE UNITED STATES, ARTICLE II, SECTION 4

In December 1998 FBI Director Louis Freeh recommended to Attorney General Janet Reno that an independent counsel investigate a "core group" of "covered persons," among them President Bill Clinton and Vice President Al Gore.[1] Freeh argued that Clinton and Gore should be investigated for possible violations of the conspiracy provisions of the federal criminal code[2] and that the independent counsel should examine a possible "conspiracy by the People's Republic of China to bribe high-ranking U.S. political figures."[3] Reno ignored the FBI director's recommendation.

Year of the Rat is about bribery, corruption, and foreign penetration of the American government at the highest levels—to an extent totally unprecedented. Since the book was first published in the fall of 1998, new revelations and developments have only confirmed what we outline in these pages. Indeed, if anything, the problem is worse than we could have imagined back in 1998, the corruption far deeper.

From the very first writing of *Year of the Rat*, we felt there was something missing—namely, how did they get away with it? Back then we could discern only the results of a massive conspiracy to obstruct justice. Now we know the details of what happened. In the new chapters, which highlight material that has emerged since the book's initial publication, the reader will be startled by the sordid picture of a corrupt and demoralized Justice Department directed from the top to cover up the actions of Bill Clinton and Al Gore.

What's more, we can now detail how the Clinton-Gore administration covered up Charlie Trie's germ warfare activities and how American investors are inadvertently financing the Chinese military's modernization.

In preparing this updated edition, as we began to review the previous material and to consider the latest revelations, we were surprised to discover how much of the administration's plan directly involved Vice President Al Gore. The administration's effort to obstruct justice was initiated to protect Gore, not Clinton. And we now know also that Gore, more than Clinton, is to blame for the administration's failure to halt massive Russian military sales to China and that John Huang's fund-raising magic on Gore's behalf was of a magnitude we never suspected.

Yes, matters are far worse than even we had realized. President Clinton was impeached, but, as you will see, it was for the wrong reason.

— Edward Timperlake and William C. Triplett II
July 2000

CHAPTER 1
THE FAUSTIAN BARGAIN

On a wall in the basement of the United States Capitol in Washington, a bas-relief depicts a Greek warrior engaged in mortal combat with a snake. The artist captures the moment when the man raises his weapon to strike the deathblow. Across the tableau is one word: *Courage.*

Artistically, physical courage is easy to depict. Moral courage is another matter. Moral courage requires taking a cold, hard look at the world and then acting, accepting the consequences, and knowing that the greatest good will ultimately be served. Moral courage demands sacrifice—the subordination of self-interest to the interests of others. To be morally or intellectually courageous requires a basic sense of honesty and integrity coupled with the will to act decisively on those principles. Moral character is of great matter in a leader and will inevitably affect the substance of his performance. Courage, character, and performance cannot be separated.

In these areas we have found President Clinton and his administration wanting. They have failed in their duty to the national interest. What is happening on Bill Clinton's watch while he serves as president and commander in chief is rapidly becoming a matter of history, and the devastating repercussions of his actions will be felt by Americans for generations to come.

Our thesis is simple: The Clinton administration has made a series of Faustian bargains and policy blunders that have allowed a hostile power to further its aims in Washington. In the main, Bill Clinton and Al Gore did it for money.

The hostile power is the People's Republic of China (PRC). It is the only foreign regime currently targeting American cities for nuclear destruction.[1]

The PRC, under the direction of the Chinese Communist Party (CCP), is engaged in four major lines of activities, all of which are contrary to the interests of the Chinese people, neighboring countries, U.S. friends and allies around the world, and ultimately the American people.

The Clinton administration sold out America's national security to one of our most dangerous adversaries merely to raise campaign cash.

First, arms dealers associated with the CCP's military arm, the People's Liberation Army (PLA), have transferred weapons of mass destruction and the means to produce them to terrorist nations, threatening Israel, our Gulf allies, and even Europe.

Second, the PLA itself is suppressing the Chinese people's legitimate desire for democracy and human rights.

Third, the PLA has a history of aggression against neighboring countries, including Tibet and India, and in recent times has shown a willingness to bully others, including Japan, Vietnam, the Philippines, and the Republic of China on Taiwan.[2]

Finally, the PRC's unjustified military modernization and expansion program threatens America's foreign policy interests and national security.

Before Bill Clinton took office, the United States was the prime obstacle to the CCP's ambitions to dominate East Asia. After he was elected, the CCP expressed two major needs—political and economic intelligence on the United States, and assistance with its military modernization program. The Clinton administration has met both Communist Chinese goals.

In these pages, we will show that, in order to gain and hold onto power, the Clinton administration has acted recklessly, allowing the wrong people to gain access to our most important political and economic secrets. Any number of Chinese arms dealers, spies, narcotics traffickers, gangsters, pimps, accomplices to mass murder, communist agents, and other undesirables will appear in these pages... all associated one way or another with the White House and money.

The most favorable explanation for this betrayal is incompetence. As the president said, "Mistakes were made." But it is far more likely that in order to gain campaign contributions and pay hush money to witnesses, the Clinton-Gore administration turned a deliberate blind eye to these threats to our national interests.

Moreover, we believe that the Clinton administration's help to the Chinese military and the cover-ups of Chinese arms proliferation were motivated by equal parts corruption and classic appeasement.

How we intend to show this rests on evidence. And here we ran into a number of initial stumbling blocks:

- Two crucial witnesses, Commerce Secretary Ron Brown and Assistant Commerce Secretary Charles Meissner, perished together in a plane crash.
- At least eighteen critical witnesses have fled the country.
- Another seventy-nine witnesses have taken the Fifth Amendment, deciding that telling what they know would tend to incriminate them.
- The higher one gets in the political structure at the White House, the more its people suffer from memory loss.
- Document tampering has been shameless. As the *New York Times* noted, "Much remains missing: Mr. Huang's* Democratic National Committee (DNC) telephone logs, most of his outgoing correspondence, his travel records, details of visits to the White House and Clinton-Gore campaign head-

---

* John Huang, a key Democratic fund-raiser and the American representative for the Riadys, a wealthy Indonesian family

quarters, and accounts of business he conducted from locations other than his office at the Democratic Committee."[3]
- Some of the most compelling evidence is highly classified and can only be discussed inferentially.
- And, we must admit, the White House has been fortunate in having incompetent members of the political opposition.

That having been said, our account is not without proof. Most of it will be direct. We have, for example, the records of John Huang's entry into the Executive Office of the president. We know how many times he went there and at least who authorized his entrance. We also know how many long distance calls he made to his former employers from his new desk at the Commerce Department. We can document at least some of his visits to the Chinese embassy in Washington. We can document the wire transfers to the DNC from Macau criminal syndicate figure Ng[4] Lapseng. We have the Treasury Department records of the hundreds of thousands of dollars in cash Ng brought into the United States and his trips to the White House.

Other evidence will be circumstantial. A common layman's misunderstanding is that circumstantial evidence is in some way lacking. On this point the courts are clear: The United States Court of Appeals has ruled, "A conviction can rest solely on circumstantial evidence, which is intrinsically as probative as direct evidence."[5] We will present a mountain of circumstantial evidence to show corrupt motivation and opportunity to harm the national interests of the United States.

Did the Clinton administration sell out America's national security to one of this country's leading and most dangerous adversaries merely to raise campaign cash? In the pages that follow, we will prove our answer, which is: yes.

PART ONE:
LIPPO LIES

CHAPTER 2
LIPPO AND THE RIADYS

Who was the biggest contributor to the Clinton-Gore ticket in 1992? Not a corporation, not a labor union, not a Hollywood mogul, but Indonesian businessman James Riady and his wife, who gave $450,000 to elect Bill Clinton.

During the final weeks of the campaign, the Riady family, its associates, and executives at Riady companies gave an additional $600,000 to the DNC and Democratic state parties.[1]

The patriarch of the business empire is Mochtar Riady, a frequent visitor to the United States. Of his three sons, James was a permanent resident of the United States, Stephen was educated here, and Andrew worked in California in the early 1980s. All, however, have fled the United States. Any Riady employee with detailed knowledge of the family's activities in the United States has likewise stolen away in the night. Even James Riady's secretary has vanished.[2] Only John Huang, the family's former U.S. operative, remains in the United States—and he has pleaded the Fifth Amendment, maintaining that telling what he knows might incriminate him.[3]

Who are the Riadys? They originally come from China's coastal province of Fujian, opposite Taiwan; the Riady family's Chinese name is "Lee." At some point the family relocated to Jakarta, the

7

capital of Indonesia. Ethnic Chinese make up 5 percent of the Indonesian population but control at least 75 percent of the corporate assets in the country, a dangerous combination.[4] Ethnic Chinese have often been targets in times of unrest, and the May 1998 riots protesting Indonesian President Suharto quickly became anti-Chinese riots, forcing hundreds of desperate ethnic Chinese to flee to Jakarta's international airport.[5] The ethnic rioting in South Jakarta destroyed a branch of the Riady-controlled Lippo Bank,[6] and elsewhere in the country, the Indonesian army had to send 360 soldiers to protect Riady property from anti-Chinese mobs.[7]

The twenty-year friendship between James Riady and Bill Clinton has spread a web of intrigue, financial corruption, and foreign influence into American government.

Mochtar Riady has a new Bell helicopter with long-range fuel tanks. If things go bad in Jakarta, he can easily fly to Singapore six hundred miles away.[8] Son James's three-story manor house and helicopter pad in Jakarta are ringed by a moat.[9] The Riadys aren't taking any chances.

The Riady empire, centered on its Lippo Group, is, as one financial analyst in Jakarta describes it, "a carefully balanced house of cards."[10] *Newsweek* has noted, "Moving cash around the globe in tangled webs of transactions has always been the Riady way," and the *Asian Wall Street Journal* accuses the Riadys of "ramping"—buying large numbers of shares in their own companies in order to support prices.[11]

In Indonesia the Riadys have gone in for grandiose development projects where their connections can facilitate governmental approval of crucial licenses and permits. For example, their billion-dollar "Lippo Village"[12] project is a walled community for opulent Indonesians with its own private school, country club, and other amenities. Tuition at the school runs to $15,000-a-year, way out of reach for ordinary Indonesians, but attractive to the super-rich who don't want to educate their children abroad.[13] The school even has a horse show ring.[14] Interestingly, the school received its operating license after James Riady took the Indonesian education minister to the White House for an Oval Office visit.[15]

The Riadys' corporate flagship is the Lippo Group. "Lippo" is a Chinese word that means "energy."[16] The Riadys began in banking, branched out into securities, and later into land development. In Indonesia, the company has its fingers in many pies, making textiles and electronics, mining coal, selling insurance, and building shopping centers, housing developments, and hospitals.[17] Though precise figures are difficult to determine due to the complex relations among Riady-associated companies, the Lippo Group as a whole has been quite successful, and the Riadys are extremely wealthy.

Dr. Mochtar Riady[18] (also known as "Dr. Man Tjin Lee"[19]) has moved from chairman of various Lippo entities to "honorary chairman," reflecting his declining health. His second son, James, runs the Indonesia operation, while the youngest son, Stephen, is in charge of Hong Kong and China affairs.[20] The mysterious oldest son, Andrew, is alleged to have lost millions on the foreign exchange markets, and has disappeared from view completely.[21]

In 1977 Mochtar Riady tried to buy the National Bank of Georgia. He failed, but one of the brokers in the deal was Jackson Stephens of Little Rock, Arkansas, who tried to interest a disappointed Riady in joining Stephens, Inc., one of America's largest private investment banks outside of Wall Street—and one with which the Riadys would have an extended relationship, as we will see. Mochtar Riady agreed, and his son James, then aged twenty, arrived to intern at Stephens, Inc.[22]

Through Jackson Stephens, James Riady met a rising politician, Arkansas Attorney General Bill Clinton. Thus began a friendship that has lasted twenty years, and has spread a web of intrigue, financial corruption, and foreign influence into American government.

In early 1984 James Riady and Jackson Stephens became co-owners of Arkansas's largest bank, the Worthen Bank. James was installed as the bank's chief operating officer,[23] and a whole team of ethnic Chinese from Indonesia came to work in Little Rock.[24]

In the first year under Riady/Stephens management, the bank lost tens of millions of dollars in Arkansas State pension funds through a risky out-of-state investment scheme. Legally, Worthen could have passed the loss to the state. But that disaster would have ended then-Governor Clinton's political career by demonstrating his professional incompetence. Instead, Jackson Stephens wrote a personal check for $32 million to bail out the bank—and Clinton.[25]

But the Riadys and Stephens also began to have trouble with federal regulators who discovered that Worthen had transferred $7 million—in increments of just under $10,000 each—to a Hong Kong bank controlled by the Riadys. And almost all the transfers were placed under phony names.[26] Because they were under $10,000, the transfers, by law, did not have to be reported to the Treasury, but the intent to deceive was clear. Later, regulators found a pattern of self-dealing that involved sweetheart loans by Worthen to Stephens-owned companies, and to Riady associates, for office buildings in Indonesia.[27] Exposed, the Riadys were forced out of banking in Arkansas.[28]

However, they retained enough influence at Worthen to come to Bill Clinton's aid at a critical moment. In the spring of 1992 Clinton was facing a crucial primary in New York, and he was out of money. According to one ex-Worthen executive, James Riady "persuaded" the bank to issue the Clinton campaign $3.5 million worth of letters of credit. This was the first of two interventions in the American political system that the Riadys would make in 1992 to help elect the Clinton-Gore ticket.[29]

The Riady-Clinton connection is more than financial: it is personal. James Riady has met and often hired many of Bill Clinton's closest Arkansas cronies. Joseph Giroir[30] and Webster Hubbell, both former law partners of Hillary Clinton, are or have been on the Riady payroll, as have Clinton golfing buddy Mark

Grobmyer[31] and ex-White House aide Mark Middleton.[32] It was Clinton's golfing partner Paul Berry who helped the young Arkansas governor obtain an unsecured loan of $20,000 for the Whitewater development project.[33] After the election, Berry joined a Washington lobbying firm, Global USA, that worked with the Riadys.[34] Global USA sent pictures of Berry with Clinton to its Asian clients. Attached was a letter claiming that "Paul's long association with President Clinton and many of his top staff will provide you with unique and fresh insight into the workings of the Clinton administration."[35]

The Riadys have also invested in California, starting in the 1980s. They purchased a small bank, the Bank of Trade, in Los Angeles's Chinatown, making it the Riadys' American headquarters. James Riady bought an estate in the exclusive Brentwood section of Los Angeles and became the chief executive officer of the bank.

John Huang, a Taiwan native employed by the Riadys in Hong Kong, was brought to Los Angeles to be James Riady's number two man. In time, Huang would become the Riadys' U.S. representative. Whether because of neglect or malfeasance, the Bank of Trade, renamed "LippoBank," soon became a target of federal regulators who found that its "problem loans" were seven times the average for a bank of its size[36] and that LippoBank procedures were an "invitation for abuse by [a] criminal element."[37] The Federal Deposit Insurance Corporation (FDIC) issued a cease-and-desist order against the bank and placed it under strict supervision.[38]

By the late 1980s James Riady was a permanent resident of the United States and thus could make legal campaign contributions. His debut was at an April 22, 1988, fund-raising dinner at his Brentwood estate for the Democratic Senatorial Campaign Committee. As the *Los Angeles Times* noted, "At every table, like a centerpiece—only better—was a United States senator primed to welcome wealthy Asian donors, both citizens and permanent residents, as valued participants in the Democratic Party."[39]

The dinner was organized by John Huang and Democratic activist Maria Hsia, and it raised $110,000. But there was an added twist to this event, which we would see repeated over and over again in fund-raising associated with the Riadys, Huang, and Hsia. The *Los Angeles Times* called it a "flirtation with deft book-keeping."[40] Federal election law requires that the source of a donation be disclosed, but attached to one $5,000 check from an Asian-American contributor was a note, perhaps in Maria Hsia's handwriting, stating, "cannot report what appears on the check. He will be very upset if his name appears at anywhere [*sic*]."[41]

In raising money for Democratic senators, James Riady had his own agenda. A few days after the fund-raiser, he wrote to Maria Hsia, giving her a list of "issues [that] needs to be followed up" with the senators.[42] One of James's prime goals was senatorial pressure on Taiwan, where he wanted to open a branch of the Bank of Trade/LippoBank. But Taiwan would have required him to open his books, and Riady must have feared that if he did he wouldn't get a banking license. Riady thus wanted Democratic senators to "impress upon Taiwan" the need to open its doors to someone of his importance, no matter what the books disclosed.[43]

By August 1992 the Clinton-Gore ticket was desperately raising money in order to be competitive in certain key states for the fall election. As he had done just before the New York primary, Clinton turned to his chief moneyman, James Riady. In the middle of August, Clinton and Riady took a limousine ride together. Soon thereafter, a cascade of Riady money—nearly $600,000—made its way to the DNC and to a number of Democratic state parties where the election was considered a toss-up. Undeniably Riady's funding played a key role in Clinton's election to the presidency: the Clinton-Gore ticket ultimately won five out of the six state races where Riady money played a factor. In Georgia, one of the states targeted for Riady funds, Clinton and Gore edged out the Bush-Quayle ticket by a mere 13,000 votes out of a total 2.4 million cast. Clinton and Gore also squeaked by in Ohio, always considered a "must-win" state for Republicans; it was their closest margin of any large state. This was the second time James Riady would come to Clinton's rescue.[44]

The Clinton-Gore inauguration in mid-January 1993 was another opportunity for the Riadys to open their wallets. James Riady and John Huang each gave $100,000 to cover the cost of inaugural parties.[45] The Riadys brought a number of friends from Indonesia to Washington for the swearing-in ceremony.[46]

Their generosity continued. At the direction of Mochtar Riady, Joe Giroir—a Lippo partner and Arkansas "Friend of Bill" (FOB)—bestowed a life-sized bust of Clinton upon the National Portrait Gallery.[47] Giroir has personally contributed $200,000 to the DNC since 1993, something made easier by his $500,000-a-year compensation from Lippo.[48]

In return for such generosity, the Riadys and their friends were given unparalleled access to the White House. In Jakarta, James Riady likes to brag about where he was on the afternoon of April 19, 1993. On that day eighty members of the Branch Davidian religious cult were holed up in their compound outside of Waco, Texas, when it was shattered by a tank-led assault. By the time the FBI and Treasury's Alcohol, Tobacco, and Firearms agents had completed their work, seventeen American children had burned to death.[49]

> In return for their generosity, the Riadys and their friends were given unparalleled access to the Clinton White House.

As might be expected, the White House was a busy place that afternoon, and the president was preoccupied. Clinton was not too distracted, however, to chat with his leading contributors—James Riady, John Huang, and Mark Grobmyer—in his little study off the Oval Office.[50] Riady later told Indonesian diplomats that, during their chat, a television in the corner showed the Waco compound burning over and over as CNN repeated its coverage.

Clinton even took time to show his visitors the White House Situation Room, then on full alert.[51] White House entry logs confirm that Riady and his companions were in the presidential offices (West Wing) of the White House that day. They apparently also dropped in on Robert Rubin, now secretary of the treasury, who was then a White House economics official.[52]

How many other presidents, in the middle of such a tragedy, would have spent their time giving major donors a White House tour?

THE BEIJING CONNECTION

During the congressional investigations of campaign fund-raising, Senate Democratic staff found a curious document in John Huang's files.[53] On Lippo stationery is a memo dated March 9, 1993, from John Huang to James Riady, regarding "Mr. Chen Xitong from China." Huang is attempting to coordinate a trip to Atlanta by Mr. Chen. Huang assures Riady, "I have already stressed the importance of this visitor to all of us."

We were initially puzzled by this memo. At the time it was written, Chen was a CCP Politburo member, ranking eighth in the hierarchy. He was also mayor of Beijing, and Beijing was competing with Sydney, Australia, for the right to host the year 2000 Summer Olympic Games. Atlanta, of course, was preparing for its own 1996 Summer Games, and it would make sense for Chen to have a look around.

But how could Chen possibly get a U.S. visa? Short of the late paramount leader Deng Xiaoping and ex-Premier Li Peng,[54] it would be hard to find a more notorious and corrupt CCP official than Chen, or one with more blood on his hands from the June 1989 Tiananmen Square massacre. Chen must be counted as at least an accomplice, if not a party, to mass murder, for it was he who instigated the state terrorism that was inflicted on his own people in Beijing. In April 1989, while some Party officials advised at least limited accommodation to the students' demands for democracy and human rights, Chen prepared an internal report for the Politburo urging an immediate crackdown.[55] As the PLA prepared its assault on the city, Chen signed the martial law decrees justifying the use of tanks and flamethrowers against unarmed civilians.[56] After the streets had been cleared of blood, Chen gave the official verdict on the massacre in a report to the Standing Committee of the National People's Congress. He blamed the murder of thousands of innocents on a conspiracy originated by "some political forces in the West."[57]

Of all the PRC officials who wanted to visit the United States in 1993, why did the Riadys and Stephens, Inc., feel they had to help such an obviously high-profile villain? Why did Huang have to remind his boss of "the importance of this visitor to all of us"?

The answer is Wangfujing Street, just three short blocks east of the Tiananmen Square and Forbidden City tourist sites. In 1993 Wangfujing Street was a typically seedy, run-down commercial area of Beijing, but it had three things going for it: location, location, location. Because of the many government ministry buildings in central Beijing, there was no comparable commercial area available for redevelopment. Getting in on the ground floor of the Beijing municipal government's plans for Wangfujing Street would be like having a license to print money. And the totally corrupt mayor of Beijing, Chen Xitong, was the gatekeeper.

In March 1993 a Riady subsidiary "signed a letter of intent with the Beijing municipal government on the land-use rights for two parcels of land in Wangfujing, the commercial and shopping centre of the capital," in the words of the *South China Morning Post.*[58] The Riadys intended "to retain a majority stake in the projects and build retail and office properties,"[59] including the Lippo Tower, with 1.7 million square feet of rental space. The overall Wangfujing Street project will involve about $6 billion. Another major investor is Hong Kong billionaire Li Ka-shing.[60]

But there was one hitch in the Riadys' plans: American fast-food giant McDonalds. In the aftermath of the Tiananmen massacre, a number of foreign firms pulled out of China. Chen was so desperate to keep foreign investors in his city that he granted McDonalds a twenty-year lease on the best corner of Wangfujing Street,[61] which drew locals and tourists visiting the square and the Forbidden City. It soon became the company's most profitable outlet worldwide.[62] But now the Riadys and Li wanted Chen to break McDonalds' lease.

The CIA knows that James and Mochtar Riady have had "a long-term relationship with a Chinese intelligence agency."

McDonalds fought him for almost two-and-a-half years, but in the end Chen broke the lease. The company took a small face-saving amount ($12 million) in compensation and departed for less-green pastures.[63] The Riadys' Wangfujing Street projects are scheduled for completion in 1999, in time for the fiftieth anniversary of the founding of the PRC.[64] Chen's "importance" to the Riadys is now apparent.

The Riadys were beholden to Chen for buying off McDonalds and paving the way for the Wangfujing Street deal. Actually, they are beholden to government and Communist Party officials all over China. In 1997 a senator asked the Central Intelligence Agency (CIA) to comment on the relationship between the Riadys and Beijing officials. The CIA said that almost all of the Riadys' joint ventures in China are "with local, regional and central governments in China."[65] The CIA added, "Lippo has substantial interests in China—about US$2 billion in the Riadys' ancestral province of Fujian alone. These include real estate, banking, electronics, currency exchange, retail, electricity, and tourism."[66]

After noting Lippo's involvement in large-scale public works projects in China, the CIA added these very important and carefully chosen words: "Lippo has provided concessionary-rate loans to finance many of these projects in key [Communist] Party mem-

bers' home areas."[67] While China is not a democratic country, a
politician, even a communist politician, who can bring home the
bacon to his constituents with below-market loans for big public
works projects would probably feel some obligation to the
lenders. This combination of networking and exchange of obligation is called "guanxi"[68] in Chinese. It is an important part of the
way business is conducted in many parts of Asia.

The mutual back-scratching between the Riadys and Chinese
Communist officials became vital to the family in the summer of
1995. The Indonesian real estate market had taken a severe
downturn, and the Riadys' chief property company, LippoLand,
found itself seriously exposed. Worse than that, LippoLand owed
a great deal of money to LippoBank. If one faltered, the other
was equally in trouble, a domino effect that could bring down the
entire Riady empire.

And LippoLand was definitely faltering. After July 1995 Lippo
sold very few of its residence units. In September, Lippo executive
Michael Farley jumped to his death from the sixteenth floor of an
office building in Lippo Village (Lippo Karawaci). The market
dropped 40 percent, and the Riadys started selling properties in a
desperate effort to keep afloat.[69] After LippoBank missed a
required payment there was a run on the bank, and the
Indonesian Central Bank had to arrange support from a consor-
tium of four other banks to keep it viable.[70]

What truly saved the bank was a timely purchase of Lippo
shares by the Riadys' chief Chinese partner, China Resources. The
share purchase was not large—5 percent of LippoLand—but it
was enough to restore confidence and bring in other investors.[71]

China Resources, the Riadys' white knight, is an arm of
Chinese military intelligence.

With as much money as the Riadys have at risk in China and
their level of integration into government and Communist Party
circles, it is inevitable that they would have dealings with

Chinese intelligence. The Riadys' chief partners in China (including Hong Kong)—China Resources and the China Travel Service—are government-owned companies that accommodate or serve as an extension of Chinese military intelligence.[72] Regarding the Riadys' relationship with Chinese intelligence, an investigating Senate committee learned the following from the CIA:

> The Committee has learned from recently-acquired information that James and Mochtar Riady have had a long-term relationship with a Chinese intelligence agency. The relationship is based on mutual benefit, with the Riadys receiving assistance in finding business opportunities in exchange for large sums of money and other help.
>
> Although the relationship appears based on business interests, the Committee understands that the Chinese intelligence agency seeks to locate and develop relationships with information collectors, particularly with close association to the U.S. government.[73]

What this means as a practical matter is that the Riadys and Chinese intelligence engage in a series of exchanges that exemplify the concept of guanxi. China's intelligence service provides the Riadys with lucrative business opportunities in China—crony capitalism in its rawest form. But Chinese intelligence is no less corrupt than any other part of the Chinese political system. The Riadys are filling Chinese intelligence officers' pockets with "large sums of money" and providing the service itself with "other help." The CIA defines this "other help" as information collected from the American government.[74] If the CIA is right, and we believe it is, what the Chinese intelligence service wanted from its Indonesian agents was not so much a policy tilt in its direction, but information from Riady sources close to the United States government, which is the main target of Chinese intelligence operations. It was simply classic espionage. The Riadys were in a position to satisfy their Chinese intelligence allies and help themselves at the same time.

COLLECTING FOR THE COMRADES

It is said that in his private Hong Kong office Mochtar Riady keeps two gold-framed pictures, one of Bill and Hillary Clinton, the other of Chinese Politburo member Li Peng.[75] One ex-Lippo executive commented on the Riady-Clinton connection: "Riady's goal was to sell his relationship with Clinton to two governments, Indonesia and China."[76]

We believe that Riady actually intended to exploit his relationship with Mr. Clinton in several ways. First, to make money and enhance his own prestige. That was always the first order of business. Then he could sell his Clinton relationship to the Indonesian and Chinese governments. Finally, he might use his White House connection to advance his American friends at Stephens, Inc.

That leads to the question: What precisely did Riady have to sell? Was it policy changes benefiting himself and his clients, or was it more likely to be information? We believe it was some of the former and a lot of the latter.

It is important to bear in mind that the Riadys are bankers, first and foremost. All else—the land deals, the stock brokerage, the insurance company—is derivative of their banking operations. In addition to LippoBank in Indonesia and LippoBank California, they are partners with China Resources in a medium-sized Hong Kong bank. Before "Lippogate" surfaced as an issue in the American press, the Riadys were in the market to purchase a large American bank.[77]

Information is vital in the banking business, both to judge risk and to find opportunity. First, a banker wants to know everything he can about a deal before the depositors' money goes into it. Second, if a banker has more accurate and timely information on investment opportunities than his competitors have, his bank will have an edge over them. An edge, even a small edge, means money.

Information collecting by bankers is quite similar to information collecting by an intelligence service. A classic of the espionage business is *The Craft of Intelligence* by the late CIA Director Allen

Dulles. Dulles shows how great financial fortunes have gone hand in hand with intelligence gathering. The merchant princes of Florence, the Fuggers of Germany, the Rothschilds of Europe, and the British East India Company all combined investment strategies with accurate intelligence. He points out that in the sixteenth century the Fuggers were the first banking house to understand and exploit information collection: "That the Fuggers made few errors in the placement of their investments was in large measure a result of the excellent private intelligence they gathered."[78] According to Dulles, the Rothschilds perfected the Fuggers' system to the point that "one of the great intelligence services of the nineteenth century in Europe was maintained not by a government but by a private firm."[79] Finally, Dulles comments that the Rothschilds "benefited their clients as well as themselves by their superior intelligence-gathering abilities."[80]

At the end of the twentieth century, information collection is even more vital to banks than it was in the past. Cutthroat competition is not just local or even regional but global. At the same time, large international banks continue to have governments as clients, and, in the case of the Riadys, one of those governments is an ambitious communist dictatorship with an insatiable appetite for intelligence, especially about American security, American technology, and American foreign policy.

We believe we can show that the Riadys were in a position to help themselves to American intelligence, as well as satisfy the desires of their Chinese intelligence-service partners for information. Because of campaign contributions to President Clinton and Vice President Gore, as well as financial support to Clinton friend Webb Hubbell at a crucial moment, they were able to place one of their representatives, John Huang, in a position to collect vital American political and economic information. This information was immensely valuable to themselves and to others, including the security services of Communist China.

On the day Bill Clinton and Al Gore were inaugurated, we could say this about the Riadys of Indonesia:

- They were knowing, participating agents of the CCP and its intelligence services.
- They had talent-spotted Bill Clinton fifteen years earlier, when he was an obscure politician from Arkansas.
- They were instrumental in gaining the Democratic presidential nomination for Clinton in 1992.
- Through illegal campaign contributions, they became the number one contributors to the Clinton-Gore ticket in the 1992 national election, and they targeted their funds at key states that were ultimately vital to Clinton and Gore's election.
- Presumably, they were not bailing out Clinton and Gore simply out of the goodness of their hearts; they expected to be paid off.

CHAPTER 3
JOHN HUANG THE MAGICIAN

The late CIA Director William Colby once said that the ideal spy is "the traditional gray man, so inconspicuous that he can never catch the waiter's eye in a restaurant."[1] John Huang, the Riadys' man in America, fits the profile.

We don't know where he was born, or even when. His U.S. government employment and security forms list his place of birth as China's coastal province of Fujian. Fujian is also the Riady family's home province. But another account of Huang's life, which he seems to have encouraged, lists his birth in the Chinese province of Zhejiang.[2] And whereas on his employment form he lists a birth date of April 14, 1945, on visa applications for China and Korea he claims to have been born in 1941. Mistakes? Clerical errors? Maybe. But these kinds of discrepancies seem to sprout around Mr. Huang.

Huang's father was a military official of the Nationalist Chinese government, and the family moved to Taiwan with the communist takeover of the mainland in 1949. He is often described as warm, personable, and well liked. His CIA briefers would later point to his adept social skills, particularly politeness and manners. He speaks, reads, and writes excellent English and claims fluency in five dialects of Chinese.

In the grim competitive environment on Taiwan in the late 1960s, Huang would not have stood out among the young men.

He had no serious family connections, which is extremely disadvantageous in Chinese society. He was also at a disadvantage in the matter of university degrees. In the Greater China[3] area it is common to put one's alma mater and degree on one's business card; the more prestigious the better. In respect to status and opening career doors, where someone went to school is often more important that what he knows. Huang's college, Taiwan's Tatung University, a technical college sponsored by an electric fan maker, doesn't get someone as far in Chinese society as would a degree from Yale or Harvard. For Huang to rise in that time and that place, he would have to work hard, he would have to be lucky— and above all, he would have to have a patron.

In 1969, after his required military service in Taiwan's air force, his family managed to send him to the University of Connecticut for his MBA on a work-study program. While he was in school, he worked in the accounting department of a local manufacturing concern. He became an American citizen in 1977.

Huang's first known contacts with the Chinese government began in the late 1970s. He had begun his banking career in Washington with an entry-level position at the American Security Bank. He was the bank's principal contact with the Chinese Liaison Office,[4] and took Chinese dignitaries to visit American business facilities, such as Bethlehem Steel's Sparrows Point plant outside Baltimore.[5] From American Security he rose to a higher position with the First National Bank of Louisville.[6] While there he accompanied its chairman to China for meetings with the Bank of China.[7] His early experience as a business tour guide and translator would serve him well later.

In the early 1980s Huang received two lucky breaks. First, in 1980 he met Mochtar and James Riady in Little Rock at a Harvard-sponsored seminar.[8]

Next, he signed up with the Union Planters Bank of Memphis, which by coincidence happened to have a correspondent relationship with LippoBank and other business ties to the Riadys.[9] Union Planters sent Huang to Hong Kong in September 1983 to open a representative office. While stationed in Hong Kong he traveled widely in Asia, broadening his contacts with officials in China, Japan, and Korea.[10]

Much as Huang tried, there was not enough agricultural trade business to sustain the Union Planters office in Hong Kong.[11] When it closed a little more than a year later, Huang was adrift in Hong Kong without prospects. He needed a lifeboat—and the Riadys picked him up.[12] Apparently he was hired at least partly to keep an eye on James Riady. The family seems to have considered him smarter than James and he was older as well; therefore, the Riadys felt he was the ideal man to keep the Riady empire's heir out of trouble.

Huang had found his patrons. But there is a downside to having a patron: it creates a strong dependency and a constant need to please one's benefactor.

Huang spent the next two years with Lippo's banking operations in Hong Kong, holding several titles, including vice president and Far East area manager of the Worthen Bank of Little Rock, then under the management of the Riadys.[13] He seems not to have had a home in Little Rock but commuted between Hong Kong and Arkansas.

By all disinterested accounts, Huang is an extremely competent banker with specialized knowledge and experience in the fields of international trade and finance. We say "disinterested" because the more senior Clinton appointees to whom Huang nominally reported while at the Commerce Department would later claim they had walled him off from work relating to China because he was "not up to" it. This version of events is, we believe, self-serving and self-protective on the part of the former Clinton Commerce officials.

The Riadys apparently recognized that Huang had a special talent. His social skills make him ideal for what is sometimes known as "business development." In a law firm, he would be called a "rainmaker," the person who opens the door and brings in new business.

In March 1985 Huang pointed out the sights of Hong Kong to Arkansas Governor Bill Clinton, who was by then a Riady family friend.[14] He would meet the governor again in 1988 when he escorted Riady clients to the Democratic National Convention in Atlanta.[15]

In late 1986 the Riadys transferred Huang to their banking operation in California.[16] He spent a couple of years there, then two more years looking after Riady interests in New York,[17] returning to California by the beginning of 1990.

HUANG THE FUND-RAISER

The Huang story hit the public in September 1996 with a *Los Angeles Times* story about his illegal fund-raising.[18] By early October, Huang was on the front page of every newspaper, every day. As might be expected, the Republicans were in full cry.

Just a week before the presidential election, a conservative legal foundation called Judicial Watch took the only deposition ever given by Huang. Under intense pressure, he answered a number of tough questions, but two stand out. He was asked if he had done any significant fund-raising for the Democrats before he went to the DNC in 1995, and he was asked if he had had any relationship with the president before being appointed to the Commerce Department in 1994. He denied both. He claimed that he had been merely a "participant"[19] in Democratic fund-raising, and stated he had met Clinton only briefly, once in Hong Kong and once in Atlanta.[20]

But the Democratic members of the Senate Governmental Affairs Committee later concluded, "He [Huang] raised money for President Clinton's campaign in 1992."[21] Actually, he began as a Democratic activist and fund-raiser on his return to the United States eight years earlier. In 1988 Huang, Riady, Democratic activist Maria Hsia, and others formed the Pacific Leadership Council in an effort to attract Asian-Americans to the Democratic Party.[22] Huang and Hsia are credited with organizing the April 1988 Democratic fund-raiser at James Riady's home in Los Angeles.[23] They were also tour guides for a January 1989 trip to Taiwan, Hong Kong, and Indonesia by Senator Al Gore and California Lieutenant Governor Leo McCarthy.[24] The later-famous Hsi Lai Buddhist Temple paid for Gore's trip.[25]

Late in the 1992 election cycle, Huang began to demonstrate the fund-raising talents that would prove to be so crucial for Clinton and Gore. On August 12 he directed that a $50,000 check from Hip Hing Holdings be sent to the "DNC Victory Fund."[26] Hip Hing was a Riady-owned shell company under Huang's control.[27] Five days later Huang requested reimbursement from Jakarta,[28] and inside of a few weeks it arrived. This check was only the beginning

What is so significant about Huang's 1992 fund-raising and his relations with Bill Clinton that he would risk a charge of perjury to deny them?

of a cascade of Riady money flowing to the Democrats. Within days, hundreds of thousands of dollars came in from family members and employees in Hong Kong and other places, ultimately making the Riadys the leading source of money for the Democrats in 1992. In 1993 Huang duplicated the DNC donation/reimbursement cycle with three $15,000 checks from Riady shell companies.

If he had not taken the Fifth Amendment, Huang would have been asked if he had directed this worldwide outpouring, and at whose request.

If Huang in his Judicial Watch deposition was being less than candid under oath about his fund-raising, what about his denial of a Clinton connection before he went to Commerce? Here the evidence is even more overwhelming. Between March 15, 1993, and his first day at Commerce (July 18, 1994), John Huang entered the White House at least forty-seven times, according to Secret Service records.[29] Nine of the visits were listed as with the president—most in the first family's quarters in the White House. Copies exist of letters to the president signed by Huang that discuss meetings and visits that took place well before July 1994.[30]

What is so significant about Huang's 1992 fund-raising and his relations with Bill Clinton that he would risk a charge of perjury to deny them? What was he really doing for the Riadys that was so valuable it had to be kept secret?

By the summer of 1994, John Huang was living the good life in California. His U.S.-based compensation[31] was more than $200,000 per year plus bonuses. And Lippo gave him a luxury model Mercedes Benz 560 as a company car. When he went to Commerce he reported a total severance package of almost $900,000, including the car.[32] Huang traveled around the world in the highest political and financial circles, including the Oval Office. Not bad, given his limited prospects in the late 1960s. Given this luxury, one can understand Huang's desire to continue to please the Riady family.

Whatever Huang was doing, it wasn't traditional banking. His Lippo colleagues viewed him as James Riady's "man in America" and a political "fixer."

The Riadys themselves never took their American business interests too seriously. They were mostly vanities designed to promote the Riadys' personal and political agendas. John Huang oversaw these enterprises, all of which were consistent money-losers. But no one seemed to care that they weren't profitable—hardly the usual response from hard-nosed bankers and businessmen. Whenever Huang was low on money, his secretary would send a memo to Jakarta for "capital injection," and fresh money would magically appear.[33]

All indicators force the conclusion that Huang's real job in the three or four years before he went to Commerce was overseeing the Riadys' political and financial investment in the Democratic Party in general, and Governor Bill Clinton in particular. His secretary would later testify that Huang directed all the political contributions from the three Riady shell companies—Hip Hing Holdings, San Jose Holdings, and Toy Center Holdings.[34] Senator Robert Torricelli (D-NJ) counted thirty-two contributions to Democratic causes[35] by these three companies. Senator Joseph Lieberman (D-CT) added the contributions and came up with $800,000,[36] from these three accounts alone, from 1991 to 1993.

In a letter to Clinton confidant Bruce Lindsey, Democratic Party activist (and Lippo consultant) Maeley Tom described Huang as follows:

> John Huang, Executive Vice President of Lippo Bank, is the political power that advises the Riady family on issues and where to make contributions. They invested heavily in the Clinton campaign…. The family knows the Clintons on a first-name basis….[37]

Lindsey knew James Riady well. When Riady visited the White House, he used the telephone on Lindsey's desk to make outside calls.[38] Lindsey would have known that the Riadys were the leading contributors to Clinton's election as president just three months before. Whether or not Lindsey knew precisely about the Riady-Clinton limousine ride in August 1992, he would have understood very well indeed the implication of the words "invested heavily."

But the Riadys had higher ambitions for Huang. Soon he would go from being the Riady's "man in America" to their "man in the American government." But for this, Huang would need a security clearance.

Of all the mysteries surrounding John Huang, his access to American classified materials is certainly among the most controversial. Answers are still needed to the questions of how he received his security clearance, when he had it, how long he kept it, what he saw, what he heard, and, most importantly, with whom he may have shared classified information.

First, the facts regarding his security clearance, as we know them:

- At the end of January 1994 Huang received an interim "Top Secret" security clearance on the pretext that Commerce Secretary Ron Brown needed his services urgently. At that point Huang could see and hear American classified information up to the Top Secret level. Top Secret includes our best foreign intelligence. But Huang did not join the Commerce Department until July 18, 1994, meaning that for five-and-a-half months this U.S. representative of a foreign bank could legally see highly classified information.[39]

- During his Commerce career, from July 18, 1994, to early December 1995,[40] he had the access to classified materials that his position called for.

- Until Congressman Gerald Solomon (R-NY), chairman of the House Rules Committee, forced Commerce to investigate, it was not widely known that Huang had kept his Top Secret security clearance for a year after he left Commerce for the DNC. We now know that during the 1996 campaign Huang was actively seeking campaign funds for the DNC from Chinese and other foreigners who have ties to organized criminal syndicates (Triads), narcotics trafficking, gambling, prostitution, the Chinese military, and all of Communist China's intelligence services. We also know that during that same period he could have legally received highly classified information.

In his best-selling book, *Unlimited Access*, retired FBI Special Agent Gary Aldrich patiently documented the destruction of the White House's long-standing security clearance system. This kind of recklessness was also perpetrated at Commerce.[41] Immediately upon gaining office the Clinton administration overturned a very competent security system, run by dedicated professionals who took pride in protecting the nation's secrets. Now, without any kind of serious background checks, anyone who wanted one could obtain a security clearance. In this atmosphere, Huang had all the opportunity he could handle. (In light of the Huang affair, Secretary of Commerce Bill Daley has commendably thrown out the "anyone can get one" approach and returned to the pre-Clinton system of carefully doled out security clearances.[42])

> Huang could see and hear American classified information up to the Top Secret level. Top Secret includes our best foreign intelligence.

It is clear that Huang was concerned about being trapped in a security violation. His files at Hip Hing produced some interesting research he had ordered. Between the time he received his security clearance in January and joined Commerce in July, he asked someone[43] to pull together information on the Larry Wu-tai Chin espionage case (discussed in more detail in Chapter 10).[44]

Huang's legal access to American intelligence, first as a Lippo executive and later as a Democratic Party official, is totally unique. A Commerce Department security officer testified before Senator Fred Thompson's (R-TN) Senate Governmental Affairs Committee that "no other consultant on the Department of Commerce payroll was ever granted a top secret security clearance."[45]

The length to which Huang went to keep his security clearance as a DNC official suggests, of course, a serious intent to exercise it. In the American system, private contractors can have access to classified materials if a serious need can be demonstrated. If someone is a government consultant designing a stealth bomber, it makes sense that he should have access to America's best intelligence on foreign radar capabilities. But what justification could Huang show for a continuing clearance after he left Commerce for the DNC?

He certainly campaigned hard for it. According to the Thompson committee's report, he pressured his immediate superior, Assistant Secretary Charles Meissner, to massage the system at Commerce so that he could become a consultant to Commerce and receive a new Top Secret clearance. When this idea was ridiculed by his higher officials, Meissner went up the chain of command to Secretary Ron Brown's chief of staff. Huang also visited White House Deputy Chief of Staff Harold Ickes, who oversaw the running of the DNC from his position at the White House and who certainly would have wanted one of his top fundraisers to have all the tools he needed.

Huang's consultancy was never approved—but his new clearance was. Such was the overall destruction of Commerce's security clearance system that the department awarded Huang the new clearance on Meissner's mere request to Commerce's security office.

Meissner died in the same plane crash that killed Ron Brown. In the winter of 1997, a United States official in a position to know told us privately that Huang's association with Commerce created a "climate of fear" among Commerce career employees— and that "a lot of secrets died with Chuck Meissner."[46]

CHAPTER 4
THE WEEK THAT WAS (I)

There are only a few television interviewers who are particularly good at extracting information from a reluctant witness. ABC's Emmy Award–winning Brian Ross is one of them. On the evening of June 18, 1997, *PrimeTime Live* aired his interview with the late Commerce Secretary Ron Brown's mistress, Nolanda Hill. Patiently and gently Ross asked her how John Huang came to be appointed to the Commerce Department:

> **HILL:** *Ron told me that the White House put him there, and it was Ron's opinion that the White House meant Hillary in this instance.*
> **ROSS:** *That she put him there.*
> **HILL:** *He believed that she was the person that made the call.*

Initially, we were skeptical, but after our extensive research we now believe that the weight of motivation, opportunity, and evidence points directly to Hillary Clinton's intervention. And we further believe that her reasons for intervening were corrupt.

The story begins in November 1992, right after her husband's election. Like many Democratic activists, Huang was thrilled that after twelve years of Republican rule the Democrats would be back in the White House. Huang and his sponsors, the billionaire Riady family of Indonesia, immediately began pressing the Clinton transition team to appoint Huang to an important post.

For the Clinton administration, it should have been an easy call. According to his American colleagues at the Riady-owned LippoBank, Huang knew the president from Arkansas days.[2] He would proudly tell people that he was an FOB. Huang had personally raised hundreds of thousands of dollars for the Clinton-Gore team and the Democrats. More importantly, the Riadys, family friends of the Clintons, were the number one source of funds for the Democrats in the 1992 election cycle. Lippo consultant and Democratic activist Maeley Tom sent a gentle reminder to Bruce Lindsey, then head of White House personnel, that the Riadys had "invested heavily" in Clinton's campaign.[3] Given what we now know of the Clintons, that had to count for a lot.

Huang had letters of recommendation from Democratic Senators Paul Simon of Illinois (who did not seek reelection in 1992) and Tom Daschle of South Dakota (the current Senate minority leader). Democratic Senator Kent Conrad of North Dakota wrote to Bruce Lindsey: "This country would be fortunate indeed to have a man of John's caliber and integrity in the Executive Branch." On the bottom of the letter Senator Conrad added this handwritten note: "John Huang is superb."[4] On his employment form Huang listed as references Joe Giroir, former chairman of the Rose Law Firm, where Hillary had been a partner; and Curt Bradbury, president of Little Rock's Worthen Bank, a crucial source of Clinton campaign funds during the primaries. Moreover, Huang had fifteen years of experience as an international banker. People who had much less experience and had raised a lot less money than Huang received ambassadorships or other high-level appointments in the Clinton administration, and fairly promptly, too.

But for some reason it took Huang eighteen months to gain his position. And the position he did take—principal deputy assistant secretary of Commerce—was a job best described as mid-level, at an agency best described as second-line.

During the delay the Clinton administration was having more than its share of disasters. First, there were a series of embarrassments involving high-level appointees (i.e., Nannygate). In the summer of 1993 Vince Foster, deputy White House counsel and the first lady's former law partner, was found dead by gunshot. By January 1994 a three-judge panel had named an independent counsel to start poking around in the Clintons' Arkansas affairs. Around the same time, the *Los Angeles Times* and *The New Republic* ran major stories on corruption in Arkansas, featuring longtime friends and associates of the first family. In the spring of 1994 White House Counsel Bernard Nussbaum resigned under fire. Also in the spring of 1994 it became known that the Senate Banking Committee would hold serious hearings on Clinton land deals in Arkansas, and a number of Clinton appointees at the Treasury Department would leave under a cloud. In that same spring Associate Attorney General Webster Hubbell, Mrs. Clinton's former law partner and President Clinton's close friend, resigned amid accusations of stealing from his clients in Little Rock.

An eight-day period in June 1994 was a fateful time for the Clinton presidency and for the country. And it would mark the third time that James Riady would bail Bill Clinton out of trouble.

With regard to the Riadys' wish to place Huang in the government, Clinton's advisers were not blind. They knew he was trouble, and they had had enough of that already. Even if they did not know of the Riadys' long-term relationship with Chinese intelligence—and they could have simply asked the CIA to perform a background check on the Riadys—Huang's Arkansas connection itself was enough to send up red flags. Months before Huang arrived at Commerce, his supervisor-to-be, David

Rothkopf, was worrying about his links to Arkansas's Worthen Bank, which was then the subject of an unfavorable cover story in *The New Republic*.[5]

Clinton's advisers' strategy was simple: Stall Huang and hope he would lose interest. He completed the paperwork in January 1994, but throughout the spring his appointment was still going nowhere.[6]

Then, mysteriously, everything came together in one week.

THE TIMELINE

In the middle of June 1994 Clinton's close friend Webb Hubbell ran out of money. He was down to $6,780 in his checking account.[7] Having resigned from Justice under a cloud, he had no job; his legal and other debts, including back taxes and penalties, were skyrocketing; and he was on his way to jail. What's more, the Clinton White House could not afford to have another disaster of the sort that had plagued the administration until that point.

With this in mind, consider the very interesting sequence of events that took place over an eight-day period toward the end of that month:

- On Monday, June 20, Webb Hubbell met with Mrs. Clinton.[8] On the same day Mr. Ng Lapseng, financial backer of Clinton crony Charlie Trie (about whom we'll learn much more later), quietly arrived in the United States from Macau carrying $175,000 *in cash*.[9]
- On Tuesday, June 21, James Riady and John Huang visited Mark Middleton, an aide to the chief of staff and a special assistant to the president, at the White House.[10] In the evening Huang attended a Business Leader's Reception with the president on the South Lawn of the White House.[11]
- On Wednesday, June 22, Ng and Charlie Trie had lunch with Middleton at the White House.[12] Riady and Huang

made their second visit to Middleton at the White House.[13]
That evening Trie and Ng were honored guests at the head
table with President Clinton during the Presidential Gala
fund-raiser staged at Washington's Hilton Hotel.[14]

■ On Thursday, June 23, Riady met Hubbell twice, for break-
fast *and* lunch.[15] Riady returned for a third time to the
White House, and Huang made two visits on the same day.[16]
In the afternoon James Riady and John Huang visited
United States Export-Import Bank Commissioner Maria
Haley, an old friend from Arkansas. At the time the bank
was considering supporting a Lippo joint-venture energy
project in China with New Orleans–based Entergy.

■ On Friday, June 24, Riady and Huang visited the White
House twice, once to meet with Middleton and once to meet
with then–Assistant to the President for Economic Policy,
now–Treasury Secretary, Robert Rubin.[17]

■ On Saturday, June 25, Riady and Huang attended the president's weekly radio address in the Oval Office. White
House photographers recorded the event on videotape. At
the beginning of the tape Riady and Huang are shown
standing in a corner. After the address, they appear again,
but Riady has changed clothes, leading to speculation that
he may have been an overnight guest of the president. After
the president says good-bye to the other guests, Riady and
Huang remain behind. Clinton says, "Just sit everybody
down, wherever you want 'em, James." At that point the
tape goes blank.[18]

■ On Monday, June 27, the first business day after the radio
address, the Lippo-controlled Hong Kong Chinese Bank
paid Webb Hubbell $100,000 from a Riady company
account ("Hong Kong China, Ltd.").[19] Hubbell had been
expecting to receive the Riady money in four $25,000 pay-
ments over time, but for some as yet unknown reason he

received the lump sum.[20] Hubbell has refused to tell federal investigators what services he rendered for the Riadys. On the same day, Huang received a memo from the Lippo Group in Jakarta congratulating him on his new position at the Commerce Department and telling him that his severance package from them would be $468,125.[21]

On Monday, July 18, Huang started at Commerce.[22]

It is no secret that the White House has been very worried about what Hubbell might reveal to Independent Counsel Kenneth Starr about Arkansas business deals and other matters. During this same summer of 1994 internal White House documents show that administration officials were "monitoring" Hubbell's "cooperation" with Starr.[23]

They had reason to be concerned. Hubbell's office at the Rose Law Firm was next to Mrs. Clinton's. Boxes of Whitewater files made their way to Hubbell's basement during the 1992 campaign and just sat there, away from prying eyes. In December 1994, just before Hubbell was sentenced to prison for stealing from the law firm, Deputy White House Legal Counsel Jane Sherburne made a list of potential legal problems for the Clintons, and Hubbell's possible cooperation with Starr featured prominently.[24] By the spring of 1997 Starr had concluded that Hubbell's failure to cooperate with prosecutors was related to possible "hush money" payments, and the White House was directed to produce any information it had relating to Lippo Insurance Group, Stephen Riady, and Riady consultants Mark Grobmyer and Joe Giroir, old friends of the Clintons from Arkansas.[25] Stephen Riady is responsible for Hong Kong China, Ltd. (which paid Hubbell the $100,000), and it's clear that Starr is looking for more Riady money.

In March 1998 NBC obtained an audio tape that prison officials had made of Hubbell talking to his wife about keeping secrets. This set off a flurry of news stories suggesting that

Hubbell was going to be indicted for hush money–related offenses. On April 30, 1998, Hubbell, his wife, his lawyer, and his accountant were all indicted for income tax evasion–related offenses.[26] At the same time the independent counsel's office released a list of Democratic donors[27] who had provided little-or-no-work "consulting" contracts for Hubbell. As Susan Schmidt of the *Washington Post* noted, "The largest single payment came from the Lippo Group conglomerate of Indonesia."[28] Even Hubbell's attorney, John Nields, admitted that the independent counsel was squeezing Hubbell for his lack of cooperation in the investigation of the Clintons.[29] Addressing Hubbell's make-work "consulting fees," *Washington Post* columnist Michael Kelly commented sarcastically, "Perhaps the $600,000 was not hush money to the sole witness who could, perhaps, personally implicate Mrs. Clinton for involvement in a fraud and for perjury."[30]

THE TRANSACTIONS

We believe that the eight-day period from June 20, 1994, to June 27, 1994, was a fateful time for the Clinton presidency and for the country. And it would mark the third time that James Riady would bail Bill Clinton out of trouble.[31]

Riady and Ng have fled the country. Hubbell, Huang, and Trie have all taken the Fifth Amendment. So has Middleton—the only former White House aide to have done so. President Clinton has claimed various legal privileges to block crucial testimony by Mrs. Clinton and Bruce Lindsey (called Mr. Clinton's "chief fixer" by *Newsweek*).[32] In short, none of the players is cooperating.

Nevertheless, we believe that the available evidence confirms Mrs. Hill's statement to Brian Ross. Hubbell was broke. Whether he blackmailed the White House or the administration only feared he would do so, we don't know. But there's no question Clinton's team felt motivated to act. Democratic staff members on Capitol Hill assert that Mrs. Clinton—whose meeting with

Hubbell on June 20, 1994, kicked off the timeline we outlined above—is, in effect, the chief executive officer of the White House defense team and that Bruce Lindsey is the chief operating officer.[33] The evidence indicates that Hillary Clinton played such a key role during the first Whitewater hearings. And her visit with Hubbell on June 20 suggests she was in charge.

To get money for Hubbell on such short notice would not have been easy. Foreign money was the White House's best opportunity. Had Ng, Trie, Hubbell, and Middleton cooperated with investigators, they would have been asked how much, if any, of Ng's $175,000 *in cash* made its way to Hubbell. Was the breakdown $100,000 *in cash* for Hubbell and $35,000 each to Ng and Trie to allow them into the Presidential Gala fundraiser on the evening of June 22, 1994, leaving $5,000 for "incidentals"?

> **We know that Clinton crony Webster Hubbell received $100,000 in Riady money. But the Riadys would have extracted a price for their generosity.**

Of course, we do know that Hubbell collected a matching $100,000 in Riady money. But the Riadys would have extracted a price for their generosity. That price would have been Huang's presidential appointment to the Commerce Department, where he could be a source of priceless military and economic intelligence. The details could have been worked out with Middleton and possibly others during the six or seven Riady-Huang visits to the White House that week. The private meeting in the Oval Office with President Clinton on Saturday after the radio address would have been the confirmation. By Monday events were in motion.

Why was Middleton the contact point? Because Middleton is a fund-raiser by nature, just as Huang is. In the 1992 campaign Middleton raised millions for the Clinton-Gore ticket and for the Democrats, first in Arkansas and later when he had fund-raising responsibility for the entire South.[34] More than anyone else at the

White House, Middleton knew about the money, perhaps explaining why he has taken the Fifth Amendment.

The deal may have been more complex than a simple exchange of a Commerce job to Huang for a bail-out of Hubbell. The billion dollar Entergy–Lippo project in China needed a political boost. Commerce Secretary Brown would later complain to Nolanda Hill that the White House forced him to promote the project on his August 1994 China trip.[35] Lippo consultant Joe Giroir was on Brown's 1994 trade mission, and Mrs. Hill has now given a signed affidavit in which she stated that Commerce's foreign trade missions were corruptly used to elicit campaign contributions and to raise funds for the DNC.[36]

There may well have been preliminary discussions about how long Huang would remain at Commerce. Clinton and his campaign team would have been anxious for Huang to weave his fundraising magic as the 1996 reelection campaign heated up. Another crucial week of Huang–Riady–White House meetings in September 1995 put the seal of approval on Huang's move to the DNC.

There are three more pieces of evidence to consider. First, long before Nolanda Hill gave her interview to Brian Ross, Commerce Department officials had confirmed her story that the first lady had orchestrated Huang's appointment to Commerce; according to Commerce officials quoted by the highly regarded Jerry Seper of the *Washington Times*, Mrs. Clinton's involvement in the Huang appointment was "common knowledge" among department officials, and they were troubled by it.[37] Second, Huang stated in his deposition to Judicial Watch, "I knew I got the job probably sometime in late June."[38] Indeed he did, as our reconstruction of the events of June 20–27, 1994, indicates.

Finally, Huang himself confirms that his appointment was sudden. When a colleague wrote to express surprise at his appointment, he wrote back, telling her, "The decision for my current position came in a rather short and quick fashion."[39]

In the legend of *Dr. Faustus*, the protagonist sells his soul to the
devil for a promise of earthly knowledge and power. The available
evidence here points to a reckless exchange between the Clintons
and associates of Chinese intelligence. The warning signs were all
there; the Clintons chose to ignore them in order to eliminate a
threat to their power.

CHAPTER 5
"MY MAN IN THE
AMERICAN GOVERNMENT"

The Clintons expended much effort, and the Riadys spent much cash, to get John Huang his job at the Department of Commerce. The Clintons got value for their effort in the form of Lippo-financed payoffs to Webb Hubbell. The Riadys got value for their money in the form of economic intelligence forwarded to them—and, in all likelihood, through them to their associates in Chinese intelligence—by Huang. Huang truly lived up to the label James Riady gave him: "My man in the American government."[1]

This allegation was first made publicly by House Rules Committee Chairman Gerald Solomon on June 11, 1997, when he announced:

> I have received reports from government sources that say there are electronic intercepts which provide evidence confirming that John Huang committed economic espionage and breached our national security by passing classified information to his former employer, the Lippo Group.

At the Senate Governmental Affairs Committee hearings on campaign finance violations, Senator Dick Durbin (D-IL) had this exchange with a witness representing the CIA:

SENATOR DURBIN: *Did you attempt to locate the information referred to in the [Solomon] press release?*
CIA: *Yes, sir.*
SENATOR DURBIN: *What did you learn?*
CIA: *I don't feel competent to answer that question in open session.*[2]

That's as close to a confirmation as the CIA can get on the public record. If the agency had nothing to substantiate Solomon's claim, it could have said so without jeopardizing classified information, because there would have been none at risk. But if it did have secret confirmation of John Huang's espionage, it could not reveal this information in public for fear the agency would jeopardize its "sources and methods," such as the electronic intercepts to which Solomon had alluded.

Did Huang collect and disseminate American economic and political information to the Riadys and their Chinese associates? The answer to that may be found in his career as an American government official at the Commerce Department.

ITA/IEP

Huang's job was at a Commerce Department division called the International Trade Administration (ITA)—an entity whose name overstates its importance. To wade still further into the alphabet soup of Commerce bureaucracy, Huang was assigned to a subdivision of ITA called the International Economic Policy (IEP) bureau. There, Huang was the principal deputy assistant secretary, reporting to the assistant secretary in charge of IEP, Charles Meissner.

Huang's job had no special geographical responsibility. This could make it what Washingtonians call a "nothingburger"—or it could allow the holder of the job to range freely over any area that struck his fancy. Huang later said in his Judicial Watch deposition that his job was "to coordinate all geographic areas." (Because of the controversy surrounding Huang's tenure there, IEP has been renamed "Market Access and Compliance," and Huang's position has been abolished.)

Huang's position at Commerce was ideal from Lippo's point of view. During the Senate hearings, Senator Max Cleland (D-GA) observed that Huang's principal deputy assistant secretary slot, although politically appointed, was not subject to Senate confirmation, and there had therefore been "no congressional hearings to explore a lot of issues and questions."[3] Senator Cleland was exactly right. If Huang had been appointed one step farther up the bureaucratic ladder, his Lippo connections would have been open to congressional examination, and his confirmation would have been doubtful.

Another factor making Huang's job an ideal one from the Riadys' point of view was that the Commerce Department is not really all that high in the policy pecking order. Despite its enormous bureaucracy, Commerce actually has only a small slice of the policy pie. This allowed Huang to keep a low media profile. Had he walked into a higher-profile agency—say, the Office of the U.S. Trade Representative—dragging his fund-raising and Lippo baggage, the trade press would have been all over him.

Still, from the standpoint of his superiors at Commerce, Huang had to be radioactive. Consider:

- Huang was the U.S. representative of Clinton's leading contributor in the previous election. The DNC put Huang on a list of "leading national fund-raisers who are interested in service in the Department of Commerce."[4] No one to whom Huang reported was on that list.
- Huang bragged to former business colleagues that he was an FOB,[5] a claim amply validated by his numerous White House visits, not to mention his calls to FOB Harry Thomason's office at Legend Air.[6]

■ His deep Arkansas connections came up when he started receiving telephone calls at his Commerce office from Little Rock cronies of the president—for example, Webb Hubbell and members of Bruce Lindsey's law firm.

Huang therefore had political connections that none of his nominal superiors at Commerce could aspire to. All this was happening when the first Whitewater hearings were on the front pages of the newspapers. The same people who were calling Huang were also being named prominently in this affair. One of Huang's supervisors, David Rothkopf, later told the *Los Angeles Times* of his great disquiet over Huang's Lippo and Worthen Bank connections: "My concern was that Lippo, through his involvement with Worthen Bank and *potentially other activities* might prove to be a lightning rod [emphasis added]."[7] A number of Commerce Department officials, including Charles Meissner's secretary, said that Meissner initially didn't welcome Huang to Commerce for the same reasons.[8]

> **The Riadys got value for their money in the form of economic intelligence forwarded to them—and, in all likelihood, through them to their associates in Chinese intelligence—by Huang.**

Rothkopf had an additional problem. According to career Commerce employees,[9] Rothkopf was trying to establish his expertise on China. (After he left Commerce, he went to head up former Secretary of State Henry Kissinger's China operations.) But he didn't read or speak the language, had never lived in China, and his contacts with the PRC government were limited. Then, in walks Huang, who speaks and reads five Chinese dialects, with years of on-the-job training in Taiwan and Hong Kong, and with a Rolodex of PRC contacts that extended right into the Communist Party Politburo. Huang's CIA briefers said that Huang had "a sensitivity about things Chinese that you just didn't get even if you're a Chinese scholar at Yale."[10]

After Huang had been on the job a few months, his supervisors decided to cover themselves by creating a legend that Huang had been "walled off" from China policy on the grounds that he just wasn't "up to" the job.[11] The implication was that Huang was a none-too-brilliant political hack, foisted on his more expert superiors for unknown reasons, and confined by them to administrative tasks, so that nothing he did or saw on China could matter. Of course the reverse was true: Huang was so far ahead of them on PRC affairs that they could never catch up, and he simply ignored their orders. They had no choice, and so they protected themselves as best they could.

THE LIPPO CONNECTION

Just before the 1996 election, the *Wall Street Journal* asked Huang if he had had anything to do with Indonesia while he was a Commerce Department official. He answered:

> Since it would be an obvious conflict of interest to work on such matters, Lippo having been my former employer, I scrupulously avoided any contact with any Commerce Department matters involving Lippo.[12]

Before the 1996 election, Commerce Department officials also told *Time* magazine, "Huang disqualified himself from any matters involving Indonesia because of his work for Lippo."[13]

Fortunately for Huang and the Commerce officials, lying to the press is not yet a federal crime. For from day one of his Commerce career, Huang not only dove headfirst into matters related to Indonesia, but he also seems to have spent the bulk of his time dealing exclusively with matters of vital interest to his former employers. Lippo Group and LippoBank have relations around the world, but they are most active in Greater China and in Southeast Asia, the area under the jurisdiction of Deputy Assistant Secretary Nancy Linn Patton,[14] a Clinton political appointee.

Although Huang had worldwide responsibilities, on his first day at Commerce he had two meetings with Ms. Patton,[15] and not a single one with anyone from another region.

That set the pattern for his entire time at Commerce. In his first two weeks at Commerce, for example, Huang held at least seven meetings with Patton, fourteen specifically identified Asia meetings with various Commerce officials, one lunch with Webb Hubbell, one two-hour meeting at the White House, two White House evening receptions (one of which was labeled "DNC mtg"), and one "Asia strategy meeting" with Meissner.[16]

As we have already seen, Huang's geographic responsibility was not confined to Lippo's operating area; such as it was, it was global. But his desk calendar does not have comparable entries for other regions outside of Asia and the Pacific. For example, Mexico and Canada are two of our nation's biggest trading partners, and we have trade problems with them from time to time. This would have been particularly true in late 1994 into 1995 as we began to implement the North American Free Trade Agreement (NAFTA). Yet from his desk calendar it is impossible to tell if Huang ever attended even one meeting specifically devoted to Canada or Mexico.[17] His interest in trade with Japan, the European Union, Africa, or the Middle East seems likewise to have approached zero. That is, despite the geographical breadth of his nominal responsibilities, he showed no interest in any region of the world in which Lippo was not a major player.

Huang's CIA briefer testified that Huang wanted American intelligence on China, Taiwan, Vietnam, and other parts of Southeast Asia—all prime Lippo operating areas.[18] He did not show any interest in Japan, South Korea, or other areas of lower priority to Lippo.

What a person calls himself is another sign of where his loyalties lie. In December 1995, while still a Commerce employee, Huang gave a contribution to Governor Evan Bayh (D-IN). On the declaration form he listed his employer as "Lippo Group." Huang would continue this identification when he went to work for the DNC. During that time he once attended a seminar and filled out the application forms by listing his position as "Consultant to Lippo."

A look at Huang's desk calendar and his telephone records while a federal official at Commerce makes apparent his overwhelming loyalty to the Riadys:

- More than four hundred telephone calls to various parts of the Riady empire, including LippoBank, Lippo consultants, and so on.[19] A former Lippo executive told the *Washington Post* that many of the calls were "to set a time to talk to [James Riady] who was then in Jakarta."[20]
- At least forty-one of these calls were made with a Lippo corporate telephone credit card, which he retained.[21]
- There were 170 calls to Hong Kong, Indonesia, and China.[22]
- Meeting after meeting with Webb Hubbell and other Lippo consultants or Lippo-related associates.

Quite plainly, Huang never really changed employers; he only changed locations.

THE COLLECTOR

As a United States government official at the Commerce Department, Huang had access to four types of very valuable information: (1) CIA briefings, (2) CIA materials shared by others, (3) classified State Department cables on foreign economic and political matters, and (4) information that is confidential, even though not classified, collected in the normal course of business by the department.

CIA representatives testified before Chairman Fred Thompson's Senate Governmental Affairs Committee that agents gave Huang thirty-seven classified one-on-one briefings in his office at Commerce.[23] In such a briefing, Huang's CIA handlers would typically hand him intelligence documents to read. They estimate that he saw between 370 and 550 CIA-produced pieces of American intelligence.[24] According to the Commerce Department, Huang also attended an additional 109 meetings at which classified information may have been discussed, including several at the White House.[25]

At least three of the documents that the CIA showed to Huang had a special marking: MEM DISSEM. The significance of this marking, according to the CIA, is that "unauthorized disclosure [of the information contained in a MEM DISSEM] could result in the death of an asset."[26] In other words, if the information leaked, the source of the information could be killed in retribution. The CIA surely does not exaggerate when it refers to these sources as "extremely sensitive."[27]

The Thompson committee provided a list of ten types of major intelligence items Huang received—every one of which would be of intense interest to Lippo, Stephens, Inc., or the Chinese government. The list included intelligence dealing with:

- Business opportunities in Vietnam.
- Economic issues confronting Taiwan and China.
- Investment opportunities in China.
- North Korean food shortage.
- Succession of power in China.
- China technology transfers.
- Nuclear power industry in Asia.
- Investments in the Chinese auto industry.
- Investment climate in Hong Kong.
- Chinese government influence on investment in China and Taiwan.

Which Chinese agency would want which kinds of information? And Lippo and Stephens—what would they be particularly interested in? Let's see who would line up to order from the John Huang Classified Information Catalogue.

Without question, at the top of the PRC's list would have been the issue of American military-related technology transfers to China. The Chinese military is using American high technology for its military modernization program. Chinese intelligence, particularly the "Er Bu" (military intelligence), would simply love to know what and whom the CIA was watching. For example, if the Er Bu found out that the CIA knew of China's interest in certain kinds of lasers with military applications, it could put that acquisition effort into deep freeze for a while. And if the CIA did not know of a Chinese effort to acquire another kind of American high technology—encryption gear, for example—it would be full speed ahead. Anything with a nuclear application, such as nuclear power projects in Asia, would be another high priority target for the Er Bu.

> John Huang had a "safe house" at Stephens, Inc.— a secure way to transmit sensitive American intelligence overseas.

Two of China's civilian intelligence services, the Ministry of State Security and the CCP's United Front Works Department, would have been very interested in learning what the CIA knew about the succession of power in China. In 1994 and 1995 Chinese paramount leader Deng Xiaoping was in failing health, and the various Chinese leaders were contending for position in the post-Deng era. Understanding the CIA's analysis of the situation would have allowed them to manipulate it to their advantage.

The materials on "investment climate in Hong Kong," for their part, would have been of interest because of the PRC's impending takeover of Hong Kong on July 1, 1997. At the time Huang was being briefed, the Chinese government was concerned that western capital would flee after the handover. Knowledge of the CIA's thinking about Hong Kong would show the PRC those areas where it had to be on its best behavior and those areas where it could gain advantage.

Most of the other CIA items would be as good as real money to an international bank and securities firm like Lippo, or to an investment bank such as Stephens, Inc., if it had access to them. Individuals, stockbrokers (such as Lippo Securities), commercial banks, or investment banks could easily make money on the basis of information provided by Huang. The authors asked a senior economist at a foreign brokerage house to prepare an analysis of how all four groups could profit from the types of intelligence to which Huang had access. (The analysis appears in the Appendix.) Consider the economist's first example: If the CIA had advance knowledge of the Vietnamese government's plan to build a new port, all four groups (individual, stockbroker, bank, and investment house) could prosper by this information.

Almost every businessman or businesswoman on the international scene is looking for investment opportunities in China. Manufacturers are chasing them, as are brokerage firms, international banks, and consulting firms. It's an extremely competitive environment. Some projects are winners, and others are losers. Tens of billions of dollars are at stake. What wouldn't such people pay to have the CIA's special inside knowledge?

Senator Joseph Lieberman asked Huang's CIA briefers a very intelligent question: "Why is it [CIA's intelligence] more than we might read in *The Economist* or *Time* or *Newsweek* or any of the newspapers that have good economic reporters around the world?"[28] The CIA replied that it has everything the newspapers have—plus "covert sources." As the agency noted, the difference between its information and that of the newsmagazines and newspapers "is that our information is clandestinely collected from protected... it is protected information. People don't want us to get it, and that is why it becomes sensitive."[29]

Sensitive and *valuable*, extremely valuable to those few who have it and can act on it. Insider knowledge, like insider trading, gives the recipient an enormous competitive advantage over all other investors. As the insider trading cases from the New York Stock Exchange demonstrate, unscrupulous individuals will pay millions of dollars for a good tip on a single stock. Now suppose someone had all the resources of the CIA at his command? Suppose someone could tell the CIA to fetch for him everything it has on any investment opportunity? John Huang had that ability.

In addition to the classified information from the CIA that was specifically addressed to him, Huang had a second source of classified information from his immediate superior, Assistant Secretary Charles Meissner.[30] Huang had a Top Secret clearance, and he had a need to know. It is common practice in trade offices to share information. Meissner was well known as a trade official who used intelligence in his work. Commenting on Meissner's trade role in the Carter administration, the CIA described him as "an appreciative and long standing customer of CIA reports."[31] As Rothkopf noted in his deposition to the Thompson committee, "Meissner was copied on all China decisions." Whatever Meissner knew, Huang knew as well.

Then there are the State Department cables. During the first Reagan administration, one of the authors[32] held an equivalent position to Huang's at the office of the U.S. Trade Representative. Each morning his secretary would retrieve a stack of classified cables from the State Department. The cables included political, economic, and trade reporting from our embassies around the world. That is, it was what our ambassadors know about the countries to which they are assigned. The author would separate out the cables he wished to be retained in the office. Those would be filed in proper categories in a classified safe kept for that purpose. The reports not retained in the classified safe would be returned for disposal by burning. *Every* classified document given him by his secretary would be returned to her, either for the safe or the burnbag.

By contrast, John Huang's secretary, Janice Stewart, testified that "she is not confident Huang returned to her all of the cables he received for either disposal or filing."[33] That is, she got back fewer classified documents than she gave him. She did not know what became of the missing documents.

A fourth stream of information accessible to Huang, and equally valuable, was the sensitive business and trade information in Commerce's day-to-day operations. In his position Huang would have known where everyone else was on any subject. The major trade agencies—the U.S. Trade Representative, the Department of State, the Department of the Treasury, even the National Security Council (NSC)—are rarely unified, at least at the beginning. Huang would know who was on what side, information that a foreign government could exploit to its own advantage by playing up to its supporters and trying to convert the doubtful.

Huang clearly had access to commercial information that would have been of keen interest to the Riadys. For example, on his second day he attended a Trade Policy Coordinating Committee meeting on Indonesia. The agenda contains Huang's handwritten notes in the margin. In addition to the printed agenda he points to other "Pending matters [that] needed attention." These include American policy on military assistance to Indonesia ("IMET"), "East Timor" (a human rights issue), and "labor rights" (another human rights issue).

At the time all of these were extremely sensitive bilateral issues between the United States and the Indonesian government. If the Riadys had been able to present our thinking on these subjects to the Indonesian government, they would undoubtedly have been rewarded. That very night Huang called Lippo in Jakarta.[34]

At the same meeting an "Indonesia Commercial Strategy" paper was passed out.[35] Again, Huang's notes are instructive. On the first page he has noted in the "Trade Finance" section a comment by another meeting participant: "U.S. Banks need to be there." This is the only one of his marginal notes that is underlined twice. Since LippoBank's major business line is trade finance, it certainly would have liked to know if the United States government was going to press then-President Suharto to open the Indonesian financial market to competition from U.S. banks.

The classic tripartite analysis of crime fiction is: means, motive, opportunity. Given his dependency on his patrons—the Riadys—Huang had a powerful motive to please them. At Commerce he had all the opportunity he needed to fetch information of value to them. We turn now to the question of means: could he transmit his information to them in a timely and usable manner?

THE SAFE HOUSE

The Willard Hotel in Washington is a venerable old institution. They say the verb "to lobby" originated there: back in those carefree nineteenth-century days when access to the president was comparatively easy to arrange, men waiting to ask him for favors would wait in the lobby of the Willard for their appointments.

The Willard is in a prime location, dominating an elegant Pennsylvania Avenue plaza, with the Commerce Department on the other side, and the Treasury Department and the White House nearby. In the early 1980s, as the Willard's business customers began to desert it, its owners saved it from the wrecking ball by selling some of its elegant space as upscale offices. One of its tenants was Stephens, Inc., of Little Rock, Arkansas.

In the intelligence business, there's a difference between a "drop" and a "safe house." A "drop" implies passivity. A "dead drop" can be a crack in a fence, a stone, or a tin can where messages are left. A "drop" may be a flea-bag hotel where an agent picks up his mail. The night clerk doesn't know or want to know the true identity of his customers; he just hands over the mail and takes the money. But a "safe house" is active. The proprietors not only know the visitor, they are also usually participants in whatever activity the visitor is engaged in. They provide a lot more services, and they have a stake in the outcome.

New York Times columnist Bill Safire has described the Stephens, Inc., office at the Willard as a "drop" for John Huang.[36] As much as we respect and admire Mr. Safire, we believe that the services rendered by Stephens, Inc., to Huang put it more in the category of a "safe house" than a "drop."

During Senator Thompson's hearings, a former Stephens secretary testified to the following:

- Huang walked across the street to the Stephens office two or three times a week carrying a folder or small briefcase.[37]
- He received overnight packages and faxes at the office.
- He sent faxes out of the office, used the copier, and made telephone calls from a small office set aside for visitors.[38]
- She did not know Huang's correspondents.[39]

It is abundantly clear that Huang did not want anyone to know of this arrangement. While Huang put at least some of his White House visits in his Commerce Department daybook, he noted none of his visits to the Stephens office. Indeed, his own secretary testified that she had "never heard of Stephens, Inc."[40] His supervisors and his coworkers were equally in the dark about the Stephens, Inc., arrangement.[41]

The head of the Stephens D.C. office, Vernon Weaver, also had something to hide. The ex-secretary from Stephens testified that Mr. Weaver gave her strict instructions to disguise the Huang-Stephens relationship. First, she told Senator Susan Collins (R-ME) that Weaver instructed her to call Huang on his behalf "because he didn't want his name to show up on the message logs of the Department of Commerce." Next she told the senator that Weaver prohibited her from leaving a detailed message if Huang was not available to take the call. Finally, she said that Huang was the only person for whom she had such instructions.[42]

One of the great mysteries of the Thompson hearings is the kid-glove treatment given the Stephens safe house operation. All of the information to which Huang had access would have been as valuable to an investment banker like Jackson Stephens as it would have been to the Riadys. Nevertheless, Vernon Weaver, now U.S. ambassador to the European Union in Brussels, was never deposed under oath or ordered to testify.[43] Neither was Jackson Stephens; nor was his son, the president of the company.[44] From his telephone records, we know that Huang spoke frequently to a number of Stephens, Inc., officials in Little Rock,[45] but none of them was ever interviewed, deposed under oath, or called to testify. And whereas other committee targets were forced to give up all their long distance call records, the attorney for Stephens, Inc., got away with the claim that Stephens had changed long distance carriers and that, therefore, telephone records for nearly all of 1995 were unavailable.[46] In spite of the long and intimate business relationship between the Riadys and Stephens, the committee did not issue a broad subpoena for all of Stephens's books and records in Little Rock and Washington.

In exchange for bailing out Clinton and Gore on numerous occasions, the Riadys were able to insert their man into the heart of American political and economic intelligence.

Counsel for the committee did, however, make a timid attempt to show what was going on. By matching CIA briefing information with the 1994 and January 1995 Stephens telephone records, which were the only ones produced, counsel was able to make three interesting connections:

- On the morning of October 4, 1994, Huang was briefed for the first time by the CIA. Late that afternoon a fax was sent from the Stephens office to Lippo, Ltd., in Hong Kong. The Riadys' China operations are run out of this office.
- The next afternoon a fax was sent from the Stephens office to Lippo Bank in Jakarta.

■ On two other occasions CIA briefings were followed fairly shortly by faxes from Stephens, Inc., to Lippo entities.[47]

We can only imagine what would have been shown if the telephone records from all of 1995 had been available or if Stephens officials had been compelled to testify. Considering that the committee was burdened by the unavailability of the most critical witnesses, due to their flight (the Riadys) or invocation of the Fifth Amendment (Huang) or untimely death (Meissner), the failure to pursue the Stephens leads is inexplicable.

THE CHINESE EMBASSY

October 3 and 4, 1994, were two event-filled days. As discovered in the Thompson hearings, on October 3 Huang was told by Jeffrey Garten, head of ITA, that he was off the case as far as China and Taiwan were concerned. The next day Garten sent a "PRIVATE/EYES ONLY" memo to Meissner (who occupied a middle position between Garten and Huang) confirming his orders to Huang and beginning the legend of Huang's incompetence on Asia: "Neither John Huang nor Nancy [Linn Patton] are up to handling Asia in any way shape or form at this time."[48] The same day, Huang, ignoring Garten, told the CIA at his first intelligence briefing that Asia and China were his top priorities, and that evening the first fax went out from Stephens, Inc., to the Riadys' China operation in Hong Kong.

Knowing how little Asia experience Garten had, Huang treated his exclusionary orders with the contempt they deserved. Besides, he was an FOB, and Garten most decidedly was not.

Huang's insubordination continued throughout his Commerce career. His telephone records, his appointment logs, and his own visits as a whole indicate that he had more contact with Chinese officials than with those of any other country.

Nor was he particularly subtle about it. One can only wonder what went through the mind of Huang's CIA briefer on June 5, 1995, as he came out of Huang's office. There, sitting in the reception area, was Huang's next appointment: Minister Wang from the Chinese embassy.[49] Quite likely, the CIA briefer shared the opinion of most international specialists—that Chinese diplomats often double as intelligence officers under official cover.[50]

Perhaps the most interesting case occurred in October 1995. On October 11 Huang took a cab from the Department of Commerce to an evening function at the Indonesian embassy. The next day, perhaps in the morning, he took a cab back to the Commerce Department from the official residence of the Chinese ambassador.[51] We don't know if he spent the night there, but there was no Chinese embassy function listed on his appointment book for either October 11 or October 12.[52]

After intense negotiations over intelligence sources and methods, the CIA told the Thompson committee that it had at least one piece of unverified information indicating "that Huang himself may possibly have had a direct financial relationship with the PRC government."[53] A retired senior American intelligence officer has told us that Chinese intelligence would typically not allow an asset as valuable as Huang to be run exclusively by a foreign businessman (that is, James Riady). It would insist on some direct connection, even if partially shared with his patron. The connection would be money.[54]

If a leak from the Senate Intelligence Committee is accurate, Huang accelerated his interest in classified materials in September 1995. As we will see, that corresponds precisely in time to a September 13, 1995, Oval Office meeting at which it was decided to move Huang to the DNC. Perhaps Huang was uncertain that he would keep his security clearance after he left Commerce and wanted to move as much material as he could, while he could— perhaps to please his masters, perhaps to aid in his fund-raising once he moved to the DNC, perhaps both.[55]

MEANS, MOTIVE, AND OPPORTUNITY

This was the payoff to the Riadys. For services rendered in the 1992 campaign, and taking care of the Hubbell matter to the tune of at least $100,000 in 1994, they were able to insert their man into the heart of American political and economic intelligence. Their agent, John Huang, was totally beholden to them. By luck or design he was placed in a position where he would not be noticed but where he could collect American intelligence that would be immensely valuable to both the Riadys and their associates in Chinese intelligence. Collecting was not enough; he found a secure way—the Stephens office across the street—to transmit his information overseas. He had the means, the motive, and the opportunity. Intelligence information and overwhelming circumstantial evidence both indicate that he betrayed the trust that the American people placed in him when he was called to their service and put on their payroll.

CHAPTER 6
THE WEEK THAT WAS (II)

Following the massive GOP sweep in the 1994 off-year elections, Bill Clinton needed campaign money, and he needed it badly.

Although he was not on the ballot in 1994, President Clinton lost the election for the Democrats. His chief political strategist at the time, Dick Morris, claims to have told Clinton before the election that he, not the Republicans' "Contract with America," was the issue.[1] According to Morris, in September and October of 1994, "the president's approval rating was so low that any candidate for whom he campaigned would have been hurt politically."[2]

Morris also observed: "The 1994 defeat devastated Clinton.... He would talk about the defeat endlessly, ruminating on what had gone wrong."[3] Clinton even "concluded that he faced permanent defeat."[4] Morris notes that both the first lady and Vice President Gore were equally affected, with Gore "badly shaken by the defeat in 1994."[5] The opinion polls reflected Clinton's low approval rating. Right after the 1994 election he was losing a hypothetical head-to-head battle with Republican Senate Majority Leader Bob Dole by a wide margin, 33 percent to 49 percent.[6]

And yet, in the 1996 presidential election two years later, it was Clinton who managed 49 percent to Dole's 41 percent.[7]

How did this amazing turnabout occur? To a large extent, it was early and plentiful advertising. Advertising requires fund-raising, and fund-raising on such a massive scale requires pros with good connections—like John Huang.

Said Dick Morris, "Week after week, month after month, from early July 1995 more or less continually until election day in 1996, sixteen months later, we bombarded the public with ads."[8] The brilliance of Morris's plan was to hide the ads in plain sight. He exploited the tendency of the elite to assume that anything that took place outside its favorite haunts wasn't really happening. Thus, while placing ads nationwide, he was careful to avoid New York City and Washington, D.C., completely, and for the most part Los Angeles as well; as a result, the political pundits missed what was going on. But 125 million Americans saw these ads three times a week on the average.[9] When polls started showing Clinton on top of the world again, the pundits scratched their heads and began their amusing attempts to "explain" it.

For Bill Clinton, this campaign was hands-on. Morris reveals that Clinton "became the day-to-day operational director of our TV-ad campaign. He worked over every script, watched each ad, ordered changes in every visual presentation, and decided which ads would run when and where."[10] Gore was also deeply involved with the program, reviewing, modifying, and approving advertisements.[11]

It would be easy to dismiss Morris's boasting as a result of an overinflated ego coupled with a desire to regain his prestige. (Morris, of course, was forced to quit the campaign in August 1996 when his long-term relationship with a prostitute was revealed.) But there is corroborating evidence to back up his claims. First, his longtime political nemesis, White House Deputy Chief of Staff Harold Ickes, tried to take credit for the ad campaign. "Basically, it was my idea," he said.[12] Second, a number of highly respected political writers were impressed by the success of the ad campaign. For example, pundits Michael Barone and Grant Ujifusa, editors of the highly regarded biennial *Almanac of American Politics*, pronounced Clinton's "behind the scenes campaign" to be "brilliant."[13]

The authors were witnesses to the effectiveness of Morris's operation. In late 1995 and 1996, we attended a number of private political meetings at which representatives of groups allied with the Republicans complained about the ads. They pointed out, correctly, the success Morris's program was having on public opinion in the American heartland. This led to heated exchanges between the activists and various highly paid consultants and lobbyists. The activists were demanding that the ads be answered immediately and in kind. The "professionals" argued that early advertising money was wasted as the "American people never concentrate on the campaign until after Labor Day"—that is, until September 1996.[14] The consultants and lobbyists had the ear of the Republican leadership, and Morris's ads went unchallenged.

Morris states flatly that if the Republicans had answered the ads in time, they would have won the presidential election in 1996: "Whoever killed [the Republicans'] plans to advertise deserves the blame for their defeat."[15]

Morris's brilliant ads, the anti-Republican media, and the Republicans' political incompetence in failing to answer in kind constituted a triple blow from which the Republicans have never recovered. Morris boasts that "Newt saw his reputation and his career destroyed by our ads."[16] By the end of February 1996, Clinton was up to 53 percent in the polls against Dole. While his eventual victory over Dole was a few points less crushing than that, the outcome was essentially in the bag while the Republican candidates were still trudging through snow in New Hampshire.[17]

Television ads are extremely expensive. Morris reports that the DNC had spent $30 million before the Republicans ran their first ad.[18] This was money they didn't have when they started out, and so it was a major political gamble by President Clinton and his advisers.[19] Where did it come from?

As it happens, the roll-out of Morris's ad campaign coincided with the reappearance of the Riadys and John Huang in the world of campaign fund-raising, during the week of September 7–13, 1995.

Three groups were involved here, each wanting the Clinton-Gore ticket to be reelected, but two with opposing agendas. In the middle were President Clinton, Vice President Gore, and their advisers: an enthusiastic Dick Morris, a reluctant Harold Ickes, and others. On September 7, 1995, Morris met the president in the Treaty Room of the White House and told him that the entire fate of his presidency depended on whether he would agree to turn up the ad campaign massively. Morris told Clinton, "We will decide the outcome of the election right here and now."[20] Morris knew that "the DNC had no cash on hand for such spending and eventually had to borrow much of the money."[21]

> **Clinton's back was to the wall. He needed the Riadys again, and he did not care what happened as a consequence.**

On Sunday night, September 10, 1995, Clinton, Gore, Hillary Clinton, Ickes, White House Chief of Staff Leon Panetta, and DNC Chairman Don Fowler held a strategy session to decide whether to approve Morris's plan for massive advertising. It was a "go" decision.[22] Clinton and Gore were committed—but without money the Morris plan was going nowhere.

Three days later, September 13, 1995, Clinton and presidential assistant Bruce Lindsey met in the Oval Office with James Riady, John Huang, and Lippo partner Joe Giroir. They decided that Huang would move from Commerce to become a major fund-raiser for the DNC, with the title of vice financial chairman.[23] Who else would Clinton and Gore turn to besides the people who had bailed them out so many times before? John Huang's fund-raising magic would have looked extremely attractive at that crucial moment.

In the Oval Office meeting, Clinton and Lindsey probably thought they had disposed of the Huang-to-DNC issue. But, in fact, they had walked into guerrilla warfare between the highest DNC officials and the Riady group—a conflict that the president himself would have to resolve two months later.

The war actually began before the September White House meeting, when Giroir showed up in DNC Chairman Fowler's office in late August to raise the issue of the DNC taking Huang on as a full-time fund-raiser. By at least one account, the meeting didn't go well. Giroir pushed; Fowler resisted.[24] A later meeting on the morning of September 13 at a luxury hotel in Washington between James Riady, Giroir, and Huang on the one side and Fowler and his staff on the other was no more successful.[25] Later in October, Ickes called DNC Finance Chief Marvin Rosen to press the Huang appointment; but even though Ickes was running the campaign for the White House, he was no more successful than Giroir in convincing the DNC that it should accept Huang.[26]

Finally, after many more unsuccessful communications back and forth between the White House, the Riady group, and DNC officials, the president took Marvin Rosen aside at a November fund-raiser to make his views clear.[27] Huang was hired.

It was strange, on the face of it, that the DNC would show any hesitancy about hiring Huang. His fund-raising record was outstanding. Why did it take strong-arming by Bill Clinton himself to get Huang the DNC job?

And why did the Lippo contingent take the stand it did? The Riadys had lobbied hard to get Huang his Commerce job. Why would James Riady come all the way to Washington to press the case with Fowler and the president, enlisting his agent Giroir in the effort as well? By the count of Republican Senator Susan Collins of Maine, Giroir made at least nine separate passes at the White House to try to move Huang to the DNC.[28] Huang himself was in the White House sixteen times between the September 13 Oval

Office meeting and November 13, when Fowler and Rosen finally surrendered.[29] He even saw Gore and the first lady.[30]

The heat was on. Huang had to get out of Commerce in a hurry, and neither Fowler nor Rosen wanted him at the DNC. In fact, when Huang finally did come to the DNC, committee officials wouldn't even let him in the main building, where they had their own offices. They put him in a scruffy annex across the street.[31] It looks as if they wanted to put as much distance as possible between themselves and Huang. They later created a legend that they had assigned Huang to a unique training program under the DNC's general counsel, something the general counsel vigorously denied.[32]

The DNC officials had good reason to believe that Huang was poison. Even if they hadn't known that he had run illegal campaign contributions through Hip Hing Holdings back in 1992, they may have had early notice of James Riady's disrespect for American law. Found in the DNC's own files was a March 15, 1994, letter from Lippo consultant and Democratic activist Maeley Tom to a previous DNC chairman, David Wilhelm, reporting that Riady wants to organize "business leaders from East Asia" as "a vehicle to raise dollars from a fresh source for the DNC."[33] Only United States citizens and permanent residents may contribute to federal elections, so, unless these "business leaders from East Asia" were U.S. citizens or legal residents—which is highly unlikely—this "fresh source" of money amounted to serious violations of American law. Anyone knowingly participating in such a scheme could be looking at a conspiracy charge and some jail time.

The Maeley Tom letter set the stage, but we believe that what probably precipitated the Riady-DNC conflict was a feature article in the September 1995 issue of *The American Spectator* by James Ring Adams. Titled "What's Up in Jakarta?" it revealed much of what we now know about the relationship among the

Clintons, the Riadys, and Jackson Stephens in their Little Rock period. It noted that "Clinton owes" the Riadys "big time." More importantly, it threw the spotlight on John Huang: "The Riadys even have an alumnus inside the Clinton administration."

The American Spectator is not just any monthly political magazine. It is conservative, it specializes in hard-hitting investigative reporting, and by the summer of 1995 it had run a number of Clinton scandal stories, most spectacularly the "Troopergate" story introducing Paula Jones. It is also widely read in Washington. Any Democrat reading Adams's story on the Riadys would be very concerned that the daily press would pick it up and give it wide circulation. The September 1995 issue would have come out no later than August 20,[34] probably a little earlier—or just before Joe Giroir descended on Fowler. Given the magazine's history of successful attacks on Clinton's ethics, it is unthinkable that it would not have circulated like wildfire at the DNC, at the White House, and among Clinton political appointees in the government.

> **The DNC knew that at least $25,000 in funding came illegally from Chinese citizens and that another $25,000 of illegal contributions was laundered through the Hsi Lai Temple.**

In short, the week of September 7–13, 1995, was a repetition of the week of June 20–27, 1994. Clinton's back was to the wall. He needed the Riadys again, and he didn't care what happened as a consequence. As the *Los Angeles Times* would note after the election, "No possible source of big money was neglected."[35] Clinton made another Faustian bargain with the Riadys. In the same way that Clinton's personnel people tried for a year and a half to keep Huang out of the Commerce Department, Fowler and Rosen fought off appointing Huang to the DNC for at least three months. Finally, Clinton had his little chat with Rosen at the November fund-raiser. That put an end to formal DNC resistance to hiring Huang; but even after that, DNC officials tried to protect themselves any way they could, including exiling him across the street.

In the end, of course, Huang went to the DNC, with his security clearance intact.[36] Events were now in motion.

Huang hit the ground running on arrival at the DNC in early December 1995. The *Los Angeles Times* credits his fund-raising production as follows:[37]

NOVEMBER 1995	**$30,000**[38]
DECEMBER 1995	**$100,000**
FEBRUARY 1996	**$1,000,000**
APRIL 1996	**$140,000**
MAY 1996	**$600,000**
JUNE 1996	**$90,000**
JULY 1996	**$700,000**

But Fowler and Rosen's instincts about Huang were right: as of the end of June 1997 the DNC had returned $2.8 million, 80 percent of which was raised by John Huang and Charlie Trie,[39] and the Lippogate/Chinagate scandals, together with the unrelated Monica Lewinsky affair, have engulfed Clinton's second term.

The following are a few of the highlights of Huang's career at the DNC:

February 19, 1996: At a fund-raiser at the Hay-Adams Hotel in Washington, Huang put Chinese agent Ted Sioeng at the head table next to President Clinton. Since Sioeng speaks little or no English and Clinton is not known to speak Chinese, their table conversation was probably limited. By March 1996 the DNC knew that at least $25,000 of the money raised came illegally from Chinese citizens and that another $25,000 of illegal contributions was money laundered through the Hsi Lai Temple, a Buddhist monastery outside Los Angeles.[40]

April 8, 1996: After a photo op with Clinton at the Sheraton Carlton Hotel in Washington, Huang collected $250,000 in illegal contributions from Korean businessman John K. H. Lee, another non-English speaker.[41] When the *Los Angeles Times* discovered this particular transaction in September 1996,[42] it was the beginning of the end for Huang.

April 29, 1996: The infamous Hsi Lai Temple fund-raising luncheon (see Chapter 7): this time Huang seated Ted Sioeng next to Vice President Gore,[43] also not known for his ability to speak Chinese. Gore could have turned to his right, because seated there was Chinese agent Maria Hsia, who speaks at least some English.

May 13, 1996: This was a major event at the Sheraton Carlton Hotel in Washington. Here Huang sandwiched Clinton at the head table between Chinese agents Ted Sioeng and James Riady. Perhaps Clinton and Riady reminisced about old days in Little Rock. Hong Kong billionaire Nina Wang also attended this event.[44] Later in the evening Huang arranged for Yogesh K. Gandhi to meet Clinton and present him with a bust of Indian leader Mahatma Gandhi. Yogesh Gandhi's $325,000 donation was later returned.[45]

June 18, 1996: This coffee was for now-indicted Thai lobbyist Pauline Kanchanalak and her clients, the CP Group of Thailand. CP is in business with the Chinese military in China.[46]

July 22, 1996: A DNC Presidential Gala was held at the Century City Hotel in Los Angeles. Again Clinton sat between Chinese agents Ted Sioeng and James Riady.[47]

July 30, 1996: This was a small dinner at the Jefferson Hotel in Washington for Clinton and a group of mostly foreign nationals, including James Riady.[48]

CONCLUSION

The Clinton/Gore reelection campaign and the DNC (any distinction between the two was erased by Clinton's hands-on role
in the DNC ad campaign, to which Dick Morris attests) needed
lots of money very fast in 1995. The Riadys were in a position to
help provide it. Their 1992 help to Clinton had been recom-
pensed by John Huang's eighteen months of rummaging through
Commerce's intelligence cookie jar and dutifully faxing goodies
to Los Angeles, Hong Kong, and Jakarta. When the heat was on
at Commerce, his patrons arranged to move him to the DNC.
DNC professionals like Fowler and Rosen knew better, but they
were overruled. Through Huang's stellar fund-raising performance at the DNC (stellar, that is, if you ignore the fact that
much of the money was illegal and had to be returned—but *after*
Clinton was safely reelected), the Riadys saved Clinton's political
hide yet again.

That is to say, Indonesian billionaires with close ties to the CCP
saved Clinton's political hide—for the fourth time.

CHAPTER 7
WOMEN OF THE CHINA CONNECTION

T he women who figured in Watergate—Mo Dean, Martha Mitchell, even First Lady Pat Nixon—were secondary characters to that drama. But a generational shift has occurred between the Nixon and Clinton scandals: Women are no longer in supporting roles. The axis between the Clinton-Gore campaigns and the Chinese Communist Party has no glass ceiling. Three remarkable women—Democratic Party activist Maria Hsia, Pauline Kanchanalak of Thailand, and Hong Kong billionaire Nina Wang—all have money ties to Bill Clinton and Al Gore, and all three have connections to Chinese intelligence or the CCP's military arm, the PLA. As we will see, Beijing did not hesitate to exploit this connection, even face-to-face with Bill Clinton.

THE HSI LAI TEMPLE FIASCO

On April 29, 1996, Vice President Al Gore attended a luncheon at the Hsi Lai Temple, which describes itself as the largest Buddhist monastery in the United States.[1] When the media first questioned Gore about the luncheon, the vice president claimed that it had simply been a "community outreach event," not a fund-raiser.[2]

Despite Gore's initial denial, the luncheon at the Los Angeles–area temple *was* a fund-raiser, though the DNC has acknowledged only that the event was "inappropriate" and a "mistake."[3] In the two years since the press discovered the temple luncheon, Vice President Gore has been between a rock and a hard place: If he and his supporters admit that he was aware it was a fund-raiser, then he opens himself to having knowingly participated in something illegal. If Gore denies that he was aware it was a fund-raiser (when everyone else around him knew),[4] people will wonder if anyone this incompetent is fit to be president.

Today, it is much harder for Gore and his associates to claim ignorance because everyone knows that Gore's 1996 visit to the temple was not a one-time happening. Gore's relationship with the temple, and the illegal fund-raising, went back eight years. This is just one of the reasons that the temple fund-raiser was far worse than "inappropriate." The Hsi Lai Temple has been used to launder campaign funds for the DNC. Moreover, the April 1996 luncheon Gore attended was awash with Chinese Communist agents.

The organizing dynamo behind the April 29, 1996, Hsi Lai Temple illegal fund-raising event was Maria Hsia.[5] Born in Taiwan in 1951, she came to the United States in 1973 and became a U.S. citizen in 1986.[6] The 1980s were a real financial roller-coaster ride for Hsia. Although not an attorney, she learned how to help Chinese immigrants navigate the shoals of U.S. immigration law. In extremely lucrative years like 1982, she reported $637,000 in income,[7] but by the early 1990s she was struggling to earn $35,000 per year as a paralegal.[8] A former lover and business associate described her in court papers as "an ambitious, aggressive, and unscrupulous businesswoman."[9]

In the early 1980s she discovered that being active in the Democratic Party could translate into increasing her own financial gain. In 1983, for example, she ran into trouble with the Immigration and Naturalization Service (INS) but was able to persuade a number of Democratic senators and representatives to support her clients' cases.[10] Shortly thereafter, she began to raise money for them in the California Asian community. As her business partner later put it, appearing in the Chinese language newspapers with Democratic senators and congressmen at fund-raisers showed her clients that she had a "kind of extra protection, so to speak."[11]

In 1988 Hsia came into contact with James Riady and John Huang when she helped put on the April 22, 1988, Brentwood, California, fund-raiser for the Democratic Senatorial Committee.[12] Later that year she and John Huang raised money for the Dukakis for President campaign and various Democratic senators and congressmen.[13] But despite her best efforts, 1988 was not a good year for Democratic candidates, and she began to look for a new horse to ride.

Right after the 1988 election, Al Gore, Maria Hsia, John Huang, James Riady, and the Hsi Lai Temple organization began what was to be an eight-year relationship. Riady began by providing $10,000 in seed money, and the temple picked up the rest for a January 1989 visit to Asia by Gore and others. Although Taiwan was the major stop on the trip, Riady and Huang recommended that Gore meet with PRC officials of the Xinhua News Agency and China Resources Group on the Hong Kong leg.[14] (Both Xinhua News Agency and China Resources are identified as part of the Chinese intelligence apparatus in Chapter 10 of this book.)

The spring of 1989 set the eight-year Gore–Hsia–temple partnership in motion. Hsia organized numerous fund-raisers for Gore, using laundered temple money as a partial source. For example, a May 1989 event raised nearly $20,000 for Gore with active participation from the temple's monks and nuns.

In 1998 Hsia was indicted in a federal district court in Washington, with the temple named as an unindicted coconspirator.[15] The federal grand jury went back to mid-1993 and charged that Hsia and the temple "knowingly and willfully" conspired to defraud the United States with regard to a series of immigration and campaign fund-raising scams.[16] One of the crimes Hsia is accused of committing involves illegal temple donations to a September 1993 Gore fund-raising event in California for the DNC.[17] In this case the grand jury said

The CIA told the Senate that Democratic fund-raiser Maria Hsia "has been an agent of the Chinese government... [and] has acted knowingly in support of it."

that, at Hsia's direction, the temple laundered campaign funds for the DNC through three of its members. Typically, persons associated with the temple, sometimes monks and nuns, would make contributions to Democratic causes, and then they would be reimbursed by temple funds. Under U.S. law it is illegal for someone to make a campaign contribution in the name of another, and it is illegal for a tax-exempt public charity (the temple) to make political donations. But this is exactly what happened at the temple.

According to the federal grand jury, Hsia and the temple leadership participated in the following events during the 1995–1996 election cycle, all of which involved illegal money-laundering:

- *September 1995:* Clinton/Gore event at the Century Plaza Hotel in Los Angeles.
- *November 1995:* Event for Senator Edward Kennedy (D-MA) in Los Angeles.
- *February 1996:* Clinton event at the Hay-Adams Hotel in Washington.
- *April 29, 1996:* Gore event at the Hsi Lai Temple in California.
- *July 1996:* Clinton event at the Century Plaza Hotel in Los Angeles.
- *October 1996:* Event at the temple for Representative Patrick Kennedy (D-RI).

Hsia laundered almost $150,000 through the temple for Democratic candidates in the 1995–1996 election cycle, of which $116,500 went to reelect the Clinton-Gore ticket.[18]

If Maria Hsia was giving to the Democrats, she was also getting from the system she helped create. The temple established a very nice lucrative sideline business that allowed her to get "green cards" (permanent residency in the United States) for its members. Perhaps it was a coincidence, but in 1990 the U.S. immigration law was modified to create an entirely new visa category, "religious workers," which just happened to benefit the temple. According to her notes, Hsia successfully lobbied Gore to support another provision relating to family reunification, which was also important to her immigration business.[19]

We know why Hsia bored in on Al Gore. She had talent-spotted him and his presidential ambitions as early as 1988. In a letter urging him to make the Riady/temple-funded trip to Asia, she told him that "if you decide to join this trip, I will persuave [sic] all my colleagues in the future to play a leader role in your presidential race."[20] The Riadys chose Clinton as their horse in the race; Hsia went with Gore.

What we don't know is exactly when she became an agent for the Chinese Communists; we only know that she did. Her contact point with the PRC seems to have been the notorious Chinese consulate in Los Angeles,[21] the subject of further discussion in Chapter 10. The CIA told the Thompson committee:

Hsia has been an agent of the Chinese government, that she has acted knowingly in support of it, and that she has attempted to conceal her relationship with the Chinese government.[22]

And, further: Hsia worked with Ted Sioeng and John Huang to solicit contributions from Chinese nationals in the United States and abroad for Democratic causes. Hsia and Huang, in particular, worked together to identify non-U.S. citizens who might contribute money to Democratic causes.[23]

The Democrats' version of the Thompson report has the following interesting observation: "Regarding Maria Hsia, the Committee received non-public information connecting some activities she undertook while an immigrant consultant in the state of California in the early to mid-1990s to Chinese Government officials."[24] In this case "non-public information" means from the American intelligence community. Why would the PRC government want to pay for immigrant advice in the United States? To our knowledge, no other government pays to help its citizens leave their own country. What is so important about these individuals that the PRC would pay Maria Hsia to help get them into the United States? Why can't they come in through the normal U.S. visa process? And why would the CIA tell the committee that Hsia was trying to "conceal her relationship with the Chinese government"? Was there something special or dangerous about her PRC immigrant clients?

The picture of Al Gore at the Hsi Lai Temple surrounded by Communist Chinese agents Maria Hsia, John Huang, and Ted Sioeng—included in this book's photo section—represents millions of dollars in illegal campaign funds. It would be interesting to question them about this but, unfortunately, Hsia and Huang have taken the Fifth Amendment, and Sioeng has fled the country.

Once again, either Gore knew what was going on around him over all those years, or he didn't. A knave or a fool: either way, his fitness to lead this nation is questionable.

THE PERILS OF PAULINE

Consider this five-month period in 1996:

February: Chinese arms smuggler Wang Jun visits the White House for coffee and "donor maintenance." The next day he rings the bell at the New York Stock Exchange. A PLA space launch vehicle crashes onto a Chinese village with great loss of life. Engineers from the U.S. aerospace companies Loral and Hughes try to make things right.

March: The PLA tries to intimidate Taiwanese voters by throwing ballistic missiles at the island. Clinton signs an order making it easier for the PLA to launch American satellites.

April: Gore sits down to lunch at the Hsi Lai Temple with a bevy of Chinese agents.

May: Representatives of Wang Jun's company and another Chinese arms company, Norinco, are arrested for trying to smuggle automatic machine guns and "Stinger" type missiles into the United States for sale to drug gangs.

June: Clinton has coffee in the White House with a group of Thai chicken sellers. Only it isn't really a social chat; the visitors are Thai in name only, and they don't want to talk about the U.S.-Thailand poultry trade. They're lobbying Clinton to increase U.S. military-related technology exports to Communist China.

What's going on here?

Another associate of the PLA, Pauline Kanchanalak, is about to make an appearance in our little drama.

Pauline is an ethnic Chinese, born in Thailand in 1950 and educated at Stanford. She married into a wealthy Bangkok family but for whatever reason decided she liked Washington better. In the 1980s she was hanging out at the Thai embassy in Washington as an assistant to the Thai ambassador and stringing for a Bangkok newspaper. She clearly had ambitions to become a major foreign lobbyist in Washington.

Kanchanalak fled the country while congressional committees were looking her way.[25] She and her sister-in-law, a U.S. resident, have been indicted by a federal grand jury on twenty-four counts of election law violations, including conspiracy and related matters. Basically, she was a party to a scheme like Maria Hsia's to launder foreign money through straw donors to the Democrats. Sometime in the 1980s she became part of John Huang's illegal campaign fund-raising network for the Democrats. We don't know when she actually began laundering foreign campaign funds; the grand jury picked her up in the fall of 1992 with illegal contributions to the DNC and the "Wayne Owens for Senate" race in Utah.[26] Over a four-year period, the grand jury traced at least $679,000 in laundered funds to the DNC, Clinton/Gore '96, the Democratic Senatorial Campaign Committee, state Democratic parties,[27] and various individual Democratic races, including Senator Edward Kennedy's 1994 reelection effort.

We wish to emphasize that the $679,000 number is a floor, not a ceiling. That's all the FBI has been able to trace. After the 1996 reelection of Clinton and Gore, she had nearly all of her business records, including computer hard drives, removed or destroyed. She's charged with obstruction of justice, and it's entirely possible her effort to pour illegal foreign money into Democratic Party causes is substantially larger than what is known at the moment.

What did she receive from the White House for her money? A lot of attention. She went in and out of the Clinton White House at least thirty-three times.[28]

Certainly the most notorious White House/Kanchanalak episode involved White House senior adviser Ira Magaziner. He had been the mastermind of Mrs. Clinton's ill-fated 1994 health care plan. In between court appearances stemming from that disaster—during which presiding Judge Royce C. Lamberth rebuked Magaziner for conduct that was "reprehensible" and "dishonest with this court"[29]—he needed something to do. So President Clinton assigned him to form a task force to identify four or five initiatives to accelerate the growth of U.S. exports. That he didn't know any more about trade than he did about health care didn't seem to matter. As part of his new assignment, Magaziner met with Kanchanalak's clients.

As later recounted by one of Kanchanalak's business associates,[30] in March 1996 Magaziner conducted a role-playing session over breakfast with Thai executives. He made them play the role of president of the United States, and asked them what they would do if they were President Clinton. They said that they would look into "the need for the U.S. to play down the issues of human rights and regional security threats, particularly with reference to China, and to explore collaborative business ventures with the influential and capital-rich ethnic Chinese in the region."[31]

> **If Gore denies that he knew it was a fund-raiser (when everyone else around him knew), people will wonder if anyone this incompetent is fit to be president.**

"Regional security threats" is, it seems, a code word for Communist China's military aggression in Asia. At the very moment this conversation was taking place, almost every newspaper outside of China was reporting that the PLA was testing missiles off Taiwan's coast. It certainly dominated the headlines in Asia.

So why were Kanchanalak's Thai clients telling the White House to play down such a threat? Because, no matter who was traveling on what passport or what the occasion was, the game was always the same: promote Beijing's propaganda line. Certainly Magaziner would have taken the message the PRC wanted back to the president. Shortly thereafter, Beijing was able to cut out the messenger and have its agents speak directly to Clinton in the White House.

COFFEE BREAK

Everything about the June 18, 1996, White House coffee organized by Pauline Kanchanalak ultimately became controversial— who the guests were, what they wanted, where it occurred, whether money was solicited on White House grounds, and all the foreign money flowing in and around it. DNC officials must have felt uncomfortable about this event because they initially tried to fight it off,[32] but John Huang, then the financial vice chair of the DNC, was insistent. He told one DNC official, "Pauline has been a big contributor, a big supporter. It goes back to… Ron Brown, and she's very high-maintenance."[33] The DNC caved, Pauline got her way, and the CP Group of Thailand had an opportunity to meet Clinton in the White House.

So, who's the CP Group of Thailand? A business conglomerate dominated by an ethnic Chinese family, the CP Group started in the wholesale chicken business. The group paid Thai farmers to raise chickens, and then marketed the meat around the country. In some mysterious fashion, during the early 1980s the CP Group managed to accumulate enough capital for an enormous expansion of its Thai business and to move into China. By the time of the White House coffee, the CP Group was the largest foreign investor in China. Its major partner on the mainland was Norinco, the arms merchant. Other companies operating in China were in awe of the CP Group's mainland connections. The CP Group was declared "unbeatable" by one Singapore-based joint-venture partner.[34] CP Group executives served as economic advisers to the PRC government, and they sat on the Beijing-picked hand-over committee for Hong Kong.[35]

The CP Group also has other, even more questionable, foreign business ties. During the Thompson committee investigation in 1997 one senator asked the CIA if the CP Group "does business with or in Iran, Iraq, Syria or Libya." The CIA gave only a classified answer. If its information had been innocuous, it would have said so.[36] Therefore we have to conclude that the CP Group is in business with terrorist nations.

Also controversial was the overtly Asian flavor of the White House coffee. At first, Huang and Kanchanalak wanted to limit the invitation to just her clients. But someone noticed that

Clinton would be appearing before a foreign audience, none of whom could legally donate to the Democrats. At the last moment, a pair of wealthy, legal DNC donors were added, perhaps for appearance's sake. The coffee, held in the Map Room of the White House, was opened by DNC Chairman Fowler, who compared Clinton to Abraham Lincoln.[37] John Huang, for his part, made an open pitch for money to the chairman of Thailand's CP Group in Clinton's presence. He said, "Elections cost money, lots of money, and I am sure that every person in this room will want to support the reelection of President Clinton."[38] The law prohibiting campaign solicitations in federal buildings (18 USC 607) makes no exception for any room in the White House. Furthermore, since the CP Group executives were not American citizens, soliciting them for campaign funds would have been legally dubious even if done at DNC headquarters.

Apparently the CP Group executives were not shy about telling Clinton what they wanted in return. They later bragged that they had made a pitch for more U.S. high-technology exports to China.[39]

Let's stop and look at this for a moment. One month after Norinco was caught by federal agents smuggling one thousand fully automatic machine guns into the United States for sale to drug gangs on the West Coast, its business associates were in the White House receiving an illegal campaign solicitation from John Huang. Norinco's agents, in turn, made a brazen pitch for more militarily useful American high-tech exports to China. All of this was made in front of and to the president of the United States! And, on the very same day, Congress was considering the PRC's most-favored-nation trade status.

NINA'S TOWER

History has shown that the direct route to Bill Clinton's heart is by way of campaign contributions to the DNC. It doesn't seem to matter if they are legal or not. There is also another route—contributing to a favorite Clinton charity.

Hong Kong billionaire Nina Wang took the second route with a $50,000 gift toward refurbishing Clinton's boyhood home in Hope, Arkansas. White House aide and Clinton fund-raiser Mark Middleton solicited the gift after she received a private tour of the White House.[40] For her generosity Mrs. Wang received the honor of a seat at the head table at one of John Huang's notorious fund-raisers.[41] Mrs. Wang's gift to the Clinton home was perfectly legal, but we'd like to ask

The direct route to Bill Clinton's heart is by way of campaign contributions to the DNC. It doesn't seem to matter if they are legal or not.

Middleton and Huang if that's where her largesse began and ended. Unfortunately, they've taken the Fifth Amendment.

Nina seems to be in Hong Kong these days tending to her real estate empire. Probably the richest woman in Asia, in November 1996 she applied to build a tower in Hong Kong that would have been the world's tallest. She named the proposed building "Nina's Tower"[42] and planned to pay cash for the building. She had the resources to accomplish her dream because as "chairlady" (her term) of the largest privately held company in Hong Kong, Chinachem Group, she is worth billions. Hong Kong height restrictions ultimately scuttled her project.

Nina Wang's ascension to really big money began with tragedy. She took over after her husband had been kidnapped and presumably murdered at sea while the kidnappers were being chased by the PLA navy. On August 9, 1990, a member of the Sun Yee On Triad group pleaded guilty to the crime.[43] Mrs. Wang refuses to agree to a legal declaration that her husband is dead, much to the consternation of her father-in-law, who would inherit his son's estate if he were legally dead. By refusing to admit her husband is dead after seven years, Nina continues to control a $3 billion empire.[44]

Mrs. Wang has another favorite charity—the Chinese PLA. For $7 million she is funding former Clinton official Joe Nye's PLA training program at Harvard.[45] Twenty scholarships to this program have been awarded to PLA officers so they can "attend seminars with top U.S. scholars, experts and officials."[46]

As part of their training, one group of PLA officers came down to Washington in the spring of 1998 to meet with Congress. After the Pentagon quietly informed the Hill that at least two of the PLA officers had participated in the Tiananmen massacre, House International Relations Committee Chairman Ben Gilman (R-NY) made certain they weren't welcome in his offices. According to the PRC's official Xinhua news agency, the officers managed to get themselves into a dispute with the Congressional Research Service over PLA missile intimidation of Taiwan. The Congressional Research Service did a commendable job of holding its ground against the PLA officers' arrogance and sarcasm.[47] Actually, the meeting with the Congressional Research Service was fairly short, as the PLA officers seemed more interested in shopping than in how democracy works.

It's not certain why Mrs. Wang decided to fund a multimillion-dollar U.S.A. shopping tour for PLA officers. It may be that she felt it might buy goodwill for her business deals with the PLA. One of these transactions is a possible joint venture with the PRC's Ministry of Defense to manufacture satellite receivers.[48]

LIEUTENANT COLONEL LIU CHAOYING
Maria Hsia, Pauline Kanchanalak, and Nina Wang—all have clearly been active players on the scene. But they are by no means the only women of the China connection. Consider PLA Lieutenant Colonel Liu Chaoying. She

■ Has made illegal contributions to the DNC through Clinton donor Johnny Chung, as Chung has now admitted.

- Has met Clinton twice at California fund-raisers.
- Is the daughter of the PLA's former top uniformed officer.
- Is a graduate of the PLA's high-tech spy academy.
- Was an official of two Chinese companies that were officially sanctioned by the U.S. government for arms trafficking.
- Is a significant player in the controversy surrounding Chinese satellite launches.
- Is a hard-line communist with an eye for fashionable western clothes.

Lieutenant Colonel Liu cannot be ignored. She will make more than one appearance on these pages....

EQUAL OPPORTUNITY

During the 1992 campaign, the media and many Democratic candidates proudly trumpeted the "Year of the Woman." Bill Clinton and Al Gore seem to have kept that proclamation in mind throughout their administration, as they have had close money ties to several remarkable women—remarkable in that they all are connected to the Chinese Communists.

Maria Hsia, Pauline Kanchanalak, and Nina Wang have not been loath to exploit their connections to the Clinton-Gore administration. Hsia, a known agent of the Chinese government who has been indicted for immigration and campaign fundraising scams, may well have helped Chinese spies get into the United States. Kanchanalak, who has been indicted for election law violations, brought leaders of a Thai conglomerate that is in business with Middle Eastern terrorists and with China's biggest arms smugglers to the White House to lobby the president himself. And Wang has given millions of dollars to enable PLA officers to come to the United States.

Apparently the Clinton-Gore administration does not discriminate against women—as long as their contributions keep rolling in.

PART TWO:
TRIADS AND
OTHER CROOKS

CHAPTER 8
A TALE OF THREE CITIES

Even if composed of hundred dollar bills, $175,000 in cash makes quite a bundle. We can only imagine what went through the minds of Treasury Department officials as Macau criminal syndicate figure Ng Lapseng sailed through the San Francisco airport on June 20, 1994, after declaring that amount of money—in cash. Within two days Ng was dining at the White House mess with presidential aide and Democratic Party fund-raiser Mark Middleton. Later that evening Ng and his associate Charlie Trie would make honored guest appearances at a DNC-sponsored Presidential Gala.

If an investigator runs Ng's trail back to his base of operations—Macau, the Portuguese-controlled enclave on the South China coast—he lands directly in the black world of Asian criminal gangs. At least two million dollars, much of it illegal, made its way from Macau and other Asian crime centers to Clinton-Gore money projects. We think it hardly coincidental that Ng would arrive like a white knight out of the East at the precise moment that Clinton intimate (and potential FBI informant) Webster Hubbell would have a cash-flow problem of his own.[1] Or that the DNC would be holding a fund-raiser. Nor do we think it coincidental that Ng would disappear back into the murky world of Macau as soon as congressional investigators started looking for him.

Our Tale of Three Cities—Macau, Los Angeles, and Phnom Penh (the capital of Cambodia)—explains how ethnic Chinese criminal gangs, called Triads,[2] created their own money conduit to the Clinton White House, for their own benefit and for their business partners in Beijing. They visited the White House many times, made illegal contributions to the Clinton-Gore reelection campaign, and were photographed at the place of honor beside the president and vice president of the United States.

TRIADS

The portion of East Asia dominated or influenced by ethnic Chinese is rife with Triads. Their origins are shrouded in legend: some say they originated centuries ago in China as legitimate underground opposition groups, resisting the tyranny of the imperial court and clinging to secrecy to protect against imperial agents. But even if they once were reminiscent of the Alliance in George Lucas's *Star Wars* movies, they have since turned into something more like what's found in the *Godfather* series of Francis Ford Coppola. As Hong Kong Commissioner of Police H.W.E. Heath put it, "[T]he Triad member is nothing more than a run-of-the-mill hoodlum masquerading in the name of a long-dead giant."[3]

The Chinese Triads and the Sicilian Mafia share certain characteristics—they're in the same lines of business. A 1988 U.S. Justice Department report listed Triad businesses as "narcotics trafficking, money laundering, contract murders, illegal gambling, loansharking, extortion, interstate prostitution rings and alien smuggling."[4]

Triads also share similar structure and membership recruitment characteristics with the Mafia. By far the best exposition of Triads is a manual prepared by the Royal Canadian Mounted Police in 1994 with assistance from Canadian immigration authorities.[5] Their aim was to separate law-abiding Chinese persons applying

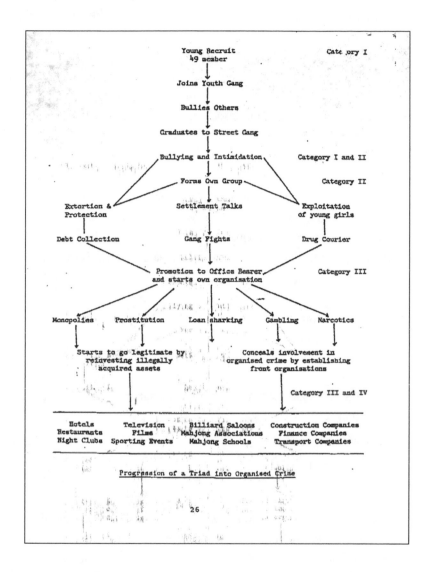

Progression of a Triad into Organised Crime

This Royal Canadian Mounted Police study shows how a Triad graduates from youthful bullying to prostitution, narcotics, loan-sharking, and gambling—and how he then infiltrates legitimate business.

for Canadian visas from Triad members. As part of the Mounties' study they created a "profile" of likely Triad recruitment and activities—"Progression of a Triad into Organized Crime." The Canadian profile shows the young hoodlum as he enters a youth gang, passes through adult activities including prostitution, loan-sharking, gambling, and narcotics, and then begins to infiltrate legitimate businesses such as hotels, restaurants, and night clubs. In carrying out their criminal activities, Triad members travel on passports of convenience, frequently Central or South American.[6]

The Mounties' report points out that, reminiscent of the Mafia, "once a triad, always a triad."[7] Once you're in, forget about getting out. In a grim ceremony, the initiate takes thirty-six oaths relative to obeying the Triad rules. The penalty for violating them is death.

As the Canadians point out, since a major goal of the Triads is to infiltrate legitimate business, their own appearance of legitimacy is important:

> Triad members work very hard at ingratiating themselves with police, government officials and politicians. The easiest way for them is by making substantial donations to charitable organizations, joining service clubs, donating funds to universities, sometimes obtaining honourary doctorate degrees, or contributing to political parties[8].... Public photographs of Triad figures with politicians is another favorite technique.[9]

The Mafia and the Triads part company when it comes to *political loyalties*. When presented with a choice between the Free World and Moscow after World War II, the Mafia went with the former. It's no longer a secret that the Mafia fought the communists to keep European docks open so that Marshall Plan goods from America could begin to rebuild the war-shattered economies of European nations. Even though their criminal activities help to undermine the social fabric of the United States (and other democracies), Mafia members consider themselves to be loyal Americans.

By contrast, the Triads appear to be more and more in the orbit of Beijing. One public signal of this was given by the late Chinese leader Deng Xiaoping when he said, "There are patriotic elements within the Triad world too."[10] The Chinese Public Security minister echoed Deng: "Not all of the Triads are bad. Some of them love the Motherland."[11] Hundreds of years ago the Triads supported the Chinese people against the totalitarian regime that oppressed them; now they've switched sides.

One way the Triads are proving their loyalty to Beijing is by facilitating the clandestine entry of PLA intelligence agents into its prime target, Taiwan. According to the Hong Kong press, Taiwan's ever vigilant intelligence service has spotted at least seventy PLA agents who have infiltrated the island through the efforts of Triad gangs.[12] There are even reports that Triad gangs have established a secret base along the China coast to train PLA agents to blend into Taiwan's free society.[13]

Chinese criminal gangs, called Triads, created their own money conduit to the Clinton White House, for their own benefit and for their business partners in Beijing.

With the rapid expansion of international trade, particularly trade originating in East Asia, the Triads have gone global. In 1995 the German newsmagazine *Die Welt* reported, "The Chinese criminal organization '14-K,' ill-famed for its brutality, has spread its international 'crime industry' to Germany, too."[14] The Germans were concerned that the Triad threat, which had been spotted in England, the Netherlands, and France, was headed their way. The specialty of the "14-K," third largest Triad in the world, is smuggling and distributing heroin, not something the German government would tolerate.

Worldwide press reports and government warnings place Triads in such diverse countries as South Africa, Romania, Poland, and even Italy, where they have been contesting turf with the Mafia. In South Korea they compete with Russian gangsters over lucrative business deals. The director of South Korea's National Security Planning Agency told his legislature, "Russian Mafias and Chinese organized crime groups armed with mass lethal weapons are trying to make inroads into our country."[15]

The Triads are now global, and they're now in the United States.[16] According to FBI Director Louis Freeh, testifying before the Senate Select Committee on Intelligence, "Asian Criminal Enterprises," including the Triads, have emerged as a significant and violent force in the United States, committing murder, extortion, drug trafficking, kidnapping, prostitution, weapons smuggling, money laundering, and home invasions.[17] The Justice Department's unpublished manuscript, *Report on Asian Organized Crime*, although circulated to law enforcement officers only, contains useful guidance for the professional concerned about Triad activity in the United States.[18]

As early as 1982, Triad leaders were trying to buy access to the Democratic Party. Before he fled the country for South America, New York City Triad leader Eddie Chan was bragging about his political contributions to former Congresswoman Geraldine Ferraro's (D-NY) reelection campaign.[19] The amount of money he actually contributed wasn't that high—$1,000, according to the *New York Times*—but it's useful to show intent.[20] A decade later—the Clinton-Gore era—the money would really begin to roll in.

But first, Macau.

MACAU

Macau ought to have a lot going for it. Just fifty minutes from Hong Kong by jetfoil, the Portuguese have managed to keep many of the pastel-colored colonial buildings from the wrecking ball. The food in family-run restaurants is excellent—Portuguese colonial with an African and Asian influence, spicy without being hot. Antique furniture from China sold in the shops on Rua de Sao

Paulo is just as good and much less expensive than on Hong Kong's Hollywood Road.

But fine dining and antique furniture are not what pay the bills in Macau. Prostitution and gambling do.

Children under twelve can stay for free at DNC-donor Ng Lapseng's Fortuna Hotel, if accompanied by their parents. But there were no children around when we visited on a Sunday afternoon in April 1998. Perhaps their parents were put off by the nearly life-sized color poster in the lobby of a stripper trying to get out of her bra. Or the companion poster of a scantily clad "table dancer" showing off her moves. The performers work upstairs at the fifth floor "night club" where women guests are not invited. The Fortuna has 20,000 square feet, plus thirty "VIP" rooms where a male guest can "enjoy your evening in a relaxed ambience along with our attractive hostesses who will offer you unparalleled attentive service."[21] According to another Fortuna Hotel brochure, the VIP rooms boast "attractive and attentive hostesses from China, Korea, Singapore, Malaysia, Vietnam, Indonesia and Burma together with erotic girls from Europe and Russia offer[ing] you an exciting and unforgettable evening with friends or business associates."[22]

The hostesses who work in and around the Fortuna are definitely "attractive." One shapely example walked into the lobby wearing black leather hot pants and matching halter top. An American woman observing this commented, "Well, her mother certainly didn't check her out when she left the house this morning!"

Through the lobby and into the back of the Fortuna's first floor is a coffee shop similar to that in any large hotel—except that it is infested with hoodlums. Evidently off duty, six Triad soldiers were gathered around a large table smoking and drinking. After a time, their squad leader, known as a "Bully Boy"[23] or "Red Pole,"[24] made his appearance. He was a powerfully built man of about thirty, with slick hair and long sideburns. When he sat down, he raised the back of his long black and silver embroidered silk shirt to reveal his working tools—pager, cell phone, and 9mm automatic pistol. Evidently he was a 1990s era gangster: traditionally, the Triad weapon of choice has been the fighting chopper or cleaver.[25]

Ng hasn't been seen on American soil since his role in the Clinton campaign money scandals surfaced, and he has refused to cooperate with congressional investigators. Before the Thompson committee began its hearings, John Pomfret of the *Washington Post* interviewed him in the coffee shop of the Fortuna. Ng wasn't there the days we visited, but Pomfret reports that Ng uses it for his office, scribbling "OK's" on credit extensions for mainland officials. Ng bragged to Pomfret, without giving details, of his mainland business enterprises, all of which are associated with Chinese government officials or the PLA. One of his major PRC partners seems to be arms dealer Wang Jun, the chairman of Poly Group.[26] He has complained to the Hong Kong press about American reports linking him to organized crime[27]—that is, to the Triads—even though his VIP rooms are reportedly under the control of one of the major Triad groups.[28]

Ng's partner in a number of business interests is another Clinton-associated figure, "Dr." Stanley Ho,[29] who has been called the "biggest gambler on earth."[30] Gambling is thought to be a particularly pernicious vice in Chinese societies, and it is banned in mainland China, Taiwan, Hong Kong, and Singapore. Therefore, any place in the region where gambling is legal, such as Macau, and any persons, such as Stanley Ho and his associates, who control the gambling licenses in Macau have a most lucrative monopoly.

In 1962 three men—Ho, Yip Hon, and Henry Fok—put together the ideal business group to take over the gambling casinos in Macau. Ho was the public face of the group; identified Triad figure Yip Hon[31] put up the money; and Fok had the vital PRC connections without which the deal would have failed. Fok first made his name by running United Nations–embargoed goods to China during the Korean War. His son was later convicted for trying to bring Chinese machine guns into the United States.[32]

But Beijing's undoubted gratitude to Fok for his Korean War service might not have been enough to protect their investment. From 1966 onward China was in the turmoil of the Cultural Revolution. Maoist madness spilled over the borders to communist-inspired riots in Hong Kong. Portugal was in no position to defend Macau and became subject to any level of extortion Beijing cared to impose. It now appears that Portuguese authorities paid the PRC "protection" money, and they did it with Nazi gold of dubious origin.

Lisbon admits that it acquired more than 160 tons of Nazi gold either directly from the Reichsbank or indirectly through Switzerland. Recently a Portuguese navy representative has confessed to having personally participated in transferring some of this gold through Macau to the mainland in 1966–1969. He and a noted Portuguese academic believe that the Portuguese government used the gold to buy off a Chinese invasion.[33] The World Jewish Restitution Organization in Israel has announced it will fully investigate these claims.

We do not, in fact, know if Ho or his partners had any role in or even knew of the Nazi gold transfer to the mainland. Had Ho been willing to cooperate with congressional investigators looking into Clinton-Gore campaign irregularities, he might have been asked about it. Whether he had any connection or not, Ho and his partners certainly benefited from the transaction even if by happenstance. An invasion of Red Guards in 1966 would have been terrible for business.

Without interference, the casino business in Macau has been excellent. The taxes Ho pays supports 30 percent of the Macau government's budget,[34] and he was still able to report a net profit of over $500 million in 1996.[35] That kind of money is certain to attract a criminal element—the Triads.

In the past few years Triad violence in and around the casinos and houses of prostitution have given Macau a Wild West reputation. Colorful characters with names like "Broken Teeth" have fought it out with rivals for control of the VIP rooms in the major casinos where the high rollers tend to congregate. Bombs have gone off, Triad soldiers have been assassinated at the doorsteps of major hotels, and attempts have been made on the lives of high-ranking Portuguese officials. Throughout, Stanley Ho has repeatedly denied any Triad connection to his casinos.[36] Or to himself.

Ho's Triad connections are really quite extensive. In addition to the seed money provided by his Triad partner Yip Hon in 1962, Ho's casinos operate in hotels owned by Triad leaders, making him their business associate, if not a partner.[37] And "Stanley Ho" appears in the Justice Department's list of Triad-associated figures.[38]

Stanley Ho and Ng Lapseng have announced their own "Rose Garden," a two billion dollar land development scheme in Macau. "Rose Garden," of course, refers to the White House Rose Garden, which Americans recognize as one of our most sacred places. Presidential initiatives to help improve the lives of all Americans are launched at this serene location just off the Oval Office. Much good for everyone has come from the president's garden. In the eyes of disabled veterans, Olympic athletes, Polish freedom fighters, and future leaders of America, the Rose Garden is seen as a touchstone of the power and majesty of the United States. Some years back, a young American Legion Boy's Nation representative, Bill Clinton, shook President Kennedy's hand in the Rose Garden. Even then, it has been widely reported, young Clinton dreamed of becoming president.

But Ho and Ng's "Rose Garden" seems to be a financial disaster. Built on reclaimed land in the old inner harbor of Macau, this "Rose Garden" is composed of a number of roughly twenty-story buildings—offices and apartments. The complex was thoughtfully designed, and decorative tiles make the buildings attractive. But when we visited there in July 1998 it was almost empty. Block after block of retail space was unleased. Looking up into the buildings we could see that inside they were mostly unfinished. Some of the construction has stopped, and grass grows through the foundations. According to sources in Hong Kong, the PRC's Ministry of State Security (China's KGB) plans to locate its southern headquarters in the Rose Garden.

The really large fortunes in Hong Kong were built on property developments. Ng and Ho evidently tried to do this on speculation, only to have seriously misjudged the market. They named their project the "Rose Garden" as an "inside joke" to demonstrate their White House connections and as a direct insult to America; we didn't see any roses planted there. Perhaps it reminded them of their time with Bill Clinton in Washington.

MACAU GOES TO WASHINGTON

As discovered by Chairman Dan Burton's House Government Reform and Oversight Committee, the connections of Ng Lapseng to Clinton and Gore are as follows:

- Ng transferred by wire anywhere from $1.1 million to $1.5 million to accounts controlled by Charlie Trie.[39] How Ng met Trie is unknown, but perhaps it was through mutually shared Triad connections. Of this amount, at least $645,000 made its way through Trie to the DNC as illegally laundered campaign contributions.
- Ng visited the White House twelve times.
- With Trie, Ng organized a function for the late Ron Brown in Hong Kong that some say became a DNC campaign solicitation event.[40]
- Ng attended a number of fund-raisers and even sat next to the president at some of them.[41] The Asian press tells us that

Ng was not able to communicate a basic greeting to the president in English, so table conversation was probably a bit limited.

Ng's bags of cash are interesting:

- *June 20, 1994:* Ng enters the U.S. with $175,000 in cash; June 22, 1994, Ng and Trie have lunch with Mark Middleton in the White House mess.
- *July 31, 1994:* Ng enters the U.S. with $42,000 in cash; he visits Middleton at the White House on August 1 and 2.
- *October 19, 1994:* Ng enters the U.S. with $25,000 in cash; he meets Middleton at the White House on October 20, 1994, the same day $99,970 arrives in Trie's account from abroad.
- *February 15, 1995:* Ng enters the U.S. with $12,000; he meets Middleton at the White House twice on the next day and finally sees Clinton in the White House residence.
- *February 18, 1996:* Ng enters the U.S. with $19,000 in cash; the next day he attends John Huang's Presidential Asian Dinner, and on February 20 he visits the White House to meet with DNC official Susan Lavine.
- *August 17, 1996:* Ng enters the U.S. with $70,000 in cash; the next day he attends President Clinton's Gala Birthday Bash, at which Trie also gives a check for $118,000.

Ng's grand total is $333,000 in suspect cash, on top of the $1,000,000–plus to Charlie Trie in wire transfers. It may be that the Fortuna coffee shop earns a profit, but at least some of Ng's money that poured into the Clinton-Gore reelection effort could have come from the degradation of women. We do not consider it coincidental that Ng would visit fund-raiser Middleton within forty-eight hours of arriving in the United States with bags of cash.

Or that this would happen repeatedly. Everyone connected to this business, even Trie's Arkansas accountant, has either fled the country or taken the Fifth Amendment. If they had been available to testify, the witnesses could have been asked if this was all the cash Ng brought into the country. (Doubtful, in our estimation.) They could also have been asked if any or all of the cash had been used for illegal campaign contributions or some other illicit purpose, including obstruction of justice or witness tampering (hush money). Ng's Triad and Beijing connections could have been seriously explored.

As we saw in the case of Nina Wang, it's not necessary to make a contribution to the DNC to come to President Clinton's notice. Consider the case of Stanley Ho: According to MSNBC News, Ho handed a $250,000 check directly to Clinton at a White House reception to support a memorial honoring President Franklin D. Roosevelt. In fact, Ho may have given as much as $500,000 to fund the memorial.[42]

According to Hong Kong sources, Ng Lapseng, Chinese agent Ted Sioeng, and others are partners in a firm called "Ang-Du International." At the request of Sioeng's daughter, two officials of Ang-Du International (Thailand), including a Macau politician serving as its president, were honored guests at a Clinton fundraiser in May 1996.[43] Micah Morrison of the *Wall Street Journal* reports that Ang-Du procures Thai women for Macau brothels.[44] Had the Ang-Du officials not fled the country, they could have been asked if the women in question were underage or had been forcibly abducted for prostitution. They could also have been asked if Ang-Du profits had made their way to the DNC as part of Ng's various illegal contributions. It would be interesting to know if President Clinton knew or cared that among the assorted Chinese agents and other undesirables supporting his reelection at Washington's luxurious Sheraton Carlton Hotel that night was a group of men who profited from the exploitation of women.

LOS ANGELES: THE CHINA CONNECTION

In the summer of 1997 one senator was dissatisfied with the pace of the FBI-CIA investigation of the "China Connection" to Clinton-Gore fund-raising. And, in truth, the investigation was out of gas at that moment. In a meeting with FBI Director Louis Freeh and CIA Director George Tenet, the senator presented them with a series of questions—in essence a road map—and asked them to follow it. They agreed.

Did President Clinton know or care that he was consorting with Chinese agents and a group of men who profited from the exploitation of women?

In mid-September Freeh and Tenet came back to Capitol Hill with their hair on fire. They had to admit that critical information on the China Connection had been in FBI files for at least two years but that, without this senator's road map, they would never have been able to find it. As Senator Arlen Specter put it in a powerful Senate floor speech, "Absent that request by [the senator]... we would not have the important link as we seek to understand the puzzle." Senator Specter went on to question whether the FBI had deliberately withheld the information or "was not competent enough to know what information it had in its own files."[45] This was the polite equivalent of a public flogging, and the bureau deserved it.[46] Shortly thereafter the newspapers began to report on personnel shake-ups at the FBI.

The subject of the FBI's embarrassment was Ted Sioeng and his family, sometimes of Los Angeles. Sioeng is a wealthy businessman with business interests in China, Singapore, Macau, and other Asian countries. His long sideburns (similar to those of the Triad squad leader in the Fortuna) make him easy to spot in photographs with Clinton or Gore. He travels on a passport from Belize (Central America).

Sioeng and his family fit the same dreary pattern we have seen repeated over and over: They are DNC donors to the tune of hundreds of thousands of dollars worth of illegally laundered foreign money; they have had close personal contact with Clinton and Gore; they have been identified by the CIA as agents of Chinese intelligence; and they have fled the country or taken the Fifth Amendment—the Riadys, John Huang, Maria Hsia, Clinton crony Charlie Trie, Ng Lapseng, Pauline Kanchanalak, Lieutenant Colonel Liu Chaoying, Clinton donor Johnny Chung, and on and on and on.

First, the money: At least $400,000 to the DNC, all illegal.[47]

Second, the personal contact with Clinton and Gore: probably Vice President Gore would prefer not to have been photographed sitting down to lunch at the Hsi Lai Buddhist Temple with Sioeng to his left, Maria Hsia to his right, and John Huang hovering in the background. Sioeng also organized three more major fund-raisers at which he sat at the head table with Clinton.[48] On one occasion, he brought forty-eight friends or business associates to a Los Angeles fund-raiser and sat to the president's immediate right. To the president's left was James Riady and his wife Aileen.[49] We do not know if either Clinton or Gore felt comfortable surrounded by Chinese agents or their representatives.

According to the CIA information given to the Thompson committee, Sioeng (1) works for the Chinese government, (2) communicated frequently with the PRC embassy and consulates, and (3) traveled to Beijing frequently for briefings by CCP officials.[50]

The Sioeng family owns a hotel in Los Angeles. Thompson committee investigators found a number of curious financial dealings between the hotel and the notorious PRC consulate in Los Angeles.[51] We surmise that the Sioeng family might be providing accommodations to important PRC nationals or some other service to the Chinese government.

At the request of the Sioeng family, an official of the China Construction Bank was included at the same Clinton fund-raiser that the Ang-Du officials attended.[52] On March 10, 1997,

Newsweek reported that the China Construction Bank had received a favorable license application to do business in the United States even though its financial status was extremely shaky. One senator asked the CIA what advice it had given to the Federal Reserve relative to the application, but it refused to give an unclassified answer.[53]

Certainly the most significant known service the Sioeng family has performed for the Chinese government is the takeover of a Chinese-language newspaper in Los Angeles. Prior to the change of management, the *International Daily News* was mildly pro-Taiwan. Afterwards, it became "breathlessly pro-Beijing," as *Newsweek* put it.[54] As the Democrats pointed out in the Thompson report, "It is untenable, therefore, to claim that Sioeng's expenditure of $3 million to purchase a money-losing newspaper was solely motivated by a desire to facilitate cigarette advertisements."[55]

Ted Sioeng and every member of his family who might know anything about this affair have fled the country. The sole exception, daughter Jessica, has taken the Fifth Amendment.[56]

Is Sioeng a communist, in the sense of a Marxist-Leninist? Doubtful, in our estimation. Not being able to ask his motivations, we have to surmise based on his circumstances. In addition to being a partner in Ng Lapseng's prostitution ring, Sioeng has other lucrative business interests. According to CIA information provided to the Senate, Sioeng was "granted government right to manufacture and export [PRC brand] Hongtashan (Red Pagoda Mountain) cigarettes throughout the world." As a result he has become a very wealthy man.[57] Not bad for an Indonesian orphan taken in by a Chinese family fifty years ago. Since PRC government concessions can be withheld as easily as given out, it would have made him very grateful to the CCP.

But Sioeng doesn't stop at pimping and running errands for the PRC. He also has ties to a narcotics trafficker.

PHNOM PENH

In the spring of 1975 the Khmer Rouge communist army took over Phnom Penh along with the rest of Cambodia. Its murderous rampage later became known as "The Killing Fields," and the capital of the country was transformed into a true "City of Death." In time the Khmer Rouge suffered internal divisions, with one faction backed by Beijing and another backed by Hanoi. At the cost of fifty thousand Vietnamese soldiers' lives, Hanoi prevailed, and its man Hun Sen rules in Phnom Penh.

But nothing is as easy as that. Hanoi's prime supporter, the Soviet Union, is no more, and now Beijing is rich. Accordingly, Hun Sen, the "former" Khmer Rouge faction chief, maintains uneasy relations with both of the communist rivals. And Hun Sen has a new financial backer, Cambodian businessman Theng Bunma.

Theng—of interest to us because he is, according to the *Far Eastern Economic Review*, Cambodia's most significant narcotics trafficker—is an ethnic Chinese with strong PRC connections, a business associate of Ted Sioeng, and a visitor to the United States.

Theng's narcotics trafficking business has been amply documented.[58] With regard to his support for Hun Sen, Theng even bragged to the press that he had financed the summer 1997 coup that consolidated Hun Sen's power.[59]

In its January 13, 1998, issue, the *Far Eastern Economic Review* (a Dow-Jones publication) revealed Theng's extensive ties to fugitive DNC donor Ted Sioeng. Reporter Bruce Gilley had discovered the two of them together at Theng's Intercontinental Hotel in Phnom Penh. The occasion was Theng's receipt of an honorary doctorate from America's Iowa Wesleyan College. The college had awarded an honorary doctorate to Sioeng at some earlier time, perhaps in exchange for donations. Theng and Sioeng also together attended a business conference in China where CCP Politburo Standing Committee member Li Ruihuan called on overseas Chinese "to act as a bridge between China and the world."[60]

Theng's notoriety has made him unacceptable in the United States, but he has entered twice on Clinton's watch. On the first occasion, in 1994, he was given a visa to attend the National Prayer Breakfast, at which Mother Teresa was the guest speaker.[61]

Since he is unavailable for testimony, we have not been able to ask him if he met President Clinton there.

> But Sioeng—who has sat at fund-raisers with both Clinton and Gore—does not stop at pimping and running errands for the PRC.

The greatest mystery surrounds Theng's second visit to Washington. In February 1994 U.S. Ambassador to Cambodia Charles Twining told the highest levels of the Cambodian government not to get involved with Theng because he was a narcotics trafficker. So the State Department was on notice of his activities. But in April 1994 the U.S. embassy in Phnom Penh granted Theng a visa to visit Washington with an official Cambodian delegation.[62] In Washington, Theng seems to have disappeared. He didn't make the rounds with the rest of the delegation. In spite of a lot of Capitol Hill pressure, the Clinton administration has never been able to explain why Theng received a U.S. visa or his whereabouts during the visit.

CONCLUSION

It is precisely on the issue of Ng's cash that an independent counsel's vigorous investigation is necessary. The appearance of large sums of cash in the political process is an important sign of high-level corruption. Federal investigators have known about Ng's affairs since at least the beginning of 1998 but, as of this writing, nothing has been done about it. Nor are we encouraged by the fact that the Justice Department chose to indict Charlie Trie for conspiring to "defraud" the DNC.[63] Making out the DNC to be in any way a victim is an absurdity on its face. There was, moreover, no mention of Ng's cash activities in the Trie indictment, leaving us to wonder about official incompetence or worse. In our view, this is of a piece with Justice's failure to prosecute John Huang for money laundering in the 1992 campaign and its failure to prosecute any high-level officials to date.

CHAPTER 9
CHARLIE TRIE

B y late winter of 1996, when the PRC was trying to derail Taiwan's democratic elections by firing missiles into nearby Pacific waters, the PLA also had nuclear missiles targeted on Los Angeles. And it threatened to use them to force the United States to back down from its historic commitment to the independence of anticommunist Taiwan. The threat worked.

It was not delivered through public or diplomatic channels, but by a fry cook from a Chinese restaurant in Little Rock, who had no serious education and no foreign policy experience. This man placed a strategic memo in front of the president at a time of international crisis, resulting in a reply that changed a long-established element of foreign policy. Only in Bill Clinton's America.

The messenger was Yah Lin "Charlie Trie," Chinese gangster, Little Rock chef, DNC fund-raiser, and current criminal defendant. To Trie, the president of the United States is "Lao Ke" or "Old Clinton."[1] According to the *Los Angeles Times*, "When they meet, the two men embrace like lost brothers."[2]

Trie belongs to a secret Chinese criminal society: he is a member of the "Four Seas" Triad gang. The authors uncovered this unsavory fact in private conversations with senior Taiwanese officials.[3] We do not make this charge lightly. We reconfirmed Trie's Triad connection after conferring with informed persons in

Taiwan and with credible media sources who for understandable reasons (Triad "soldiers" are extremely creative killers) must remain unnamed.

Trie was born in Taichung, Taiwan, on August 15, 1949; he emigrated to the United States, settling in Little Rock to work with his sister Dailin Outlaw; he worked his way up from busboy to cook to co-owner, with his sister, of the Fu Lin Chinese Restaurant.

His Taiwan background tells us more. He grew up in a military housing environment known on Taiwan for producing individuals with a somewhat casual attitude toward the law. He was one of what the *Asia Times* called "children of mainlanders who had followed the Nationalist government's retreat to Taiwan in 1949 and had begun [criminal Triad activity] by engaging in street fights and the collection of protection money."[4]

Apparently allowed to lie low in Little Rock, Trie became of service when the permanent campaign began to accelerate Clinton's political fortunes in Arkansas. He began to befriend the young and obviously ambitious politician as soon as he arrived in Little Rock. The friendship grew. It seems they traveled together to Taiwan while Clinton was governor. By the time Bill Clinton took the oath of office as president, he was perfectly positioned to help his friend Charlie, and vice versa.

As a tool for the PRC and the Triads, Trie had the advantage of not having to face the question of "where he came from." He had been in Little Rock since sometime in the late 1970s, and had known the Clintons for almost as long. His relationship with them was not something that, on its face, cried out for explanation. Thus, Trie was the perfect Triad/PRC messenger and "agent in place," ready to be reactivated without suspicion. As the Canadian study of Triad behavior points out, "Once a Triad, always a Triad."

At some point around 1992, Trie acquired a business partner— Ng Lapseng, the Triad-connected tycoon from Macau. Trie and

Ng went into the real estate business. They had no success in the U.S. real estate market, but they didn't really need it; Ng had and has plenty of successful businesses in Macau. This fact becomes important when we turn to Trie's mysterious donation to the Clinton Legal Defense Trust on March 21, 1996. Their U.S. real estate business, it seems, was a cover—a "loss leader" for their political influence.

THE UNITED STATES, COMMUNIST CHINA, AND TAIWAN

Ever since Chinese anticommunists fled to Taiwan to escape Mao's advancing armies in 1949, the United States has guaranteed Taiwan's independence against Communist China's threats of forcible "reunification."

President Eisenhower's policy was "not to let the ChiComs get away with murder in the China Sea."[5] Nor would he "sit idly by and permit the Reds to build up any large force on the mainland for an invasion."[6]

From Ike, skip ahead three decades. In March 1996 Taiwan was preparing for a national ritual that the PRC seems to find inherently menacing—elections. For the previous four months, stories had been flying in the Hong Kong press to the effect that the PRC would strike Taiwan militarily if Taiwan went through with its balloting. What the PLA did, when Taiwan's elections proceeded on schedule, was to give a precision display of the accuracy of its intermediate range ballistic missiles (IRBM): it "bracketed" Taiwan with them, firing a few into the Pacific just off the north and south ends of the island. These were "blanks," with "dummy" warheads, but all the same, the demonstration was the first time that IRBMs were ever fired in anger.

Thanks to the *Wall Street Journal*, the PRC's hostile stance toward Taiwan's elections was known in the West in January 1996. Had the U.S. response been left up to then–Secretary of Defense William Perry, there would have been none. Perry was too busy arranging a smooth U.S. visit for his PLA counterpart, General Chi. But political operatives in the White House prevailed on the president with the argument that it would be foolish to abandon Taiwanese democracy in an election year, so Clinton sent battle groups from the Seventh Fleet, including its two largest aircraft carries, the *Independence* and the *Nimitz,* into the Taiwan Straits. This time, Clinton did the right thing, even if for political reasons.

Charlie Trie was the perfect Triad/PRC messenger and "agent in place," ready to be reactivated without suspicion.

But the story does not end there. We now know that the PLA was up to far more than just local war games: *the PLA was threatening Los Angeles with nuclear weapons.* According to former Reagan Defense official Frank Gaffney, Jr., "a top Chinese official intimated to the longtime No. 2 man at the U.S. embassy in Beijing that such an attack against Los Angeles would be in prospect if the United States interfered in China's campaign of intimidation against Taiwan."[7]

In addition to this direct method of getting its bellicose message through to the United States, the PRC used one more channel— Charlie Trie carrying a letter, and a bag of money.

A DAY IN THE LIFE OF CHARLIE TRIE

On the morning of March 21, 1996, Trie dropped off hundreds of thousands of dollars to the president and first lady's favorite "charity," the Presidential Legal Defense Trust. The report of the Senate Committee on Governmental Affairs strongly suggests that then–White House aide Mark Middleton, part of the Arkansas apparat, "directed Trie to the Trust as opposed to Clinton/Gore '96 or the DNC, where the contributions would have received much greater scrutiny and been subject to FEC guidelines."[8] On the same day, Trie also delivered to the White House the letter about the situation in Taiwan. Under the circumstances, we have to consider that the money came from both the PRC and Triad activity.

The Presidential Legal Defense Trust was a legal mechanism for allowing Americans to give the president money to cover his attorneys' fees. The trustees of this fund were a blue-ribbon assembly capable of handling a broad array of possible ethical dilemmas; but one doubts that even they were prepared for a Chinese courier with nearly half a million dollars in one hand and a letter threatening a major global crisis in the other.

The Clinton administration will no doubt characterize this as yet another of the amazing coincidences that have dogged the Clintons since their Arkansas days.

Trie's first errand on March 21, 1996, was to see the fund's executive director, Michael Cardozo, at the office of G. William Miller (treasury secretary under President Carter). Trie opened an envelope, and $460,000 in checks and money orders spilled out. As Cardozo counted the money, Trie excused himself to go to a scheduled lunch at the tony Palm Restaurant with Mark Middleton. (Middleton, of course, has since become the only White House aide to plead the Fifth.)

At the Palm lunch, Trie gave Middleton a high-priority letter to be delivered immediately to the White House. At 1:14 PM—minutes after Trie's lunch ended—Middleton faxed a letter from Trie addressed to the president. The immediate recipient was Maureen Lewis, who handled the president's personal correspondence.[9] Middleton's cover note read:

Dear Maureen,

As you know, Charlie is a personal friend of the President from L.R. [Little Rock]. He is also a major supporter.

The President sat beside Charlie at the big Asian fundraiser several weeks ago.

Thanks for your always good assistance.

Personally, Mark

The letter did get to Clinton's desk. The Thompson committee reprinted the letter in its entirety; here is its text, all phrasings and spellings preserved:

Dear President,

Regarding the currant situation in the Taiwan Strait Crisis and also the U.S. aircraft carriers and cruisers involvement, I would like to propose some important points to you in order not to endanger the U.S. interest based on the followings:

1. Any negative outcomes of the U.S. decision in the China Issue will affect your administration position especially in the campaign year.

2. Why U.S. has to sent the aircraft carriers and cruisers to give China a possible excuse of foreign intervention and hence launch a real war? And, if the U.S. recognizes "one China" policy, don't such conduct will cause a conflict for "intervening China's internal affairs?" Therefore, won't the recent inconsistent talks by the captains and some governmental officials in the mass media cause problems for the U.S. policy of not interference of China's internal affairs?

3. With the Chinese background and the recent six years business experiences in China and Taiwan, I think the U.S. senators and Congressmen do not fully know that most Chinese don't expect the intervention from the U.S.

4. Before last June, there is no conflict between the common goal of economic growth and cooperations of China and Taiwan, Li's visit [Taiwan President Lee Teng-hui's visit to his alma mater, Cornell University] is the direct cause of the crisis.

5. Has the U.S. government considered if China starts to occupy the two small outer islands (Wu Chiu and Ma Tzu), will the U.S. proclaim war against China? or just withdraw its ships?

6. The complication of China's internal problems of military challenges to the Jiang Tze-Ming adminstration, together with other possible independence movements from Tibet, Inner Mongolia, Xin-Jiang

and the returning of Hong Kong issue, the bluff to Taiwan Independence issue, Will U.S. be involved in such complicated internal matter by showing up the military ships at present moment?

7. Once the hard parties of the Chinese military inclined to grasp U.S. involvement as foreign intervention, is U.S ready to face such challenge?

8. It is highly possible for China to launch real war, based on its past behavior in sino-vietnam war[10] and then Bao-Tao war with Russia.[11]

I hope the president will carefully consider these issues and make the decisions that are beneficial to the U.S./China and Taiwan altogether.

Yours sincerely,

Charlie Y.L. Trie

It doesn't take a degree in international relations or military strategy to see in this letter a direct threat against the actions of the United States should it act in accordance with its long-established commitment to defend Taiwan. Robert L. Suettinger, an Asia hand on the NSC staff, wrote a memo to then-NSC Director Anthony Lake characterizing the Trie letter as "a rather provocative letter about U.S. actions taken prior to the presidential election on Taiwan." "The reply," Suettinger continued, "reassures Trie that the U.S. has no hostile intentions toward the PRC, and the situation has returned to a calmer state."[12]

The PLA was up to far more than just local war games: the PLA was threatening Los Angeles with nuclear weapons.

Despite the odd grammar and syntax, which make the letter sound as if it had been translated from Mandarin by someone with one year of English and a dictionary, the reasoning has a steely precision. It sends a number of related strategic messages: Get out of the PRC's face or it'll cut off your campaign allowance; the presence of the Seventh Fleet in the strait is an "intervention in China's internal affairs"; "hardliners" in the PRC are about to get really mad; they just might "launch real war."

But is it "they"—or "I"? Is this really a back-channel letter from the highest political and military authorities of the PRC or is it a letter from Bill Clinton's neighborhood chef and fund-raiser?

Viewed from the point of view of English composition, the letter just might have been written by Trie. But from the point of view of reasoning, that's all but impossible. Trie's work-product— the "Trie Report,"[13] as some have generously called it—from his service on the Commission on the United States Pacific Trade and Investment Policy, to which President Clinton had gone to great lengths to appoint him, makes clear his limitations as an abstract reasoner.[14] The report was labeled by other commission members as "superficial, grammatically deficient, and generally unhelpful."[15] One witness interviewed by the Thompson committee called it "completely incomprehensible."[16] But the letter he sent to Clinton via Middleton is different. While the "Trie Report" is airy, the letter is blunt. While the report means nothing, the letter means business. And—more to the point—while the report rings with biz-school clichés, the only clichés in the letter are those all too familiar from official statements emanating from Beijing. One of these is "intervening in China's internal affairs," a standard Beijing byword for outside criticism of its miserable human rights record, or for international concern for the independence of Taiwan—which, of course, is not an "internal" matter at all, except in the PRC's fantasy world, in which Taiwan is a "renegade province" of the mainland.

On reading the letter, Clinton must have known instantly that its contents did not originate with Charlie Trie. Perhaps that is why he took it so seriously.

Besides the possibility that Clinton recognized an order from Beijing and responded accordingly, there is one other explanation, a Clinton administration favorite—the White House ineptitude defense. This explanation would imply that the Clinton foreign policy team—the president included—is a bunch of lightweights who folded like bedsheets when threatened by Trie. Only in Bill Clinton's Washington would this be a theory for the *defense*. Frankly, we would like to think better of those who make our country's foreign policy. They are not stupid: they are just doing their job for a man who has lost—if he ever had one—his moral compass.

Clinton's NSC drafted a reply by Clinton that, unfortunately, marks a humiliating retreat from the historic American policy of guaranteeing the independence of Taiwan from Communist China. The president signed it, and it was sent to Trie—and, we must assume, to whatever paymasters Trie was serving when he sent his letter to Clinton. The letter in response, sent on April 26, read as follows:

> Dear Charlie:
> Thank you for the letter you sent me via Mark Middleton.
> I hope that events since you wrote have clarified U.S. policy, but let me mention some additional points. U.S. policy at the time, particularly the redeployment of the *Independence* and the *Nimitz*, was intended as a signal to both Taiwan and the PRC that the United States was concerned about maintaining stability in the Taiwan Strait region. It was not intended as a threat to the PRC. Moreover, we made clear to both sides that U.S. interests were engaged in the region, and that we wished for PRC-Taiwan disputes to be resolved through peaceful means.
> We all are glad that tensions in the Strait have receded since that time, and the actions we took played a part in that development. It was good to hear from you.
> Sincerely,
> Bill Clinton

This letter was a precursor to the complete sell-out of Taiwan that Clinton announced during his July 1998 trip to China. If the letter had stopped after "maintaining stability in the Taiwan Straight region," it would not have signaled any fundamental change in U.S. policy toward Taiwan. But it went on to say that the U.S. carrier battle groups deployed to the Taiwan Strait were, in the words of "Old Clinton" to his good friend Charlie, "not intended as a threat to the PRC."

Then why were they there? To threaten Taiwan?

Adding that sentence exposed the United States' real Taiwan policy. The import of Clinton's reply is that the Clinton administration will no longer be prepared to deter Beijing in any menacing actions it may care to take toward Taiwan. Formerly linked to Taiwan by a shared rejection of communism, the United States now views Taiwan and the PRC as morally interchangeable entities ("both sides") who just happen to have an inexplicable quarrel that could threaten "U.S. interests" if not "resolved through peaceful means."

Clinton folded in the face of pressure from Beijing, delivered in a letter by a Triad gang member who has been indicted for making illegal contributions to the DNC.

Clinton folded in the face of pressure from Beijing, delivered in a letter by a man whose previous experience was as a "made" member of a Triad gang, a fry cook, a member of the Arkansas Fire Extinguisher Board, a big-time DNC donor whose checks were returned under a cloud, who is now under indictment for violating election laws.

But do gestures like Clinton's reply to Trie, or even his public rejection of Taiwan in July 1998, really have serious consequences? Sometimes they do not—but then again, sometimes they start wars. President Truman's secretary of state, Dean Acheson, gave a speech in 1950 in which he described U.S. security interests around the world—but did not mention South Korea. This omission gave the PRC and its North Korean satellite-state the impression that the United States did not care about the future of South Korea. Six months later, the Korean War broke out. The United

States never made the same mistake about Taiwan, and, consequently, the Chinese Communists knew better than to attack that island, the refuge of Chinese anticommunists.

Now that has changed.

COVERING UP THE TRIE DONATION

Meanwhile, back at the Presidential Legal Trust, an innovative cover-up was in progress.

Cardozo and the fund trustees had cause for alarm. Cardozo and his board were smart Washington players; some of them had experience battling Richard Nixon's abuses of power in Watergate. A large donation from a Little Rock fry cook turned clientless consultant was not something they could accept in the ordinary course of business. But rather than go to the U.S. attorney, or to outside counsel, they seem to have gone to Hillary Clinton.

In an April 4, 1996, White House meeting, the first lady began by pretending not to recognize Trie's name, but then, according to the Thompson report, she "recalled him as the owner of a restaurant in Little Rock frequented by then-Governor Clinton."[17] The impression left is that the governor and Trie were close, but that the Arkansas first lady did not like Chinese food. Or perhaps it was just Charlie's cooking.

But Mrs. Clinton's vagueness was a clever ruse. Trie had interacted frequently with Bill and Hillary alike, both in Little Rock and later in Washington, including at White House and DNC dinners where they were at the president's table. In one memo the Clinton's team wanted to reward Trie at a DNC VIP fund-raiser ("B" table at minimum) because, according to one aide, "he gave 100k that I believe went to healthcare."[18] Another function honoring DNC managing trustees (those generous individuals who either raised more than $250,000 or wrote $100,000 checks to the DNC in 1994) had Trie sitting at the first lady's table on February 15, 1995.[19]

But the most telling Trie/HRC connection was a 1995 phone message in the White House just before the first lady's Beijing trip: "Mr. Charlie Tree [*sic*] of Little Rock called, spoke with HRC in Little Rock about going to Beijing. Wants to know if he can go with her."[20]

So Hillary knew Charlie a little better than she let on. All the more reason why she would recognize that his check-stuffed envelope was indeed the sort of thing that Clinton loyalists had better investigate before an independent counsel did. So the fund trustees decided to investigate the source of Trie's money, and for that purpose they hired Terry Lenzner and his firm, Investigative Group, Inc. But Cardozo put one condition on the investigation: It should not look into Trie himself, because he was close to the Clintons. The investigation turned up some allegations of money being transferred through a Buddhist sect (not the famous Al Gore fundraiser), but Trie was kept out of it. Eventually, however, the Clinton Legal Defense Trust returned the entire $640,000 that Trie had delivered.

CONCLUSION

We do not yet know, with precision, the source of Trie's donation to the Clinton Legal Defense Trust, but given what we know of Trie's background, the probability that his cash came either from the Chinese government or from Triad crime activity through his business partner Ng Lapseng, or from both working together, is high. This cash bought Trie access for his letter and respect for its message; that message in turn brought about a critical and long-sought change—long sought by the PRC, that is—in U.S. foreign policy.

Bill Clinton sold Taiwan's security to the PRC.

In January 1998 the Department of Justice handed down an indictment of Trie for campaign finance violations. But don't expect Trie to tell very much. For one thing, Janet Reno's Justice

Department is not asking very much: the indictment avoids references to the Chinese government and makes Clinton's DNC sound like a passive victim of Trie's machinations. But there is another reason why Trie will clam up. A Triad ceremony called "The Thirty Six Oaths of The Hung Mun" sets forth in detail the rules for a member of a Triad. Rule #18: "If I am arrested after committing an offense I must accept my punishment and not try to place the blame on my sworn brothers. If I do so I will be killed by five thunderbolts."[21]

PART THREE:
CHINA'S CONTINUING THREATS

CHAPTER 10
PENETRATING THE SYSTEM

I t must have been embarrassing. In March 1997 the DNC was forced to return another $37,500 in illegal campaign funds from Chinese sources.[1] The donor, Chun Hua Yeh, a non-U.S. citizen, had sat at President Clinton's table during a fund-raiser in the summer of 1996. He turned out to be the chairman of a small bank in southern California suspected by U.S. banking regulators of being controlled by foreign interests and, perhaps more important, in partnership with a branch of China's armed forces, the Commission on Science, Technology, and Industry for National Defense (COSTIND). As the *Wall Street Journal* put it, "The specter of President Clinton sitting down to dinner with a contributor beholden to China's military is another indication of the laxness of the Democratic Party's fund-raising process."[2]

"Laxness" is a generous characterization; "reckless disregard for the national security of the United States" would have been more accurate.

COSTIND has three main functions. First, it coordinates all of China's research on weapons of mass destruction—nuclear, chemical, and biological—and the missile systems to deliver them. Second, it is an arms-smuggling outfit. Third, it is one of the PRC's intelligence agencies. In the opinion of American defense specialist Nicholas Eftimiades, "COSTIND personnel engage in espionage by attempting to steal foreign technology with military applications, primarily from the United States."[3]

From both journalistic and senatorial rostrums,[4] the accusations went forth throughout the first half of 1997 to the effect that China had tried to influence the 1996 elections through donations to the DNC. Understandably, these charges, and the White House's denials, dominated the campaign finance headlines that year. We believe, however, that an important distinction needs to be made between the PRC's long-term, and mostly successful, intelligence operations aimed at the United States, and a one-time response to a particular PRC-perceived problem.

> **Chinese agents and gangsters have sat beside the president at fund-raisers. Millions of dollars in suspect political contributions have had to be returned.**

The charges made by *Washington Post* reporter Bob Woodward, Senator Fred Thompson, and others relate to the CCP's anger over a 1995 U.S. visa granted to President Lee Teng-hui of the Republic of China on Taiwan. Dr. Lee has a Ph.D. in agricultural economics from Cornell University and wished to make a nonofficial visit to his alma mater. Since Dr. Lee is the leader of a democratic country with which the United States has had friendly ties for more than fifty years, the visit seemed eminently reasonable to most Americans, the United States Congress,[5] and, ultimately, President Clinton. But the Chinese Communists went ballistic, showering nuclear-capable missiles at Taiwan in July 1995. Clearly, the Chinese Communists' rage over any courtesy extended to Taiwan was one factor motivating them to beef up their influence in Washington. All the same, we believe that the PRC's long-term penetration program was—and is—far more insidious.

TARGET: AMERICA

Since at least the mid-1980s the FBI has known that the PRC considers the United States a primary target for espionage, subversion, and illegal technology acquisition. In 1987 James Geer, the FBI's assistant director for intelligence, told a group of former U.S. intelligence officers that China's intelligence service was a growing menace. Geer told his audience that the PRC was engaged in a "massive effort to steal U.S. defense secrets and recruit Americans as spies."[6]

The following year Special Agent Harry Godfrey III, chief of FBI counterintelligence, gave an extraordinary interview with the *Los Angeles Times*.[7] First he identified China as "the most active foreign power engaged in the illegal acquisition of American technology." He then made the following claim:

> We know they are running operations here. We have seen cases where they have encouraged people to apply to the CIA, FBI, Naval Investigative Service, and other Defense agencies. They have also attempted to recruit people at our research facilities at Los Alamos and at Lawrence Livermore.[8]

For whatever reasons, Mr. Godfrey's successors have not felt free to make such strong public comments on the intelligence threat posed by the PRC.

In October 1992 U.S. Customs Service agents arrested Chinese spy Bin Wu and his associates. Wu is currently serving a ten-year term at the Federal Correctional Institution in Loretto, Pennsylvania, for illegally exporting to China the sort of night-vision devices used by American tanks in the Gulf War.[9] Wu has cooperated at least partially with federal authorities and has provided a rare and useful look at the inside of Chinese intelligence, particularly with regard to recruiting agents.[10]

Wu's story begins around the time of the Tiananmen Square massacre in Beijing (June 3–4, 1989). It is not widely known outside of China, but the pro-democracy rally that was brutally suppressed in Beijing was accompanied by similar demonstrations and uprisings around the country. The government was later forced to admit that pro-democracy rallies took place in 123 Chinese cities during the spring of 1989.[11] Bin Wu, according to his narrative to the FBI, was a participant in one of these local movements, while serving as a lecturer at a university in central China. As a result of his political activities, he found himself under investigation and out of a job—not an unusual predicament for Chinese dissidents. Nor is it surprising that he decided it was time to leave the country.

But in order to leave China, one needs a passport and an exit permit. While waiting for his documents to be approved, Wu was ordered to the office of the Communist Party's United Front Works Department at his university. There he was told that "it would be impossible" for him to leave the country unless he cooperated with Communist authorities. Then he was passed on to recruiters from the Ministry of State Security (MSS), China's KGB. They put it to Wu directly: "If you [cooperate] we will allow you to go; if not, we can't." Wu knew there was no way out and agreed to cooperate. Within a week, he had his passport and his exit permit.

Before he left the country, Wu had a long meeting with a senior MSS official brought down from Beijing. "The old man" (later identified to Wu as the chief of North American Operations) laid it out for Wu:

- He would "develop over a long period of time."
- He would work his way up and "meet U.S. congressmen and women."
- He would "report on U.S. political developments and obtain political intelligence."
- He "must find a way to get into the White House."
- He was given a three-page list of restricted American military technologies, including a "superlow radar system" that the MSS wanted.

After this final briefing, the Chinese spy agency gave him $500 in U.S. currency and sent him on his way.

RIGHT UP TO THE TOP

That the PRC should be engaged in a clandestine and illegal effort to obtain U.S. military technology is not surprising. The PLA is engaged in a massive military buildup, and it needs our secrets to catch up.

What is profoundly surprising, however, is the targeting of the American political system—right up to the White House. Ever since Harry Truman cleaned Stalin's friends and supporters out of the executive branch, no communist government has ever felt it worthwhile to spend precious assets on that kind of penetration effort. The Soviets mostly confined themselves to traditional espionage-military technology, code-breaking, and counterintelligence (identifying our spies in Moscow). By contrast, the PRC obviously thinks it has a reasonable chance of success in an espionage assault on Washington's political leadership itself. As the MSS told Wu, "Don't worry... we have our own people there [in the U.S.]."

A second warning concerning the PRC's political schemes came in February 1992. Democratic Representative Nancy Pelosi of California, a consistent critic of the PRC, indicated during a congressional hearing that the Chinese government was attempting to make contributions to members of Congress through intermediaries.[12] Pelosi told the press that these attempts occurred before 1992 and were "not necessarily related to elections."[13]

At that point, the FBI had already interviewed Bin Wu. Therefore, well before the 1992 election, both the executive branch and the legislative branch of the federal government were on notice of the PRC's intent to penetrate the American political system. Because of Pelosi's courageous revelations, public notice had been given. There was no excuse, that is, for the kind of ignorance and recklessness we were to see in 1995 and 1996.

CHINA'S SPY AGENCIES

Communist China's two principal intelligence agencies are the MSS and the Er Bu, the military intelligence arm similar to the Soviet GRU. Both the MSS and the Er Bu are heavily "mobbed up," with close and intimate ties to Chinese organized crime syndicates, the aforementioned Triads. The MSS is in partnership with the Sun Yee On Triad, which controls night clubs and sex services in the Kowloon area of Hong Kong. The Shui Fong (Water Room) syndicate, a major Triad in gangster-ridden Macau, is connected to the Er Bu.[14]

There are at least three other important PRC intelligence agencies: (1) the CCP's United Front Works Department, which recruited Bin Wu and which mainly targets overseas Chinese, (2) COSTIND, the PLA-associated organization, which targets the foreign scientific community, and with which DNC donor Chun Hua Yeh was associated; and (3) the PLA's Liaison Department, which is under the control of one of Deng Xiaoping's daughters and specializes in deep undercover work and psychological warfare, primarily against Taiwanese military targets worldwide.[15]

In addition to these official intelligence agencies, there are the so-called "internals": heavily compartmentalized operations run by powerful Politburo members for their own use.[16] Chinese President Jiang Zemin has his own internal spy service called the "central social and political work research team," with both domestic and external responsibilities.[17]

According to the State Department, "The People's Republic of China is an authoritarian state in which the CCP is the paramount source of power."[18] That's a diplomatic way of saying that China is a nation of captive people under the dictatorship of the Chinese Communist Party. Since the Chinese spy agencies were established by Soviet experts loaned by Stalin, it should not be surprising that they look a lot like their Soviet-era counterparts.[19] The Soviet KGB had responsibility for stifling internal dissent; the Chinese

MSS has the same mission. The MSS has been particularly successful in harassing post-Tiananmen Chinese democrats in exile. In addition to operations in the United States, the MSS has gone after Chinese student groups in Japan[20] and Australia.[21]

The MSS often operates out of the education department of a Chinese embassy or consulate.[22] The education department of the PRC consulate in Los Angeles was the headquarters for its 1996 illegal campaign contributions operation. For at least ten years our law enforcement community has known that the Chinese consulate in Los Angeles is a nest of spies[23]; the FBI strongly opposed allowing it to open in 1988. By one account,

For at least ten years our law enforcement community has known that the Chinese consulate in Los Angeles is a nest of spies.

there was a "major battle" between the Justice and State Departments over this issue.[24] As James Geer of the FBI told the *Los Angeles Times*, "The opening of the consulate in Los Angeles gives them one more platform. One of the things we know about the Chinese is that they will use every means at their disposal in intelligence gathering."[25] The current PRC consul general is thought to have special connections to the top of the CCP leadership, in particular the notorious Li Peng, premier during the Tiananmen massacre.[26]

Again following the Soviet pattern, Chinese intelligence agencies use Chinese state-owned enterprises for nonofficial cover and accommodations. Chinese newspapers and the Xinhua News Agency are common fronts for the MSS.[27] For many years the upper floors of the Xinhua building has been the MSS station in Hong Kong.[28] In anticipation of Hong Kong's transfer to PRC control on July 1, 1997, the MSS set up a new southern headquarters—believed to be located in Macau—to handle Hong Kong and Macau affairs.[29] Chinese foreign trade companies, banks, insurance companies, and ocean-shipping companies[30] provide cover abroad for MSS agents from the Second (Foreign) Bureau.[31] The

Er Bu has a special arrangement to place its military intelligence agents in the Everbright Group—a state-owned enterprise commercial conglomerate active in Hong Kong—and the Bank of China Group, the PRC's primary foreign exchange bank.[32]

Two cover organizations, the China Resources Group and the China Travel Service, deserve special mention for two reasons: (1) they are the prime PRC partners of the Indonesia-based Riady family, owners of the Lippo Group banking empire; and (2) both organizations serve the Er Bu. China Resources is a major state-owned enterprise conglomerate under the control of the Ministry of Foreign Economics and Trade. It owns department stores in Hong Kong, among other enterprises. As American defense specialist Nicholas Eftimiades notes, "For example, a vice president of the China Resources Holding Company [*Hua Ren Jituan*] in Hong Kong is traditionally a military case officer from Guangzhou [Canton]."[33]

The case of the China Travel Service is much more ominous. Shortly after the Tiananmen massacre, two platoons of PLA agents infiltrated Hong Kong to "cause trouble" for Hong Kong democratic leader Martin Lee. The China Travel Service loaned the PLA one of its Hong Kong hotels as operational headquarters. Fortunately, agents from the Special Branch of the Hong Kong police spotted them and were able to provide round-the-clock protection for Mr. Lee, with two separate teams of machine gun–toting officers. Mr. Lee took special precautions, such as sending his staff to safety.[34]

The China Travel Service also has a propaganda function. It operates a theme park in Florida "where every corner is a riot of joyfulness," according to a brochure.[35]

China's intelligence services have been quite successful, particularly in operations against the careless and the stupid. In the fall of 1993, for example, they raided a room and copied CIA documents that Dr. Mitchell Wallerstein, a Clinton appointee to the

Department of Defense, had left in his Beijing hotel room.[36] Apparently the Clinton administration did not learn from the Wallerstein debacle: Four months later, an aide to Clinton's Treasury secretary, Lloyd Bentsen, lost an important document from her room, which was guarded by Chinese security during her absence.[37]

They have also had some success in the area of military espionage:

- American laser expert Dr. Peter Lee is serving a year in prison for passing nuclear technology to Beijing.[3]
- Chinese agents penetrated the United States army's premier facility for weapons experimentation at Aberdeen Proving Grounds, Maryland.[39]
- In 1996 Chinese intelligence was recruiting laid-off aerospace engineers from Pratt & Whitney in an effort to obtain the secrets of the "hot section technology" for F-15 and F-16 jet engines.[40]
- After the Russians found to their horror that the Chinese had stolen nuclear secrets from their Minatom nuclear weapons facility, they had to restrict access to their labs.[41]
- The Ukrainians were also victimized when the Chinese stole documents for Intercontinental Ballistic Missile (ICBM) engine design and development.[42]
- In the 1970s French military intelligence officers observed Chinese agents, posing as tourists, dipping their ties into a special photographic process on display by the German firm AGFA. Presumably they cut off the ends of their ties and sent them to Beijing for analysis.[43]

The worst known case of theft of the American military occurred in the mid-1980s, when Chinese agents successfully stole technology critical to production of their own neutron bomb. Apparently there was a major penetration of our weapons lab in Livermore, California. The neutron bomb is a special device that will destroy humans but will leave buildings and other facilities intact. When word of this weapon leaked out during the Carter administration, there was a worldwide outcry against it. Consequently, neither the United States nor any other nuclear power ever deployed such a weapon—until the Chinese military detonated one in September 1988.[44]

The most damaging long-term penetration of United States security prior to 1996 that we have discovered was the Larry Wu-tai Chin case. As the Senate Select Committee on Intelligence reported in 1986:

> Larry Wu-tai Chin gave the Chinese an inside view of U.S. intelligence reporting on China and related topics for decades, first as a translator for the U.S. Army and then as a translator and foreign media analyst for the CIA. Chin was a "plant" who received intelligence training before his employment by the Army in 1943. His reporting was highly praised by Chinese officials.[45]

Chin worked for the United States government from 1943 to 1981, always in association with our military or intelligence services.[46] In 1985 he was indicted on six counterespionage-related offenses. Defense specialist Eftimiades believes that Chin was in a position to help the PRC to:

- Identify American agents operating against the PRC here and in China.
- Determine the accuracy of U.S. intelligence assessments against "China's intelligence, political, economic, and military infrastructures."
- Compromise a number of American intelligence and counterintelligence programs.

- Learn about "American intelligence requirements and foreign policy initiatives towards China."

One particular coup for Chin came in 1970: he passed to
Beijing the classified documentation on
President Nixon's secret plan to open rela-   **To obtain intelligence, the**
tions with the PRC. Therefore, well before   **PRC has successfully tar-**
Secretary of State Henry Kissinger   **geted the American politi-**
approached the PRC, Beijing knew our   **cal system—right up to the**
intentions and was able to extract the max-   **White House.**
imum political benefit from the visit.[47]

Ethnic Chinese overseas are a particular target for recruitment
by the Chinese spy agencies. Eftimiades notes: "The MSS appears
to be far more comfortable recruiting persons of Chinese descent
as opposed to non-Chinese foreign nationals."[48]

The FBI hastens to add that the overwhelming majority of
Chinese-Americans are loyal to the United States and that most of
the bureau's successes against PRC spying have come from tips
provided by the Chinese-American community.

The use of long-term "plants," as exemplified in the Wu Bin and
Larry Wu-tai Chin cases, is a common technique of Chinese intelligence. In 1996 the Chinese defense minister gave a pep talk to the
intelligence services in which he recommended "lying in wait for
years on end" in order to steal foreign military technology.[49]

By 1992 what did the federal government know, or what
should it have known, about intentions and capabilities of
Chinese intelligence? It should have known at least the following
about Chinese spies:

- They are extremely capable, with numerous successes as
  proof.
- They are engaged in a massive effort to penetrate the
  American government, Congress, and the White House itself.

- They are looking for political, economic, and military intelligence, and will take anything that's not carefully protected.
- They specialize in "plants"—that is, long-term sleeper-type agents.
- They are in partnership with Chinese organized crime (the Triads).
- They recruit extensively from the ethnic-Chinese community, at home and abroad.
- China Resources, China Travel Service, and China Ocean Shipping Company (COSCO) are all known to be associated with Chinese intelligence operations.
- The Chinese consulate in Los Angeles is a particular problem for American counterintelligence.

But instead of living up to its responsibilities, the Clinton administration has acted as if it knew none of these things. Chinese agents and gangsters have sat beside the president at fund-raisers. Millions of dollars in suspect political contributions have had to be returned. And, with no concern for the consequences, the Clinton administration went so far as to grant a Top Secret security clearance to an individual associated with Chinese intelligence—John Huang—and give him access to some of our most important secrets.

By 1995 the Chinese were within sight of one of their main espionage goals—a goal the senior MSS official had laid out for Bin Wu: They had been able to "find a way to get into the White House."

CHAPTER 11
APPEASEMENT AT ANY COST

O n November 17, 1938, soon after British Prime
Minister Neville Chamberlain returned from
Munich having tried to appease Germany's Adolf
Hitler, Winston Churchill assessed the situation:

> By this time next year we shall know whether the Prime Minister's view
> of Herr Hitler and the German Nazi Party is right or wrong. By this
> time next year we shall know whether the policy of appeasement has
> appeased, or whether it has only stimulated a more ferocious appetite.

By November 17, 1939, the world was at war. The Nazis and
the Soviet Communists had joined hands to dismantle Poland and
the Baltic countries; the North Atlantic was a watery battle-
ground; and soon the French, Dutch, Belgians, Luxembourgers,
Danes, and Norwegians would learn what it was like to live in an
occupied country. Churchill offered an epitaph for Chamberlain's
policy of appeasement: "A sad tale of wrong judgements formed
by well-meaning and capable people."[1]

Today the dictionary definition of "appease" is very unflattering: "to buy off an aggressor by concessions usually at the sacrifice of principles."[2] So, for the editors of the *Jerusalem Post* to
accuse the Clinton administration of appeasement, as they did on

May 29, 1998, is worthy of note. They write that the Clinton foreign policy "encourag[es] a range of nations to test America's will,"
and that "[t]here is a thread running through all these policies:
There are no consequences to threatening American interests."
Regarding China, they point to broken promises on "weapons proliferation" and missiles "stationed in Tibet." Finally, there is this
prediction: "If the United States does not change course now, the
world is likely to be a more dangerous place a few years from now,
especially for Israel."[3]

The Clinton-Gore policy toward the Chinese Communist Party's
military arm, the PLA, is nothing less than the encouragement to
dictators that Churchill would have instantly recognized. What follows is an examination of three areas—proliferation of weapons of
mass destruction (a term of art in military circles, usually capital-
ized, and often abbreviated as WMDs), exports of military technology, and military-to-military contacts—in which the Clinton-Gore
administration has already made the world a more dangerous place.

PROLIFERATION

As a presidential candidate in 1992, Bill Clinton declared, "I per-
ceive the biggest threat in the future to be, as I've said earlier, the
proliferation of nuclear technology, as well as other weapons of
mass destruction, to other countries." In October 1994, as president, Clinton proclaimed, "There is nothing more important to
our security and to the world's stability than preventing the spread
of nuclear weapons and ballistic missiles."[4]

Clinton's analyses are correct; unfortunately, the Clinton
administration's performance in light of the dangers posed by
Chinese proliferation activities makes one wonder whether the
president has grasped the import of his own statements.

The proliferation of WMDs[5]—ballistic missiles and advanced
conventional weapons, including cruise missiles—began with the
communist revolutionary families who established the PRC in

1949. The late Deng Xiaoping called these families "clans" because of their family-before-national-interest outlook.[6] Orthodox communists may have considered them ideologically retrograde, but long after the revolution their influence is still felt. Family representatives—called "princelings," male and female—still dominate the highest levels of the Chinese arms-smuggling companies. Wang Jun, the chairman of China's leading arms merchant, Poly Group, is the son of China's former vice president, and the president of Poly is Deng Xiaoping's son-in-law. The companies themselves are either owned directly by the PLA or closely associated with it.[7]

Consider the case of Lieutenant Colonel Liu Chaoying. She is the daughter of General Liu Huaqing, until 1997 China's premier PLA officer and an old revolutionary communist soldier. She's a graduate of the Electronics and Computer Department of COSTIND's National Defense Technology University in Changsha, China's leading military science and technology facility. She also has a degree in political economy (Marxism-Leninism) from the Chinese People's University in Beijing, a major training center for future Communist Party officials. According to the Hong Kong press, her husband is reputedly the behind-the-scenes sponsor of *Looking at China with a Third Eye*, a Maoist polemic published in 1994.[8] She began her military intelligence career with Chinese navy intelligence.[9] She has been, in succession, assistant to the presidents of the China National Precision Machinery Import-Export Corporation and the China Great Wall Industries Corporation, both of which have been sanctioned twice—in 1991 and 1993—by the United States government for ballistic missile sales to Pakistan. She is presently vice president for international trading of the China Aerospace Industrial Holdings Ltd. (CASIL) and, as we will see in Chapter 13, she made illegal campaign contributions to the Clinton-Gore ticket in 1996.

Colonel Liu is a communist; she's a high-tech spy; she's an arms broker; and she met Bill Clinton at a California fund-raiser.[10]

In his memoirs, former Secretary of State James Baker explained why it was so difficult to gain Chinese agreement to stop problem arms sales: "I suspected why: the Chinese had signed lucrative contracts to deliver missiles to Pakistan. In all probability, several senior government and party officials or their families stood to gain from the performance of those contracts."[11] In another case, Polytechnologies (owned by the General Staff Department of the PLA) is thought to have made two billion dollars in net profits off a single sale of missiles in the Middle East. Most of the profits from arms sales go back to the PLA and related defense industries to finance the PLA's military modernization program, but the princeling brokers get a cut. Their money, in hard currency, is used by family members for education abroad, travel, and as a hedge against China becoming a democratic country.[12] In case accountability ever sets in, they want to have their nest eggs handy.

James Baker saw through the smoke screen put up by Chinese officials. But other Americans have shown a staggering naiveté leading to ludicrous scenes in which they appeal to high-ranking Chinese for restraint, only to learn later that the same Chinese officials have a flourishing side-business brokering arms deals.

Since Baker had seen classified materials, he had to clear his memoirs with the Clinton administration. In 1995, his collaborator on the book, Thomas DeFrank, wrote a revealing article in *The Weekly Standard* called "Sinapologists."[13] He vividly described the Clinton administration's frantic efforts to remove any reference to Chinese leading families making money as arms smugglers. The administration didn't challenge the truth of Baker's assertions, only that they were "insulting" and "would harm relations" with the communist regime. Baker rightfully rejected the censorship, and DeFrank made a telling comment on the process: "This administration, despite some positive movement in the relationship, still thinks that covering for

Beijing passes for a China policy."[14] Cover-up, appeasement—it's all the same.

THE PATRIOTS

DeFrank is a veteran White House correspondent, and his point is dead on: There is an underground war going on in Washington between patriots hidden away in the American national security apparatus and the Clinton administration's efforts to appease the PLA. American patriots wish to shine the spotlight on the Clinton China policy, especially how it tolerates PLA arms-smuggling operations. Since typically nothing gets done about the illicit PLA arms transfers, the patriots make certain the media find out about them.[15] The Clinton administration then tries to square the circle and explain why a Chinese WMD arms transfer to a terrorist country is not really a violation of American law.

As vice president, Al Gore has been totally silent on the issue of arms sanctions against the PRC and has made no effort to enforce or defend his own legislation.

For example, when the administration could no longer deny that PLA-associated companies had transferred M-11 ballistic missiles to Pakistan, it began suggesting that the missiles might not be "operational."[16] Toward the end of his tour as State Department spokesman, Nicholas Burns took to screaming "Leaks!" whenever the *Washington Times*'s Bill Gertz printed a highly classified U.S. document showing that the Chinese were engaged in selling WMD equipment to terrorist regimes, that the Clinton administration knew about it, and that it was covering up for the Chinese.[17]

Dr. Gordon Oehler, never a leaker, was the CIA's proliferation czar. His politically incorrect mistake was delivering an unclassified report to Congress in the summer of 1997 that stated, "During the last half of 1996, China was the most significant supplier of Weapons of Mass Destruction related goods and technology to foreign countries."[18] In the fall of 1997 Oehler returned from vacation to find his authority seriously weakened.[19] He took early retirement.

The timing of Dr. Oehler's problems at the CIA is quite interesting. He departed just as Chinese President Jiang Zemin arrived for the first-ever state visit by a Chinese Communist leader. Highlighting the Jiang visit was the announcement that the United States planned to transfer American nuclear technology to China. CIA reports of continuing Chinese nuclear sales to terrorist countries would have spoiled that little garden party for sure. On March 13, 1998, less than five months after Dr. Oehler's departure, both the *Washington Post* and the *Washington Times* ran front-page stories, indicating that U.S. intelligence had discovered that PLA companies were trying to sell nuclear weapons-making equipment to Iran and Pakistan.

Another group of patriots held out at the Office of Naval Intelligence (ONI). In the spring of 1997 these officials produced a series of unclassified pamphlets designed to alert the American public to the dangers our servicemen and women face in the Middle East from secret Chinese arms sales to Iran:

> Discoveries after the Gulf War clearly indicate that Iraq maintained an aggressive Weapons of Mass Destruction procurement program. A similar situation exists today in Iran with a steady flow of materials and technologies from China to Iran. This exchange is one of the most active WMD programs in the Third World, and is taking place in a region of great strategic interest to the United States.[20]

We note that ONI said "from China to Iran," not "from China *and other countries* to Iran." After the pamphlets began to be quoted by the press, the admiral in charge of ONI was replaced by Rear Admiral Lowell E. Jacoby. We cannot confirm a *Washington Times* claim that Admiral Jacoby has a "self-professed" reputation for not wanting to offend the PLA, but it is true that the pamphlets have not been reissued for 1998.[21]

In this space it is not possible to do justice to the tidal wave of WMD proliferation that the corrupt Chinese princelings have loosed upon the world. What follows are some recent highlights of Chinese arms smuggling, drawn from unclassified sources:[22]

- *Iran:* Nuclear weapons technology,[23] biological weapons-making equipment,[24] chemical weapons materials and technology,[25] ballistic missile technology,[26] specialty steel for ballistic missiles,[27] cruise missiles.[28]
- *Syria:* Chemical and biological warheads for ballistic missiles,[29] ballistic missile fuel,[30] ballistic missile guidance systems.[31]
- *Libya:* Poison gas-making components,[32] ballistic missile technology.[33]
- *North Korea:* Ballistic missile components and training.[34]
- *Pakistan:* Equipment to make fissile (nuclear) materials,[35] nuclear weapons development,[36] ballistic missile fuel,[37] a complete ballistic missile factory.[38]

Every one of the above transfers took place on the Clinton-Gore watch. Since this is only the *public* list, it's fair to assume that the CIA knows of other Chinese arms smuggling operations that have not yet been leaked to the *Washington Times* or the *Washington Post.* Beyond that, there is the question of how many princelings have deals even the CIA doesn't know about yet. We can only wonder.

AL GORE'S SILENCE

Special attention needs to be given to the role of Vice President Al Gore and the issue of Chinese cruise missile sales to Iran.

The Chinese have a particularly deadly antishipping cruise missile designated the C-802. It's both a copy of and an advance on the sort of missile that killed thirty-seven American sailors aboard the U.S.S. *Stark* in the Persian Gulf in 1987.[39] The C-802 is produced in three models—a ship-board version, a land-based battery, and an air-launched version. Lieutenant Colonel Liu's former employer, the China National Precision Machinery Import-Export Corporation, produces it, and all three types have been exported, in substantial numbers, to the Iranian Revolutionary Guard since 1995. A United States military officer traveling with Defense Secretary Bill Cohen in the Gulf was quoted as saying, "You now have a 360 degree threat," referring to Chinese cruise missiles that could be fired at U.S. forces from the land, the sea, and the air.[40] China Precision correctly describes the C-802's performance as follows: "Good maneuvering, mighty attack capability, great firepower."[41]

In 1992 then-Senator Al Gore (D-TN) joined with Senator John McCain (R-AZ) to pass the Iran-Iraq Arms Non-Proliferation Act.[42] The legislation placed severe sanctions on foreign countries that exported advanced conventional weapons, including cruise missiles, to Iran or Iraq. At the time of passage in 1992, Senator Gore addressed the president of the Senate as follows: "[I]t is abundantly clear that we need to raise the stakes high, and we need to act without compunction if we catch violators."[43]

Although the State Department has admitted to Congress that there is "evidence" of the Chinese shipments of C-802s to Iran,[44] and fifteen thousand American servicemen and women are within range of these weapons, the administration has refused repeated congressional demands to enforce American sanctions. The vice president has been totally silent on the issue and has made no effort to enforce or defend his own legislation.

MILITARY TECHNOLOGY TRANSFERS[45]

It seems pretty sensible that governments should not allow their citizens to put money ahead of the national interest and sell war material to hostile powers. For example, in 1561 Queen Elizabeth I issued a decree prohibiting the export of armor to Russia.[46]

Yet money talks, and inevitably there is tension between those who wish to earn profits and those charged with guarding our national security. Too often money wins out. At the time of World War II British Prime Minister Neville Chamberlain was completely wedded to the idea that exports should not be hampered by questions of national security; he argued, "Trade, like religion, should recognize no frontiers."[47] As a consequence, the British

Under the Clinton administration, almost every senior PLA officer in a command position at Tiananmen made a triumphal tour of Washington.

were still selling high-performance aircraft engines to Germany even as the Nazis rolled over Poland.[48]

The Clinton-Gore campaign in 1992 sounded more like Elizabeth I than Chamberlain on this issue. Clinton, for example, accused President Bush of allowing American militarily-useful technology to flow to Iraq before the Gulf War and criticized Bush for not restricting high-tech flows to China.[49] In an October 19, 1992, campaign speech, Al Gore complained, "President Bush really is an incurable patsy for those dictators he sets out to coddle."

In office, however, Clinton and Gore have governed according to the principles of Neville Chamberlain. In the spring of 1993 the administration began unilaterally to dismantle COCOM; COCOM was the Western Powers' longstanding system of export controls, first established in World War II and later expanded to prevent WMD-related goods from being sold to terrorist countries.[50] The administration finally extinguished COCOM at the end of March 1994. In a January 4, 1995, story headlined, "High-Tech Goods Flood Into China As Controls Ease," the *Wall Street Journal* reported on the glee in the American high-tech community. According to the *Journal*, after the death of COCOM, AT&T was able to sell previously restricted high-speed telecommunications equipment to China without being monitored by Western intelligence agencies. Motorola, IBM, and Digital Equipment Corporation officials were similarly jubilant.

On September 29, 1993, President Clinton announced a massive lifting of controls on supercomputers, and another round of liberalization came through in October 1995. Gary Milhollin, director of the University of Wisconsin Project on Nuclear Arms Control, immediately denounced Clinton's decision, accusing the administration of a payoff to California-based supporters and predicting that the Chinese would inevitably divert their American supercomputers to military uses.[51] There was no indication that the administration acknowledged Milhollin's prediction when it admitted in 1997 that, in fact, he was right: A U.S. supercomputer exported to a Chinese "civilian" project turned up in the hands of the PLA.[52]

DR. WILLIAM PERRY

Dr. William Perry is one of America's most brilliant military scientists. In the Carter administration he was a high-ranking Defense Department official instrumental in the development of advanced weaponry, including stealth technology. During the Reagan/Bush years Dr. Perry was a consultant to a number of defense contractors and headed the Defense Science Board in 1988.

Somewhere in his career, probably in the Carter years, Dr. Perry met PLA General Ding Henggao. Ding is a missile engineer and graduate of the Leningrad Institute of Precision Machinery and Optical Instruments.[53] More importantly, General Ding was, until 1997, the head of COSTIND. On June 22, 1991, *China Daily* reported that COSTIND "is responsible for scientific research and testing of weapons for all of China's armed forces. During the past thirty years they have successfully developed an atomic bomb, a hydrogen bomb, intercontinental missiles and submarine missiles, telecommunications and weather satellites and a four-stage rocket."⁵⁴ At the time of the PLA's spring 1996 missile intimidation of Taiwan, Ding was featured in communist publications calling for the use of force against the island.⁵⁵ During the period from 1981 to 1992, Perry apparently made a number of trips to China.⁵⁶ It is not known if he visited General Ding or if they ever had a business relationship.

Perry's spring 1993 arrival in the Clinton administration as deputy secretary of defense caused an immediate reversal when it came to the Chinese military. The normally hard-line Pentagon became friendly toward the PLA, and State Department diplomats, traditionally sympathetic to the foreign governments they deal with, were forced into the unaccustomed role of guardians at the gate.⁵⁷

The spring of 1993 also brought a visitor to the Pentagon. An old Perry crony, Stanford University Professor John Wilson Lewis, had started a sideline business to sell telecommunications equipment to China. There were just two problems with the deal: (1) His corporate partner on the Chinese side (Hua-Mei) was owned by COSTIND, and (2) it looked as if the U.S. National Security Agency, part of the Department of Defense, was going to block his export application.

Lewis's first order of business was to neutralize any possible Defense Department opposition to the license. On April 26, 1993, Lewis sent a letter to Frank Wisner, then awaiting confirmation to the post at the Defense Department that oversees export controls.⁵⁸ Attached to the Lewis letter was a four-page memo defending the sale to China. At the time, the Clinton administration was three months old, and Wisner was a career State Department officer who had been kept on and promoted by the new team. Just to make certain Wisner didn't miss the point, Lewis used Perry's name four times in a single page. When Wisner was confirmed by the Senate, Perry would be right above him. Traditionally, the deputy secretary of defense has the prime management functions in the department, and Wisner would have known that his line of authority led through Perry.

After dismissing the Lewis memo as "misleading," the Defense Department replied along the following lines: (1) the equipment in question is controlled by COCOM, (2) it is only produced in COCOM or COCOM cooperating countries,[59] (3) it has never been licensed for China, and (4) "any approval would require a policy change at the N[ational] level." Fortunately for Lewis, at this point the export controllers didn't know he was in partnership with the PLA, or their reply would have been even more pointed.

But despite these strong arguments against the deal, within a year Lewis had won, and the national security experts had lost. First, the Clinton administration unilaterally killed COCOM, so there were no problems from that quarter. Second, the administration raised the level of what could be exported to China to the point that the goods in question no longer even needed a license.

(In one meeting with national security experts, Lewis picked up the phone and called Perry, and, in front of the entire group, apologized that he would be late for lunch. The group got the message.[60])

In January and February 1996 the *Far Eastern Economic Review* (a Dow-Jones publication) ran an excellent exposé of the Hua-Mei case, pointing out the military implications of the Hua-Mei transfer.[61] As the story noted, the PLA's military modernization program required battlefield communications that combined the functions of "command, control, communication, computers and intelligence." The article also revealed that General Ding's wife Nie Li was cochairman of Hua-Mei. Nie Li, a weapons scientist in her own right, was also a princeling. Her father, the late Marshal Nie, was responsible for China's nuclear and missile programs.

In the April 1996 issue of *The American Spectator*, Kenneth Timmerman wrote an extensive and, overall, unflattering look at Perry and China. These magazine stories may have hastened the departure of Professor "Late-for Lunch" Lewis from the Defense

Policy Board to which he had been appointed by Secretary Perry. But why was he there in the first place? We wonder about the appointment of a PLA business partner (Lewis) to a government board where he would have access to our most sensitive intelligence on China.

After Dr. Perry became secretary of defense in 1994, he showed up in another controversial China deal: the U.S.-China Defense Conversion Commission. About the same time that Defense Department and State Department officers began sharing their private concerns about Perry's attitude toward the PLA, this commission began to be discussed around the government as Perry's personal project. On its face, the idea of the Defense Conversion Commission had merit: assist the PLA industries to convert swords into plowshares. The problem was that this was never the Chinese view of the project. They wanted to convert some surplus military production into civilian goods, export them for hard currency, and invest the profits in modernizing their military lines. If they could also absorb some sophisticated American military technology along the way, they wouldn't mind at all. After interviewing a COSTIND official, University of Hong Kong Professor John Frankenstein came to the conclusion that "China's defense conversion is actually diversification in support of defense modernization."[62]

Perry and Ding announced the commission with great fanfare in Beijing, but Chairman Floyd Spence (R-SC) of the House National Security Committee stopped it dead in its tracks.

MCDONNELL-DOUGLAS

Instead of telecommunications gear, the McDonnell-Douglas case involved the kind of sophisticated machine tools necessary to produce military aircraft and missiles.

On the edge of the Columbus, Ohio, airport there is a U.S. government–owned plant that produced airplanes during World War II. The plant is a government-owned, contractor-operated plant, and over the years a number of defense contractors have moved in, produced war material, and moved out when their contracts were concluded. In the 1980s and 1990s North American Rockwell made parts for the B-1 bomber. The Minuteman missile was assembled there, and McDonnell-Douglas built parts for the F-15 fighter and the C-17 airlifter.

Giant computer-controlled strategic machine tools capable of grinding metal along five axes of travel, and to minute tolerances, are the heart of the plant. These machines allow the operators to get into corners and remove weight. A retired American aerospace engineer explained to the authors that a Russian MIG-29 has 15 percent to 18 percent excess metal weight over an American F-15, because our computer-controlled machine tools are superior. This is not just a factoid for control-freak engineers; it has tactical, even strategic, implications. It means a MIG can carry less ordnance; has a shorter range; requires heavier, stronger engines; and has less agility. Because Russian machine tools can't remove metal as well on the inside of aircraft structures as American machine tools can, Russian aircraft can't carry as many internal avionics packages, including electronic countermeasures to divert enemy missiles.

> **Thanks to the Clinton-Gore foreign policy of appeasement, we now live in a much more dangerous world.**

Since the Columbus machine tools are so versatile, they have in a number of cases been sold from one contractor to the next. But then what happens when a contract ends, the Cold War is over, defense budgets are downsized, and there is no successor?

McDonnell-Douglas faced just this problem and solved it by selling the guts of one of America's most important military aircraft plants to the purchasing arm of the Chinese PLA.

In theory, strangers can't just walk into an American defense plant and start taking pictures. That's why the place is surrounded by high fences and guards are posted at the gate. Imagine, then, the astonishment of Columbus plant workers on August 24, 1993, when Chinese officials walked in and started videotaping the plant and equipment. A Columbus worker we interviewed told us that word went around quickly and the workers tried to block the PRC visitors with overturned tables and filing cabinets.[63] In light of such opposition, McDonnell-Douglas officials rescheduled future visits for Sundays, when the plant was shut down.[64]

The following are excerpts from a June 1994 unclassified U.S. Department of Defense strategic assessment of the Columbus transfer:[65]

- 90 percent to 95 percent of the plant was defense related.
- At least 275 semi-trailers were used to transfer equipment from Columbus to the West Coast for retransfer to the PRC.
- This represented a total turnkey transfer of a military aerospace factory because it includes metal treatment, measurement, testing, transportation, and evaluation equipment as well as the machine tools.
- Doubts were raised about the facility to which these machines were to be delivered in China and information already indicated the equipment would be trans-shipped to PLA military factories.

By 1995 it was abundantly clear that both of the last two concerns were exactly right. The facility the Chinese claimed was being built in China was a phony—it never existed—and at least some of the machine tools made their way to a PLA cruise missile plant.

How did this happen? To begin with, McDonnell-Douglas was desperate. Both its military business and its civilian airliner sales were in decline at the same time. After World War II Douglas DC airliners flew 90 percent of the free world's civilian passengers. By the 1990s the company had 10 percent of the market. While the Fausts at McDonnell-Douglas were brooding in their study, up popped Mephistopheles in the form of the China

National Aero-Technology Import and Export Corporation (CATIC), the PLA's primary aerospace purchasing and advanced product facilitator. In return for McDonnell-Douglas's selling it the Columbus plant, CATIC would agree to a joint venture in China to produce short-range aircraft ("trunkliners"). In essence, CATIC was dangling a billion-dollar deal in front of McDonnell-Douglas.

Not everyone at McDonnell-Douglas was willing to sell the company's soul for a PRC promise. Sometime in mid-September the company dug in its heels. As the Chinese acknowledged, it was a stalemate. But on September 30, 1993, CATIC sent McDonnell-Douglas a thinly veiled threat: No Columbus plant, no trunkliner. McDonnell-Douglas caved.

What really made the deal go through, however, was the change from the Bush administration to the Clinton administration. In 1989 CATIC tried to buy MAMCO, a machine shop in Seattle that supplied metal parts and components to Boeing civilian airliners. MAMCO had far less sophisticated three-axis machine tools than the five-axis models at Columbus, but President Bush, citing strategic concerns, halted the purchase. (This is the same President Bush, by the way, whom vice presidential candidate Al Gore would call a patsy for his supposed subservience to China.)

CATIC had to have an export license to get the Columbus plant transferred to China. Application for the license set off a major war between Ron Brown's Commerce Department and the national security specialists at the Defense Department's Defense Technology Security Agency. Initially, Commerce won out because Secretary Perry would not support his own troops. But in the long run, the Chinese got most of the gear; the promised trunkliner project was scaled back to a fraction of what was promised;[66] McDonnell-Douglas was absorbed by Boeing; and the entire mess went before a federal grand jury.

MILITARY-TO-MILITARY RELATIONS

In the twentieth century, the world has had negative experiences with rising militaries directed by nondemocratic governments, Imperial Japan and Nazi Germany being the most obvious examples. Today, China is an occupied country, under the boot of homegrown thugs who go by the title of the CCP and its military arm, the PLA. The United States policy toward the PRC should be quite simple: To the extent possible, we should be promoting democracy and human rights in China while doing everything we can to hold back the modernization of the PLA. This is a commonsense approach to a potential adversary that threatens us and our friends. We owe this to the region, to those threatened by proliferation, to the long-suffering Chinese people, and to ourselves.

The Clinton-Gore administration has adopted the very opposite policy—discourage Chinese patriots struggling for democracy in their own country and promote the prestige and capabilities of the PLA. Nowhere do we see this more clearly than in the Clinton-Gore military-to-military policy toward the PLA.

On June 4, 1989, the PLA made a major assault on China's capital city that involved as many as twelve divisions. Colin Nickerson of the *Boston Globe* wrote, "Chinese troops massacred unarmed civilians this morning, cutting a bloody swath through Beijing and rolling into student-occupied Tiananmen Square with tanks and armored personnel carriers."[67] Just west of the square, young students from four of Beijing's most prestigious universities—Beijing University, Beijing Agricultural College, the Beijing Institute of Aerospace Engineering, and Beijing People's University—and the Nanjing Medical College[68] died with their school banners flying.[69] Something on the order of four thousand to six thousand Chinese people died.[70] Unknown numbers of others were wounded. Survivors who were not arrested fled into exile.

Congress reacted immediately, forcing President Bush to cut off all military-to-military exchanges with the PLA. There matters stood for the next four years—until reversed by the Clinton administration. Assistant Secretary of Defense Chas Freeman led a military team to Beijing in the fall of 1993. When Dr. Perry became secretary of defense in the spring of 1994, the exchanges really took off, until by 1997 there was one major delegation going to China or coming from China almost every month.[71]

We do not oppose every single U.S.-China military-to-military exchange. But such exchanges should be guided by two standards: (1) do not rehabilitate those senior PLA officers with personal responsibility for murdering their own people, and (2) do not assist the PLA to project force.

The Clinton administration has violated both of these principles. While Dr. Perry was secretary of defense, almost every senior PLA officer in a command position at Tiananmen made a triumphal tour of Washington. Typically they received a nineteen-gun salute from an honor guard at the Pentagon, a tour of American military facilities, and meetings with top American officers. General Chi Haotian, who was in operational command on June 4, even had his picture taken with President Clinton in the Oval Office. All this was covered with maximum propaganda at home and served to bewilder Chinese patriots.

The United States military also has something useful to impart to mid-level Chinese officers, such as good military citizenship, the implications of the use of force in a democratic society, and environmental cleanup of abandoned military facilities.

Instead of these kinds of limited but useful exchanges, the administration seems to have deliberately chosen to educate the PLA in modern warfare. The Clinton-Gore administration has:

- Shown senior PLA officers our most modern military facilities.
- Shown PLA air force officers one of our "Red Flag" exercises (similar to the navy's "Top Gun" school for fighter pilots).

- Shown them a Marine amphibious landing exercise.
- Shown them around our latest guided missile cruiser.
- Given the PLA chief of staff a tour of the Blue Ridge, our national military command center in the Pacific.
- Escorted the PLA chief of staff around an American nuclear attack submarine.

The administration's biggest mistake in military-to-military relations is its obsession with training the PLA in logistics. During the American Civil War the United States army and navy developed modern logistics. We're very good at this—the world's best. Logistics is the basis for maintaining a deployed force and power projection. Any analysis of the PLA will show that modern logistics is one of its major weakness, a weakness we should not want to see fixed. Logistics is real war fighting capability. But the Clinton administration has quietly welcomed a number of PLA logistics teams to the United States. For example, the PLA was told that FedEx's system of package distribution at the Memphis, Tennessee, airport is about 95 percent similar to the U.S. military's wartime logistics system. Senior PLA officers have been to Memphis repeatedly since the fall of 1996.[72]

What's the purpose of all this? Dr. Perry may have let the cat out of the bag in early 1998.

Although he resigned in 1996, former Defense Secretary Perry has been active, this time leading a team of retired officials to the PRC and Taiwan. The idea would be for the officials to serve as mediators between the two sides. For this, the team would have needed some credibility on both sides of the Taiwan Straits. But a number of the participants were either in business on the mainland or known to be hostile toward Taiwan's democracy. Perry didn't help his case when he was quoted in his Beijing stop by the PRC's mouthpiece, Xinhua, as saying that he hoped "that the United States would be able to assist the modernization drive by

China's army."[73] Taipei's diplomats received the Perry delegation politely and sent it on its way.

GENERAL XU'S VISIT TO WASHINGTON

Under the Freedom of Information Act, we have obtained a number of previously classified "Secret" documents[74] that report on the August 1994 visit of PLA General Xu Huizi to Washington. These papers more than amply illustrate why the Clinton administration's China policy has a worldwide stench.

First, General Xu. On the night of the Tiananmen massacre, June 3–4, 1989, General Xu was, according to a U.S. army general, in "tactical control" of the PLA troops in and around Beijing.[75] At 4 PM on June 3, he gave the "mount up and move out" order to the armored and mechanized units, thereby shouldering more responsibility for the deaths of his countrymen than any other officer in the PLA. Under his orders, children as young as three died from PLA gunfire.[76]

With General Xu's bloody hands in mind, what follows are highlights of his visit garnered from the declassified documents:

- The Clinton administration tried to keep Xu's visit a secret. For obvious reasons, it was not announced to the public.
- In case the visit was found out, the administration was prepared to say that Xu was just following orders at Tiananmen.
- Defense Secretary Perry stood in the rain to meet his guest at the Pentagon entrance. Upon his arrival, General Xu received a nineteen-gun salute from a U.S. military honor guard.
- Perry revealed that he had led a delegation to China in 1980, during the Carter administration, "to begin discussions on military technology cooperation." Perry's host in Beijing was General Liu Huaqing, Lieutenant Colonel Liu Chaoying's father.

■ Perry told General Xu that his visit had "great symbolic significance."

■ Perry pledged to Xu that, during his own upcoming visit to Beijing in October 1994, he "will brief the PLA on the U.S. strategy and plans for the years ahead."

■ The American taxpayers paid $13,200 for General Xu and his party to have a four-day visit to Hawaii. They were "housed in a secluded area of the Hilton Hawaiian Village Hotel."

At the 1992 Democratic National Convention, Bill Clinton attacked President Bush for coddling dictators from "Baghdad to Beijing." Even if we make allowances for campaign rhetoric, it is hard to understand how Clinton and his minions could descend to this point: A secret visit by a Chinese war criminal that ends up with a taxpayer-funded Hawaiian holiday? It's not a question of losing one's moral compass; it's having no moral values at all.

So far as we can tell, General Xu was the first Chinese general to be welcomed to the Pentagon after the Clinton administration reversed President Bush's no-contact policy. What perverted logic led the Clinton-Gore administration to single out General Xu for these honors, we honestly do not know. It is beyond our understanding.

Unfortunately, civilians cannot be prosecuted for having promoted the Xu visit. But we believe that any United States military officer who was actively involved in the Xu visit should be subject to a general court martial under the terms of the Uniform Code of Military Justice (Conduct Unbecoming of a Military Officer).

Finally, the Xu visit leads to other intriguing questions. At his own visit to Beijing two months later, did Secretary Perry fulfill his pledge to brief the PLA leadership on "U.S. strategy and plans for the years ahead"? If so, what did he tell them? We have filed a new Freedom of Information Act request on precisely this issue.

CONSEQUENCES

What are the consequences of the Clinton administration's adopting Neville Chamberlain's foreign policy of appeasement? In 1939 all of Europe paid the price of Chamberlain's folly. Thanks to the Clinton-Gore appeasement foreign policy, we now live in a much more dangerous world.

South Asia is at the top of the list. On Clinton and Gore's watch, more than ten nuclear weapons have been tested by Pakistan and India—all within the space of a few weeks in 1998. Modern ballistic missile delivery systems are being readied for Armageddon. This did not have to be. Without Chinese intervention, there would be no Pakistani nuclear program. Without Chinese intervention, there would be no Pakistani ballistic missile program. In his speech to the world announcing Pakistan's first nuclear tests, Prime Minister Sharif said, "We are very proud of our neighbor, China, for all its help."[77] Without Pakistani ballistic missile tests, there might have been no Indian tests. The Clinton administration had the responsibility and it had the tools—American sanctions law—to put a stop to PLA arms proliferation into South Asia. It chose instead to cover up PLA bad behavior. It even signaled the Indian side that the threat of nuclear war in South Asia was no longer its top priority: "We think... the economic and commercial investment part of our relationship should be the centerpiece of our relationship with India," declared Karl F. Inderfurth, assistant secretary of state for South Asian Affairs.[78] Chamberlain would have been proud.

Taiwan is the next concern. In 1995 and 1996 the PLA tried to intimidate the country with missile tests right off the coasts. Its intentions were plain to everyone on the island. Making the PLA's equipment more reliable and giving it an enhanced ability to project power—modern military logistics—only ratchets up the temptation to use it.

The Chinese people also suffer from a policy of appeasement

and *de facto* U.S. support for PLA modernization. After all, they have been the most recent victims of PLA-enforced state terror. It must have been shattering to the cause of Chinese democracy to see the very perpetrators of crimes against them received as honored guests at the White House.

Israel is especially vulnerable to the American government's failure to address Chinese proliferation of WMDs and ballistic missiles to terrorist countries. Once this sort of technology is transferred, it can't be retrieved. WMDs, including germ warfare, are particularly attractive as terrorist weapons by subnational groups willing to strike civilian targets without warning.

> **The United States, in the end, may be the biggest loser from a policy of appeasement. Our cities have become the targets of more reliable nuclear-tipped missiles.**

Japan was enjoying its improved security situation when the Soviet Union disintegrated and North Korea declined. Tokyo cannot be happy to see the rise of another militarized dictatorship on Japan's doorstep.

America's Gulf allies must wonder why the American government does not take Chinese cruise missile sales, particularly to Iran, seriously. This is certainly true given the presence of so many U.S. service personnel in the area.

Democratic countries in Southeast Asia have already seen one of their number, the Philippines, become the victim of PLA aggression in the South China Sea. In February 1995 there were Chinese flags on small islands and reefs in the territorial waters of the Philippines. At the time there was much speculation that this was a trial by Beijing, since Manila is acknowledged to have the weakest navy and air force in the region. So, in light of such the PRC's demonstrated aggression, why would the nations of Southeast Asia want the PLA to have enhanced ability to project power?

The United States, in the end, may be the biggest loser from a policy of appeasement. Our cities have become the targets of more reliable nuclear-tipped missiles. And our troops are within range of C-802 cruise missiles in the hands of the Iranian Revolutionary Guard Navy. If the PLA, modernized by the United States, attacks one of our friends in Asia, what then?

The only winners from a policy of appeasement are the dictators and those who make money supplying them with war material.

CHAPTER 12
MILSPACE

One of the worst fallouts from the "year of the rat" is the assistance the Clinton-Gore administration has given to Communist China's space program, a program that directly threatens America's security.

MILITARY SPACE: U.S.A.

Shortly before he retired, Lieutenant General Howell Estes, commander in chief of the U.S. Space Command, allowed himself to be quoted as follows:

> "It's politically sensitive, but it's going to happen. People don't want to hear this, and it sure isn't in vogue... but—absolutely—we're going to fight *in* space. We're going to fight *from* space and we're going to fight *into* space when [orbital assets] become so precious that it's in our national interest" to do so [emphasis in the original].[1]

The mere mention of "military space"—or "milspace," as it is sometimes called—raises images of a futuristic universe and the Starship *Enterprise*. In fact, milspace is here now and has been around for at least two decades. In the summer of 1998 President Clinton was expected to release a National Security Strategy report reaffirming "a U.S. commitment to space control."[2]

Why are we trying to control space?

The United States has billions of dollars invested in space assets—from satellites to projected space stations—and we want to protect them. The American military has four major types of defense satellites. They are:

- Remote sensing satellites, which are designed primarily for early warning of missile attacks and for intelligence gathering. Included here are photo-reconnaissance satellites that take pictures of political hot spots from thousands of miles up. Other intelligence satellites target the infrared (heat) signatures of missile launches or use special radar to look through the clouds or even under the oceans.
- Military communications satellites, which are the irreplaceable link in the "command, control, computers, communications, and intelligence" of a modern battlefield.
- Military weather satellites, which, among other reports, can provide up-to-date, militarily useful information about weather affecting landing zones and drop sites.[3]
- Navigational satellites, which allow our military forces to orient themselves in places like the featureless desert of western Iraq. In addition, new navy geological satellites will be able to measure the height of the sea's surface down to the centimeter so that task forces can avoid strong currents and make faster time.[4] When a crisis occurs, timing is critical. Mere hours in the movement of a carrier battle group can make the difference between victory and defeat.

An enemy—which the PRC potentially is—would want to (1) disable United States space assets by using antisatellite weapons or through "information warfare" that would cause computer and other electronic systems to shut down or, in some cases, give false readings; and (2) protect its own.

Bottom line: The United States is going to lose any future conflict on earth if its opponent controls space.

MILITARY SPACE: THE PRC

The PRC expects to place at least one astronaut, perhaps two, in orbit by late 1999. It hopes to have a "space spectacular" in time to "celebrate" fifty years of communist rule in China.[5] Massive expansion is under way at its military launching facility on the edge of the Gobi desert. And over the last two years, a number of Chinese pilots have been undergoing cosmonaut training in Russia. At this point it is unclear whether the Chinese will use one of their existing space launch vehicles or a heavier lifter now under development. If they use existing launchers, they will probably be limited to one astronaut, similar to the U.S. Mercury program of the early 1960s. If the new rocket is available, they will be able to lift a two-man team, similar to our Gemini program, the follow-up to Mercury.[6] Early in the next century the Chinese expect to have a "space plane" and a lunar lander.[7] A trip to Mars is also being considered.[8]

The father of the PLA's missile and space launch corps was Qian Xuesen,[9] an MIT-educated scientist and Cal Tech professor who was deported to China in 1955 as a suspected communist. In China he became as notorious for denouncing his colleagues for being insufficiently Maoist as he was adept at creating modern missiles and space launch vehicles.[10] He began with missiles, and on October 27, 1966, China launched one of Qian's creations with a live nuclear warhead, the only country ever to attempt anything so dangerous.[11] It detonated in the atmosphere over western China; local casualties, if any, are unknown.

Qian and his colleagues successfully tested an intercontinental ballistic missile in the South Pacific in May 1980, bringing the United States in range for the first time.[12] Chinese intermediate- and short-range missiles are capable of reaching neighboring

Asian countries including Japan, India, and the nations of Southeast Asia. The PRC is the only country ever to fire a nuclear-capable missile at another country, as the PLA demonstrated in 1995 and 1996 when it bracketed Taiwan's northern and southern coasts. Chinese intermediate-range missiles have been sold to Saudi Arabia, and Chinese short-range missiles have been delivered to Pakistan. COSTIND is developing two new, mobile, solid fuel, long-range missiles, and a new submarine-launched variant. These missiles have not yet been deployed.[13]

In April 1970 Qian and his colleagues turned their hands to space and successfully sent up the PRC's first satellite.[14] By 1975 they could accomplish a satellite recovery, and in 1981 they conducted their first multiple satellite launch.[15] They have a limited military reconnaissance satellite capability at present, but expansion of this program is a high priority.[16] Their military communications satellites have been a troubled program. Fixing that program is a top priority.

We know that the PRC shares the same view of milspace that the United States does: You can't win without it.

One excellent source of PLA attitudes is *Chinese Views of Future Warfare*, edited by Dr. Michael Pillsbury and published by the U.S. National Defense University in 1997. In one of the articles, a PLA navy captain argues that "mastery of space" and "mastery of outer space" will be "prerequisites for naval victory."[17] A PLA air force major general suggests that "one who controls outer space can control Earth."[18]

In September 1994 the U.S. Office of Naval Intelligence (ONI) issued a "Top Secret" report on Chinese spy satellites.[19] The report noted that the Chinese are already using existing remote sensing data from commercial satellites like the U.S. Land Satellite (LANDSAT) and "undoubtedly are exploiting the data for military purposes."[20] The report also predicted that by the year 2000 the PLA will have its own spy satellite program in place and that this "will greatly complicate U.S. navy mission planning in the future."[21] Translated from navy bureaucratese, this means the PLA will be able to detect any U.S. navy carrier battle groups sent in defense of Taiwan, Japan, or the democracies of Southeast Asia, including the Philippines. Finally, the report noted that COSTIND's space program is heavily dependent on western technology and components, acquired through "international cooperative efforts"[22]—a prime example of capitalists selling communists the rope with which to hang themselves.

In space, weapons follow reconnaissance. Recently, Chinese military writings have discussed the development of exotic weaponry with space applications. For example, on Christmas Day 1995 the PLA's daily newspaper pointed to various kinds of "beam technology" such as "plasma weapons," "microwave weapons," and "subsonic weapons" as "superstars" of the future.[23]

A particularly chilling development in PLA thinking has been increased discussion of "preemptive strikes" in "limited high-tech warfare"[24]—that is, a kind of space-age Pearl Harbor. This sort of strategy would mean a massive assault by long-range precision strike weapons (ballistic and cruise missiles) coupled with information warfare designed to shut down an opponent's power grid, disrupt military and civilian communications, and create industrial and financial chaos. Space-based assets would be crucial for success.

In short, until China becomes a democratic country, the West should do everything possible to hinder the PLA space program and blunt its military threat. Unfortunately, what "should be" and what "is" are opposites in this case.

THE CHINESE SATELLITE CONTROVERSY

We are not going to claim that the Clinton-Gore administration initiated assistance to the PLA's milspace program. This gross stupidity goes back at least to the Carter administration in 1980, when we allowed the PLA's leading rocket scientist into the U.S.

for two years of graduate study.[25] Nor do we think the Reagan and Bush administrations should have permitted American satellites to be launched by the PLA. We do believe, however, that a program begun in error, but with some controls, has been grossly expanded—because of the scent of money.

One of the inherent dangers involved in the space launch issue is the applicability of space launch vehicle technology to ballistic missiles. The CIA has even prepared a comparison for Senator Thad Cochran (R-MS), showing how a space launch vehicle such as the Chinese "Long March" series has a lot in common with an ICBM-airframe, engines, staging mechanisms, and so forth.

> **The U.S. should do everything possible to hinder the PLA space program and blunt its military threat. Unfortunately, what "should be" and what "is" are opposites in this case.**

At a May 21, 1998, Senate hearing, Dr. William Graham, former deputy administrator of NASA and science adviser to Presidents Reagan and Bush, told Senator Cochran, "Intercontinental ballistic missiles can be considered space launch vehicles whose orbits intersect the earth at the target."[26] Dr. Graham pointed out that most American space launch vehicles "are derived from current and previous ballistic missiles," as are their Russian counterparts.[27] "In the case of China," he said, "the Long March 3 [space launch vehicle] is based on DF-5 ballistic missile technology." According to Dr. Graham, ICBMs and space launch vehicles share the following:

- Propulsion—mostly liquid fuel, but some solid fuel.
- Structure—"the same premium on materials, design and fabrication."
- Staging—"since staging occurs during the powered flight part of ascent, it is identical for SLVs [space launch vehicles] and ICBMs."

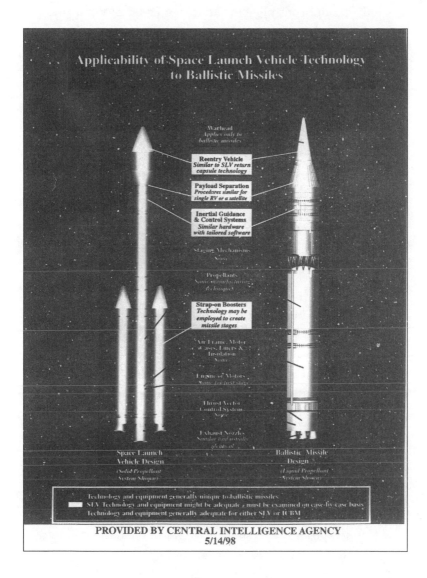

Applicability of Space Launch Vehicle Technology to Ballistic Missiles

Warhead
Applies only to ballistic missiles

Reentry Vehicle
Similar to SLV return capsule technology

Payload Separation
Procedures similar for single RV or a satellite

Inertial Guidance & Control Systems
Similar hardware with tailored software

Staging Mechanisms
Same

Propellants
Same manufacturing techniques

Strap-on Boosters
Technology may be employed to create missile stages

Air Frame, Motor Cases, Liners & Insulation
Same

Engines or Motors
Same for first stage

Thrust Vector Control System
Same

Exhaust Nozzles
Similar and usually identical

Space Launch Vehicle Design
(Solid Propellant System Shown)

Ballistic Missile Design
(Liquid Propellant System Shown)

Technology and equipment generally unique to ballistic missiles
SLV Technology and equipment might be adequate ; must be examined on case-by-case basis
Technology and equipment generally adequate for either SLV or ICBM

PROVIDED BY CENTRAL INTELLIGENCE AGENCY
5/14/98

This CIA document, prepared for Senator Thad Cochran, demonstrates the similarities between space launch vehicle technology and ballistic missile technology, revealing the danger of helping the PRC improve its space launch capabilities.

- Guidance and control—"for attacking cities, SLV guidance systems are sufficiently accurate for ICBM use."
- Ground support and launch equipment and procedures— "SLV ground crews are automatically capable of being ICBM launch crews."
- Overall system integration—"Measures taken to increase the performance and reliability of SLVs translate directly into performance and reliability improvements for ICBMs."
- Payload deployment—the release of single and multiple satellites is similar to the release of missile warheads.
- Development testing, engineering, and facilities—"The testing, engineering, and facilities required for SLV development are the same as those required for ICBM vehicle development."

The principal national security argument against allowing United States or European satellites to be launched by Chinese space launch vehicles is the possible transfer, even inadvertently, of technology to the PLA's missile and space launch development. The key point is *reliability*. If we have made Chinese space launch vehicles and missiles more reliable, we have enhanced their missile force and their ability to get into space consistently. In light of the PLA's threat to incinerate Los Angeles with nuclear Armageddon,[28] no one would want to improve the PLA's nuclear option. But at the same time, given what we know about the PLA's intentions to use space for military purposes, it is equally important not to help COSTIND's space launch program. In short, it is not in the national interest to help either China's missile or its space program.

But that's exactly what our country is doing.

Former Defense official Henry Sokolski points specifically to the question of the transfer of technology associated with space launches[29] that "help make much more reliable, efficient military solid-rocket motors" than what China currently has.[30]

The Natural Resources Defense Council's study of Chinese nuclear weapons notes that China's DF-5 intercontinental ballistic missiles and its CZ-2 space launch vehicle "have an identical airframe" and "it is not easy to distinguish them during their production phase."[31] Consequently, it is argued, allowing COSTIND to launch Western satellites inevitably gives the PLA both the hard currency to produce new missiles and the economies of scale resulting from a longer production run. Launching foreign satellites is incredibly lucrative for the PLA. We estimate that COSTIND will gross almost $1.5 billion in launch fees over the next few years, much of which gets plowed right back into the PLA's missile and milspace programs.

Until the *Challenger* disaster, the U.S. government discouraged American rocket firms from entering the commercial launch field. NASA wanted satellite launches to be a shuttle monopoly. After the disaster, NASA encouraged American firms to invest large sums of money in new production facilities for space launch vehicles. General Dynamics, McDonnell-Douglas, and Lockheed-Martin answered the call only to discover they would have to compete against subsidized launches from the PRC.

In 1988 the launchers took their case to Capitol Hill. The result has been a ten-year war. On the one side are the satellite makers looking for a cheap launch. They have been supported by the softer end of the State Department. On the other side has been the launchers, supported by the pro–national security side of Congress.

In March 1992 twenty-two senators, including Al Gore (D-TN), Edward Kennedy (D-MA), Jay Rockefeller (D-WV), Jeff Bingaman (D-NM), Alfonse D'Amato (R-NY), Jesse Helms (R-NC), and Chris Dodd (D-CT), signed a letter to Secretary of State James Baker urging the administration to enforce a pricing agreement the PRC had signed in 1989 but never lived up to.[32]

Others, particularly Congressman Gerald Solomon and Senator Helms, were not satisfied with a pricing agreement—they wanted to block COSTIND's foreign launch operation completely. They got their chance, first in 1989 and later in 1990, when Congress reacted to the Tiananmen massacre by preparing a list of sanctions. One of them, sponsored by Congressman Solomon and Senator Helms, denied permission to export satellites to China without a presidential waiver.

At midnight, on the last day of the congressional session in 1990, Senator Bingaman, under unanimous consent, slipped a series of sanctions against missile proliferation into the Defense bill. The Bingaman sanctions would prohibit the export of "space systems or equipment" to dangerous missile exporters—like China. Just to make certain everyone knew the intended target, in the summer of 1991 Senator Helms adjusted these sanctions to apply to proliferators from "non-market economy countries which have never been a member of the Warsaw Pact."[33] China had never been a member of the Warsaw Pact.

Nearly all the attention has been on the launcher, but the second controversial area is the satellite itself. Just as the launchers are derived from ICBMs, the satellites, in most cases, are derived from military satellite programs. This is true even if the satellite is a commercial telecommunications satellite. All American satellite makers are major defense contractors, and some civilian satellites have technology identical or related to military hardware. For example, the satellites contain encryption technology designed to prevent outsiders from using the satellite services without paying for them. This technology, in the PLA's hands, would enhance its ability to encrypt its communications. As commercial satellites become more sophisticated, they more closely parallel military satellites. Therefore, these satellites are on the Munitions List, kept by the side of the State Department that listens to the Pentagon, and they require a State Department export license.

Aside from the *launchers* and the *satellites*, there is the question of the *operators*. The first American satellites cleared for launch were owned and operated by Australia. No problem there; the Australians are American allies. The next batch was sold to ASIASAT, a Hong Kong–registered company with Chinese government participation but dominated by the British telecommunications firm Cable and Wireless. In the summer of 1998 we went to Hong Kong, looked up the officers and directors of ASIASAT in the Companies Registry, and interviewed persons knowledgeable about the firm. We are satisfied that this is a purely commercial operation.

Following the sale to ASIASAT, American satellites were cleared for sale to the Asia-Pacific Telecommunications Company (APT), another Hong Kong–based firm and a rival to ASIASAT. This is an entirely different operation. Based on our examination of APT's stock prospectus in the Hong Kong Companies Registry and our interviews in Asia, it is fairly clear that APT is the PLA in civilian dress. In contrast to ASIASAT's boardroom dominated by businessmen, APT's executive suite includes an executive from the "Ministry of Weapons." According to sources in Hong Kong, the president of the company, He Kerang, is called "General He" by American satellite engineers.[34] And many of the executives come from COSTIND.

At least APT is registered in Hong Kong, where some of its operations are a bit transparent. But what happens when a satellite—particularly a satellite with very special capabilities—is sold to a murky Chinese government–dominated firm in Singapore? Or when a satellite is sold to a Beijing-registered firm that is half-owned by China's most important arms trafficker?

We believe that the current congressional investigations should look at the *launchers* (from both a missile and space launch perspective), the *satellites*, and the *operators*. This last has been somewhat overlooked. For example, from the summer of 1991 onward, in order to launch Western satellites, COSTIND has faced a triple hurdle: (1) an *export license* from the hard-nosed side of the State Department; (2) a presidential case-by-case waiver based on the *Tiananmen sanctions*, and (3) some sort of presidential intervention to block *proliferation sanctions* whenever PLA companies got caught delivering missiles or missile technology to the wrong people. All of these were aimed at the *launchers* and to protect the *satellite*. There was no serious examination of the *operators*.

LORAL

President Bush waived the Tiananmen sanctions at the end of 1989 on the grounds that National Security Adviser Brent Scowcroft had obtained a commitment by the Chinese not to sell certain missiles in the Middle East. Three satellites were cleared for launch by COSTIND. By the spring of 1991, the CIA discovered that PLA companies had been selling short-range missiles (M-11 models) to Pakistan. New antiproliferation sanctions were then imposed, but they were lifted in late winter 1992 when the PRC gave new and improved antiproliferation promises. During the nine months from June 1991 to February 1992, there were no waivers for Chinese launches of American satellites. Then, in September 1992, President Bush granted more Tiananmen waivers. For this, Bush was criticized by Clinton,[35] and Candidate Gore called Bush "an incurable patsy for those dictators he sets out to coddle."[36]

Which brings us to the Clinton-Gore era.

In the early morning hours of February 15, 1996, a Chinese Long March 3B space launch vehicle rose a short distance off the launch pad and then fell over onto a local village with an incredible explosion. According to an Israeli engineer who witnessed the disaster, "thousands of corpses were loaded in dozens of trucks

> Since space-launch technology is often nearly identical to missile technology, by helping Communist China improve its satellites we help improve its missiles.

and buried in mass graves."[37] A COSTIND spokeswoman denied the Israeli's charge: "These are lies."[38] But an American aerospace official we interviewed at the time confirmed the Israeli's account.

Loral Space Systems, the builder of the February 15 satellite, had a problem. So did the Chinese launchers, who had such a poor reputation for reliability that they were uninsurable.[39] Without insurance, Loral and the other U.S. firms could not use Chinese rockets to launch their satellites. Something had to be done to make the Chinese rockets more reliable if the satellite makers were going to save a dollar or two on launch fees. Of course, since the Long March space launch vehicle was nearly identical to a Chinese intercontinental ballistic missiles, what made one more reliable made the other equally reliable. This is precisely the kind of technology transfer the U.S. government (or some parts of it) didn't want.

On April 4, 1998, the *New York Times* ran a major story by investigative reporter Jeff Gerth—"Grand Jury Probes 2 Firms Ties to China Missile Program"—that linked Loral and its partner, Hughes Electronics, to China. Gerth came back with follow-up stories on April 13 and April 16. Gerth is a highly respected reporter who broke the Whitewater story in 1992 and was instrumental in bringing the Riady–Huang–Clinton connection to light right before the 1996 election. Policy-makers in Washington take Gerth seriously, and by mid-May the White House was reeling. Under pressure from Congress, the National Security Council was forced to release a series of documents it would have preferred to keep secret. The substance of the allegations is as follows:

■ Without obtaining a proper license from the State Department, engineers for Loral and Hughes helped the Chinese make their rockets reliable. Not only did the engineers solve the immediate cause of the February 15 accident, they also recommended improvements to other areas of weakness in the Long March.

- In May 1996, after the federal government found out about this, the U.S. Air Force did a classified study of the event and concluded that "United States national security has been harmed."
- After a number of delays, the Justice Department began a federal grand jury investigation.
- In February 1998 the Justice Department was closing in on Loral and Hughes when President Clinton approved a waiver allowing the free transfer to China of the same technology that Loral and Hughes were accused of transferring under the table. This severely undercut Justice's case.
- National Security Council documents show that, although at the time of the February waiver National Security Adviser Sandy Berger knew Loral's conduct was "criminal, likely to be indicted, knowing and unlawful,"[40] he did not recommend against what amounted to a get-out-of-jail-free card for Loral.
- Adding to the overall concern, the encoded portion of the Loral satellite was missing when the Chinese returned the debris from the February 1996 explosion. NBC has shown pictures of PLA soldiers picking through the crash site while U.S. officials were kept away for five hours.
- Finally, after the Loral-Hughes fixes, the Chinese launch program now has a perfect record for reliability.[41]

Then there is the question of the money. Loral Chairman Bernard Schwartz claims that it is only a "coincidence" that he, his family, and his employees were large donors to the Clinton-Gore cause and subsequently received favorable treatment from the administration.[42] Maybe. Maybe not. It's the timeline that's crucial.

In the 1991–1992 election cycle, Schwartz personally donated $12,500 to help elect Clinton and Gore—not much for a man of his wealth.[43]

After Clinton and Gore were elected, they had something Schwartz wanted. In the summer of 1994 he wrote a check to the Democrats for $100,000. Two months later he was on Ron Brown's trade delegation to China.[44] Brown arranged meetings between Schwartz and Chinese officials. In the 1993–1994 cycle, Schwartz contributed a total of $112,000 to the Democrats. Schwartz has denied to the newspapers any connection between the $100,000 and the Brown trade trip to China. The Commerce Department, however, has been in the courts defending claims by Judicial Watch that the late Secretary Brown sold seats on his trade missions for $100,000 donations to the DNC. The case is not over yet, but Commerce is losing.

Then, in the 1995–1996 cycle, three things came together: (1) Clinton desperately needed money for Dick Morris's TV advertising blitz, (2) Schwartz needed antitrust approval from the Clinton administration's Justice Department for his spinoff of some parts of Loral to aerospace giant Lockheed, and (3) Schwartz desperately needed Clinton support (and later, cover) for his China satellite program. He wanted granting-authority for the export licenses he needed transferred to the user-friendly Commerce Department. He also wanted regular waivers of the Tiananmen sanctions on satellites, and, to avoid the proliferation sanctions, he had to persuade the Clinton administration to ignore Chinese missile sales to Iran.

Everyone got what he wanted. Bernie wrote a lot of checks. His personal contributions rose to an amazing $586,000 in the Clinton-Gore reelection cycle of 1995–1996. As of May 1998 Schwartz had contributed $421,000 to the Democrats' 1997–1998 campaign cycle. That makes him the number one contributor to the Democrats in both the 1995–1996 and 1997–1998 campaign cycles. Between 1992 and 1998 he has given the Democratic Party $1,131,000. His family, his companies, and his executives have given another $881,565 to Democratic candidates. Finally, he has contributed $217,000 to the Democratic Leadership Conference, a Clinton-associated think tank.[45] Grand total: More than $2.2 million to the Clinton-Gore ticket, Democratic candidates, and Democratic causes. If we were to graph his contributions, his 1991–1992 contribution of $12,500 would take one inch; the $2.2 million since contributed would take fourteen feet.

Bernie got his antitrust exemption for Loral. On March 12, 1996, Clinton overturned an October 1995 decision by Secretary of State Warren Christopher and transferred authority for satellite export licenses to the Commerce Department.[46] Tiananmen waivers became routine for Clinton. As we saw in Chapter 11, America's first line of defense against missile proliferation was dismantled. Loral would have gotten off the hook with the February 1998 Clinton waiver if somebody hadn't tipped off Jeff Gerth of the *New York Times*.

Equally important, Clinton and Gore were reelected.

Is it a "coincidence" that Bernie went from a $12,500 contributor to a $2.2 million contributor as soon as he needed something from the Clinton-Gore administration? Or that he got everything he needed? Or that the number one contributor in the 1991–1992 Clinton-Gore election cycle (the Riadys) and the number one contributor in the 1995–1996 Clinton-Gore reelection cycle (Schwartz) both had China on their minds? Two special congressional committees and a federal grand jury will have to sort this one out.

HUGHES ELECTRONICS

Put yourself in the shoes of PLA General Shen Rongjun:

- As deputy director of COSTIND, you're in charge of the PLA's military satellite programs.
- You and General Liu Huaqing, China's highest-ranking uniformed officer, have publicly stated that satellites are crucial to the development of China's military capabilities.

- You are quietly telling subordinates of your plans to use satellites to gather information.
- Satellites are failing, and General Liu has let you know how he feels about failure.
- As a stopgap measure you lease space for PLA encoded messages on an American-built commercial telecommunications satellite operated by your friend General He at APT.
- You contract with Hughes Electronics of Los Angeles to purchase a set of very expensive satellites ($650 million) with special antennas that might be used to spy on Asian military forces as well as handle PLA encrypted telecommunications. Such antennas have been used only for American spy satellites and have never before been cleared for export.
- The operator of the satellite is going to be the Asia-Pacific Mobile Telecommunications Company, a murky outfit registered in Singapore but under your control.
- But you're worried that the Americans might put something aboard the satellite that will give them the capacity to listen in on PLA communications. The solution? Get Hughes to name your own son as a manager on the project.
- Everything is going fine. President Clinton signed an expedited waiver and export license in June 1996. The satellite is nearing completion.
- Then, on June 18, 1998, Jeff Gerth throws your whole game on the front page of the *New York Times*. Even your picture (supplied to the *New York Times* by Timperlake and Triplett) is in the paper. Your son is immediately blocked from the project due to what State Department spokesman Jamie Rubin calls "information that has recently been brought to our attention that we're not at liberty to discuss publicly."[47]

General Shen's project with Hughes Electronics now has a big question mark over its head and may or may not lift off in the year 2000. Ostensibly, the satellites are going to be used to bring mobile telephone service to consumers in China and parts of Southeast Asia. To put this to the test, in the summer of 1998 the authors went to Asia to interview the telecommunications expert of a leading European merchant banking house. The expert noted that (1) Chinese cities are already well covered by ground-based mobile telephone systems (i.e., "cellphones"), (2) ground-based mobile systems have some technical advantages because satellite systems are affected by clouds and tall buildings (blind spots), (3) the market is currently "quite flat" for the sort of service being offered by General Shen, (4) a number of competitive satellite-based services such as Motorola's multibillion-dollar Iridium program are coming on stream very shortly, and (5) General Shen's project at $650 million is much too expensive, considering any possible commercial return on the investment. Without being pressed, he volunteered that the most likely customer for the Hughes project would be a "government" client, not consumers, and further, the government client would be operating in "rural areas." We did not discuss the special antennas.

Based on our military and intelligence experience, we believe that, if the Hughes project goes forward, its functions—whatever the cover story—will be (1) to give the Chinese military signals intelligence (SIGINT) against allied armed forces in Asia,[48] and (2) to provide command and control communications for the PLA. That is, an American satellite built by a major U.S. defense contractor will be misused to spy on our friends and allies in Asia. Prime targets for PLA SIGINT operations would be the military services of India, Taiwan, Japan, South Korea, the Philippines, Malaysia, and Singapore.

This is a military communications satellite (in disguise), and it would markedly enhance the PLA's command and control capabilities down to the small unit level in both foreign and domestic operations. Such a satellite, for example, would be all but vital in any PLA assault on Taiwan. This would be true whether the assault took the most likely form—a massive attack with information warfare and precision guided weapons on Taiwan's command and control structure—or a more traditional invasion.

The PLA has a paramilitary sister organization called the "People's Armed Police" whose prime function is to maintain Communist Party power in China. The Hughes satellite could conceivably be used by the People's Armed Police to coordinate forces in order to suppress pro-democracy demonstrators in outlying towns and villages before they could unite to become a serious force for change.

Is it a coincidence that Bernard Schwartz became a $2.2 million contributor as soon as he needed something from the Clinton-Gore administration?

Hughes, the world's largest satellite maker, has a number of political and possibly legal problems. First, it was a partner with Loral in the spring 1996 rocket fixes. It does not help its case that the Loral scientist who led the inspection team is under suspicion for improperly transferring the technological report to the Chinese, and that he is now working for Hughes. Second, there is question of why General Shen's son was appointed manager of a Hughes satellite project. Third, Hughes was involved in a previous Chinese rocket fix in 1995. In this case the company informed the Commerce Department, but Commerce failed to inform the State or Defense Departments.[49] Finally, congressional investigators will want to look at how former Hughes CEO Michael Armstrong lobbied the Clinton administration.

Armstrong, now the CEO of AT&T, has an aggressive personality and drove the system to obtain the results he wanted—not necessarily what was good for the country, in our opinion. For example, under the Bush administration, officials from the Defense Department were sent to China to keep an eye on the Hughes satellite. One firm we interviewed in the spring of 1998 said it paid for Pinkerton guards and the per diem of Defense Department officials sent to monitor the satellites and its launch. According to the *Washington Post*, Armstrong persuaded the Commerce Department to allow Hughes much more free access to private discussions with Chinese rocket scientists. "We just didn't want somebody from [the Department of Defense] looking over our shoulder," Hughes said.[50] This is exactly what the national security apparatus didn't want to happen. When congressional pressure forced Clinton to sanction Chinese firms in 1993 for flagrant missile proliferation, Armstrong hit Clinton with thinly veiled political threats, in writing, urging that the sanctions not be applied to his projects. Clinton responded: he not only excluded the Hughes satellites from coverage under the antiproliferation laws, he also named Armstrong to head his Export Council.

THE LOCKHEED-MARTIN AFFAIR

On May 30, 1998, a Chinese Long March rocket sent up a Lockheed-Martin telecommunications satellite called "China-Star 1." As of this writing there are no allegations that Lockheed made any improper technology transfer to COSTIND associated with the launch or that the satellite has any exceptional capability. The issue is the *operator*.

Over the course of the past eight years there has been a steady trend in satellite operators from Australians, to legitimate commercial interests in Hong Kong, to COSTIND in civilian clothes in Hong Kong, to something mysterious in Singapore, and now to a Beijing-registered, PRC government–owned firm, China Orient Satellite Telecommunications (COSAT). According to published reports, COSAT is a joint venture between the Chinese Ministry of Posts and Telecommunications, and Polytechnologies.[51]

Polytechnologies is the problem. It is owned by the General Staff Department of the PLA and headed by Deng Xiaoping's son-in-law. Poly is China's leading arms smuggler and the conduit for Russian arms transfers to China. Poly was also one of two

Chinese arms smugglers caught by U.S. Customs agents trying to sell fully automatic machine guns to U.S. drug gangs in 1996.

With regard to ChinaStar, Poly is alleged to have arranged with Lockheed to ensure that the satellite downlinks "passed through missile launching sites" in western China.[52] The operating assumption is that this is going to be primarily a command and control satellite for the PLA and for PLA business interests.

We have asked American military sources about COSAT but have been told that it is "too sensitive" to discuss. Congressional investigators will want to ask Lockheed and the administration, "What did you know, and when did you know it?" If it was known to a foreign wire service as early as 1995 that COSAT was a front for the notorious Polytechnologies, why did the Clinton administration grant approval for the deal? Is this another example of the Clinton administration's under-the-radar-screen effort to build up the PLA? Or is something else involved here?

DAIMLER-BENZ AEROSPACE

Sometime in the late 1970s or 1980s the German aerospace firm of Messerschmitt-Boelkow-Bloem (MBB) became involved in a secret project to develop a ballistic missile called the "Condor II" for Iraq and other countries. The aim was to produce a mobile, solid-fueled, nuclear-capable missile with a range of six hundred miles—long enough to strike Israel. Israeli intelligence estimates that US$2.4 billion was ultimately spent on the project. The United States and other concerned countries managed to shut down the Condor II program, but not before United Nations inspectors found fourteen missiles and one mobile launcher in Iraq after the Gulf War.[53]

MBB, now absorbed into Daimler-Benz Aerospace, has been working in China since the early 1980s.[54] MBB/Daimler has collaborated with COSTIND in the PLA's communications satellites, the Dong Fang Hong-3 ("East is Red") series.[55] It was the failure of this series in 1994 that set off General Shen's frantic scramble for a replacement. The Germans managed to get a DFH-3A model up on a Long March launcher in May 1997,[56] but it does not have anything like the capability of General Shen's project at Hughes.

SINS OF OMISSION AND COMMISSION

In order to keep the U.S. satellites flowing to Chinese launchers and operators, the Clinton administration had to take certain actions and avoid taking others. First and foremost, it had to avoid a formal "finding" that Chinese military companies, especially the launchers, were engaged in selling missiles or missile technology to unstable parts of the world. With the Bingaman/Helms proliferation sanctions in U.S. law (and no hope of their repeal), any such findings would automatically block the satellite deals. Early in the life of the administration, in August 1993, Chinese missile proliferation was so flagrant and Congress was so upset about it that the administration had to take action. It sanctioned the very companies that launch satellites for Armstrong, Schwartz, and the others. The screams of outrage from Armstrong and the rest of the satellite maker CEOs caused the administration to back down immediately.[57] The Clinton-Gore administration must have made a never again pledge because it has not sanctioned the Chinese again for missile proliferation, even in the face of these devastating news reports:

- In June 1995 *Defense News* reported the existence of a top secret CIA study entitled, "China-Iran Missile Technology Cooperation: A Timeline Approach."
- On February 1, 1997, the *International Defense Review* revealed that Chinese missile technicians were working at a defense complex outside Tehran, Iran.
- On June 22, 1995, Italy's *La Stampa* quoted a Top Secret NATO assessment asserting that Iran would have 2,000-mile ballistic missiles thanks to a Chinese "command and control system *disguised as space technology* [emphasis added]."

- On July 23, 1996, the *Washington Times* reported on Chinese shipments of missile guidance systems to Syria.
- On August 25, 1996, the *Washington Post* revealed that Chinese companies were building *an entire turnkey ballistic missile plant* in Pakistan.
- On June 16, 1998, the *Washington Times* reported that PLA companies were transferring missile technology to Libya. At a hearing that day a senator challenged Secretary of State Madeleine Albright, and she did not dispute the *Times*'s account.

These are merely some of the highlights.

The Clinton-Gore administration, it seems, has cleverly solved the problem of how to please its aerospace supporters who were in a position to lose money because of the proliferation sanctions. It was simple. The administration just ignored reports that PLA companies (the launchers) sold missiles or missile technology to anyone.

But the Clinton administration wasn't satisfied with sins of omission; it was willing to commit a major offense. On March 23, 1998, the *Washington Times* printed the text of a secret memo: "Subject: China Missile Proposal." Until the memo was discovered, the Clinton administration was going to (1) offer the Chinese "substantial protection from future U.S. missile sanctions" and (2) actually expedite U.S. missile-related exports to China. In return the Chinese would sign a new pledge not to export missiles or missile technology to Iran, Libya, Syria, Pakistan, and other countries. Since the Chinese had made this same pledge repeatedly and violated it just as repeatedly, such an agreement would have been a one-way street: the administration would find an excuse not to sanction the PLA space launchers, and Loral, Hughes, and Lockheed would receive wider latitude to sell U.S. missile-related goods to China. Press ridicule and sharp questions from Congress have put this Clinton-Gore plan on hold—at least for the moment.

THE QUESTION OF SANDY BERGER

Samuel R. "Sandy" Berger is President Clinton's national security adviser and a true Friend of Bill (and Hillary). He met the first couple when all three were political operatives on the McGovern campaign of 1972. In the years leading to Clinton's first inauguration in January 1993, Berger was a Washington-based lawyer-lobbyist. In an interview with *Washington Post* columnist Nat Hentoff, Representative Nancy Pelosi (D-CA) pointed out, "Sandy Berger was the point person at the Hogan and Hartson law firm for the trade office of the Chinese government."[58] So far as we can determine, this statement has never been denied by Mr. Berger.

> **The Clinton administration's decisions have contributed, little by little, to China's ability to conduct space warfare in the twenty-first century.**

Under these circumstances, we believe that Berger should have recused himself from anything having to do with the PRC, certainly anything to do with trade. But in the same way that John Huang dove right into matters involving his Riady clients, Berger seems to be around whenever Clinton administration decisions are made that, in our opinion, favor PRC trade ties over American national security interests.

Example One: We now know that it was Berger who led the charge to repeal export controls on satellites for China. According to White House documents released to Congress, in 1995, as soon as Secretary of State Warren Christopher made his decision to keep the controls, Berger—then the deputy national security adviser—"began campaigning from the White House to reverse the decision."[59] The campaign wasn't particularly subtle. Attached to the memo Clinton finally signed reversing Christopher was another memo from then–National Security Adviser Anthony Lake and Laura D'Andrea Tyson, then head of the National Economic Council; the attached memo said, "Industry should like the fact that they will deal

Indonesia's Mochtar Riady and his son, James, whose cascades of money ensured victory for Clinton and Gore in 1992. The CIA has confirmed that the Riadys have long been connected to Chinese intelligence.

Hillary Clinton hobnobs with Mochtar Riady, whose "generosity" has bailed out her husband on at least four occasions.

President and Mrs. Clinton pose with major Democratic contributor Ng Lapseng. Did the Clintons know that Ng is a member of a Macau criminal syndicate and that he profits from prostitution?

President Clinton shakes hands with John Huang, the Riadys' "man in the American government." Huang received Top Secret clearance from the Clinton administration, giving him access to American intelligence, which he could pass along to the Riadys.

This still frame from a White House video shows President Clinton with his arm around John Huang. To Huang's immediate left is James Riady.

President Clinton with a group of Asian business leaders. In the foreground is Pauline Kanchanalak, a Thai businesswoman and major Democratic fund-raiser. She has pleaded guilty to election law violations.

At this White House coffee, President Clinton sits at the middle of the table, and John Huang is at the head. Huang reportedly made a blatant pitch for money at a coffee, which would violate the law prohibiting campaign solicitations in federal buildings.

Yah Lin "Charlie" Trie—Friend of Bill, felon, and member of a secret Chinese criminal society. Trie gave nearly a half-million dollars to Clinton's Legal Defense Fund on the same day he delivered a letter demanding the president to change U.S. policy on Taiwan.

Maria Hsia, longtime fund-raiser for Al Gore. Hsia was found guilty of attempting to hide illegal campaign contributions.

AP PHOTO/JOE MARQUETTE

Vice President Gore gazes intently at the temple's Buddhist master. Maria Hsia is on the far left, and Ted Sioeng—a major Democratic donor who is a Chinese agent—is seated on the right. John Huang hovers in the background, between two Secret Service agents. Sioeng has fled to Beijing.

AP PHOTO

Gore walks with Master Hsing Yun and event-organizer Maria Hsia outside the temple.

During a September 4, 1997, Senate committee hearing, Buddhist nuns from the Hsi Lai Temple testify about the April 1996 luncheon for Al Gore.

In this still frame from a White House video, Johnny Chung presents President Clinton with a gift in the Oval Office. Chung's largesse gave him extraordinary access to the White House.

Johnny Chung, far left, poses with the first lady, the president, and Chinese beer company officials at a 1994 White House Christmas party. Chung has cooperated with American authorities to reveal the truth about Communist Chinese penetration of the Clinton-Gore administration.

with the more 'user-friendly' Commerce system"[60]—that is, Ron Brown's Commerce Department.

Example Two: We also now know that it was Berger who was deeply involved in saving Bernard Schwartz's Loral Space Systems from the bloodhounds at Justice. Even though Berger's own staff was informed by the State Department that Loral's offenses were "serious" and "knowing" and that Loral "was likely to be indicted," he recommended going ahead with the presidential waiver. Berger is a smart lawyer; it is hard to imagine he did not know the effects of this on Justice's case.

Example Three: In the spring of 1997 one of the authors[61] had a private conversation with Berger on Chinese cruise missile sales to Iran and on the Gore-McCain Act to punish such sales. This issue had been publicly debated for more than fourteen months, and the State Department had even told Congress that there was "evidence" of these missiles being in Iran.[62] When one of the authors mentioned the threat to American servicemen and servicewomen in the Gulf, Berger contemptuously declared, "Never heard of it!" and stormed out. As of this writing the Clinton administration has never sanctioned Chinese companies for selling cruise missiles to Iran. Had it done so, satellite sales to China would have been in serious jeopardy.

On July 16, 1998, *New York Times* columnist William Safire made the following extraordinary claim:

> [FBI Director Louis] Freeh has been worried all along that secret intelligence gathered by the Bureau and the National Security Agency would make its way back to the top White House policy makers close to the Chinese operatives and [those] most interested in shutting down the investigation.

No names were mentioned, but in the Clinton-Gore administration, many spring to mind. Safire has made this accusation before, and it has never been denied.

CONSEQUENCES

Keeping Mike Armstrong, Bernard Schwartz, and the other aero-space CEOs happy has made the world a much more dangerous place.[63] Certainly the total collapse of any effort to stem PLA missile proliferation complicates the life of Israeli defense planners and makes development of the "Arrow," Israel's anti-missile defense system, even more vital. If NATO intelligence is right that Iran will have a 2,000-mile missile courtesy of the Chinese space launchers, even Rome or Moscow would be in range. And, of course, a turnkey missile plant in Pakistan does nothing to make South Asia a more stable and secure area.

When the congressional investigators and the federal grand jury complete their work, we are probably going to find that Clinton's decision to allow U.S. satellites to be launched by the PLA has made Chinese ballistic missiles and space launch vehicles more accurate, more reliable, and generally enhanced in a hundred subtle ways. All of this contributes, little by little, to China's ability to conduct space warfare in the twenty-first century.

PRC publications bluntly reveal its capabilities and intentions for space warfare. For instance, a Chinese military trade magazine called *Wide Angle* announced:

> In a crisis in the Taiwan Strait, China's reconnaissance satellites will know the exact location of U.S. aircraft carriers... as well as Taiwanese destroyers and frigates. If the satellites are used to coordinate a saturated strike by long-range anti-ship missiles and submarines, neither the U.S. nor the Taiwan naval forces could defend themselves.[64]

If General Shen gets his $650 million satellite from Hughes, the PLA's ability to wage war on its neighbors will be further enhanced, and the ability of Chinese democrats to organize freely will be set back.

And why did all this happen? Why did the Clinton-Gore administration improve the military capability of a country that has us targeted for nuclear destruction?

In the end, it all came down to money.

CHAPTER 13
RED CHINA, BLUE WATERS

U sing Clinton donor Johnny Chung as her intermediary, a PRC military officer connected to the highest military and intelligence circles in China, made contributions to Clinton's DNC and had her picture taken with the president in 1995. In short order, the Clinton administration began making policy decisions favorable to COSCO, a merchant marine that is essentially a naval arm of the PLA. We believe the relationship between Chung's donations and Clinton's policies toward COSCO is one more way in which Chinese campaign cash resulted in policy shifts beneficial to China and harmful to U.S. security.

MR. CHUNG AND LIEUTENANT COLONEL LIU

Johnny Chung, a would-be businessman from southern California, made large donations to Clinton's reelection effort despite the perennial prostration of his own businesses. Currently cooperating with the Justice Department's probe of 1996 campaign finance violations, Chung has told prosecutors that he got his contribution dollars from Lieutenant Colonel Liu Chaoying. Lieutenant Colonel Liu is the daughter of General Liu, the most senior officer in the PLA. By means of these contributions, Chung was able to arrange for a "grip and grin" photo op with the president for Lieutenant Colonel Liu.[1] He arranged the same for himself, in hopes of generating business for himself in China by showing businessmen over there that he was tight with the president of the United States.

The elder Liu, despite his title of "general," is a navy man. (The Chinese sometimes use army and navy titles interchangeably.) He fought against the Japanese invaders in World War II, then in the Chinese civil war that led to the communist takeover, after which he helped develop the Chinese navy. He was trained in the Soviet Union before the Sino-Soviet split, graduating in 1958 from the Voroshilov Naval Academy in Leningrad.[2] Following in her father's naval tradition, Lieutenant Colonel Liu was educated at COSTIND's technical university, and her elder brother was a senior official of the Chinese navy's Equipment Study Center.[3]

There is a consensus among military intelligence specialists that China is prioritizing two areas of military growth: its missile program and its navy. COSCO is essential to its naval program, and Lieutenant Colonel Liu's campaign contributions, relayed through Johnny Chung, were essential to COSCO.

COSCO: SHIPPING BAD THINGS TO BAD PEOPLE

COSCO is a major arms supplier to dictators and terrorists. On June 17, 1991, for example, a COSCO cargo ship docked at Rangoon, Burma, carrying a clandestine shipment of arms from China to the Burmese military regime. Approximately twenty T-63 main battle tanks, spare parts, and ammunition, along with a bridge-layer, were welcome additions to the arsenal of one of the most totalitarian regimes in the world. The military junta of Burma (whose name the military changed to Myanmar) used the weapons to consolidate its power. The cargo ship was the *Chi Feng Kou*. This roll-on, roll-off ship belonged to COSCO, the merchant marine arm of the PRC—and one of the largest merchant fleets in the world.[4]

Another example: on April 29, 1996, a COSCO ship was stopped by customs in Hong Kong for carrying Chinese-made rocket fuel that was, according to the *Far Eastern Economic*

Review, "headed for Pakistan's secretive Space and Upper Atmosphere Research Commission, which has been suspected for several years of developing military versions of its sounding and satellite-launching rockets."[5] As of June 1998, Pakistan's nuclear program is no longer a secret, open or otherwise.

Bill Gertz, the well-regarded national security reporter for the *Washington Times*, broke a story in early June 1998 to the effect that a COSCO ship "left Shanghai on May 26 [1998] and passed through the Strait of Malacca headed for Karachi [Pakistan]." The ship was carrying weapons materials that would enable Pakistan to develop its anti-tank missile program, which is, according to U.S. government officials, "virtually identical" to

China's Red Arrow 8 missile weapon system. Government officials told Gertz that "the Chinese are continuing to sell weapons with little regard to their impact on the region" and that "China is acting as a force for destabilization."

While U.S. officials were confirming to Gertz that COSCO was shipping weapons equipment to Pakistan, President Clinton was praising China for bringing stability to southern Asia. China's role in arming Pakistan may sit particularly poorly with the Israelis, who are not amused when an Islamic state bolsters its military capability. Both the Israelis and the American Jewish community fear, probably correctly, that Pakistan is sharing its nuclear knowledge with other Islamic countries.

Third example: in 1996 a COSCO ship called the *Empress Phoenix* was caught carrying two thousand automatic weapons into the port of Oakland, California. The cargo was seized by U.S. Customs agents. The *Empress Phoenix* was manned on that voyage by Wang Jun's arms dealership, Polytechnologies. The cargo was destined for Los Angeles gang members.[6]

Fourth example: COSCO is delivering nuclear-weapon components to Iran also.[7] Though Iran is less advanced than Pakistan along the road to nuclear capability, its intentions toward the United States and Israel are a great deal more sinister.

Yet far from doing what it can to stop COSCO's activities, the Clinton administration has been defiantly defending this arm of the PLA. Confronted with reasonable questions about COSCO, both National Security Director Sandy Berger and Navy Secretary John H. Dalton have chosen a path of evasion and dissembling. Their actions are case studies in the dangerous influence of PRC campaign contributions to the Clinton/Gore campaign and the DNC. We will look at Dalton and Berger in turn—but keep in mind who was responsible for appointing them, giving them policy direction, and protecting them as long as they were taking flak for him.

JOHN DALTON: THE NAVY'S BLUES

John Dalton is one of the true human casualties of Bill Clinton's sale of U.S. security to China. At Clinton's behest, and sure of Clinton's protection, Dalton shamelessly stonewalled Congress about the threat that COSCO poses to the U.S. navy.

John H. Dalton, seventieth secretary of the navy, is a 1964 Naval Academy graduate who entered the elite nuclear submarine force. He left active naval service to attend the Wharton School of Finance and Commerce, and became president, CEO, and Loan Committee chairman of the Seguin Savings Association. This Texas thrift failed, costing the taxpayers at least $100 million. Additionally, federal regulators concluded that Dalton had committed "gross negligence" as Seguin's president.[8]

Ten weeks elapsed between Clinton's announcement of his choice of Dalton as secretary of the navy and his forwarding the nomination to the Senate for confirmation. The confirmation process before the Armed Services Committee requires that nominees list all jobs held in the previous ten years. Dalton's form did not list Seguin; it did, however, include a stint at Freedom Capital, which was merely a corporate shell for Seguin.[9] The committee eventually looked into the Seguin matter in relation to Dalton, but in closed session. Senator John Warner of Virginia, a Republican member of the Armed Services Committee, said that "in retrospect it was the responsibility of the committee to put references to his savings and loan in the public record."[10] But the committee didn't, and Dalton was confirmed.

In office, Dalton has made many decisions based on policy judgments with which we disagree sharply. These, however, are not the ones we mean to focus on, but on others that deserve closer scrutiny. In particular, Dalton actively dissembled to Congress about COSCO, when asked about it by Chairman Gerald Solomon of the House Rules Committee.

Solomon began with a simple question, asking Dalton in a May 9, 1997, letter: "Considering [COSCO's] potential worldwide information gathering capabilities, a history as the delivery system of weapons of mass destruction to terrorist countries, and the size of this fleet under direct control of the communist PRC regime—does COSCO pose a potential global tactical or strategic threat against the U.S. Navy?"

Secretary Dalton ignored the question and tried to change the subject to COSCO's proposed business dealings in the United States, but his evasive response did not satisfy Solomon. So, on his next pitch, on May 22, 1997, Solomon threw a little harder:

Dear Secretary Dalton:

No, your May 21 letter certainly *does not* respond to my concerns about the possible threat to the U.S. Navy and American interests from the China Ocean Shipping Company (Cosco).

Mr. Secretary, I wanted answers, not the promise of a "review." I can assure you that I have been around Washington long enough… to recognize such a promise for what it is, a stonewall….

Mr. Secretary, I ask again, for the third time, and with every expectation of a prompt and complete answer: Does the China Ocean Shipping Company (Cosco) pose a potential global tactical or strategic threat to the U.S. Navy? Yes or no?…

On June 3 Solomon had to write Dalton *again* to repeat his very simple question. Stating that he did not appreciate Secretary Dalton's "evasive dissembling," Solomon concluded, "Mr. Secretary, I sincerely advise you not to make a congressional investigation necessary."

Finally, Dalton responded. On June 3 he wrote, "I do not believe that the China Ocean Shipping Company poses a tactical or strategic threat to the U.S. Navy."

Here was the secretary of the navy telling a senior member of Congress, in apparent seriousness, that China's merchant marine was not to be considered even a *potential* threat to the U.S. navy.

GERALD B.H. SOLOMON
MEMBER OF CONGRESS
22D DISTRICT, NEW YORK
ROOM 2206 RAYBURN BUILDING
WASHINGTON, DC 20515-3222
(202) 225-5614

MEMBER
HOUSE TASK FORCE ON AMERICAN
PRISONERS OF WAR AND
MISSING IN SOUTHEAST ASIA

RULES COMMITTEE
CHAIRMAN

MEMBER
HOUSE TASK FORCE ON
CHILD CARE, DRUGS,
EDUCATION AND THE ELDERLY

Congress of the United States
House of Representatives
Washington, DC 20515-3222

May 22, 1997

VIA FAX: (703) 614-3477
The Honorable John H. Dalton
Secretary of the Navy
Department of the Navy.
1000 Navy Pentagon
Washington, D.C. 20350-1000

Dear Secretary Dalton:

No, your May 21 letter certainly *does not* respond to my concerns about the possible threat to the U.S. Navy and American interests from the China Ocean Shipping Company (Cosco).

Mr. Secretary, I wanted answers, not the promise of a "review." I can assure you that I have been around Washington long enough, and have enough experience with the current administration to recognize such a promise for what it is, a stonewall.

Worse yet, Mr. Secretary, would be the conclusion your non-answer invites, namely, that the answer to my inquiry is something you deliberately chose not to answer. You were appointed to your position to know such things, or to employ assistants who do.

I find it particularly offensive that I should receive such a non-answer from you at the same time you prepare to address the new class of graduates at the U.S. Naval Academy, including appointees from my district. These new ensigns have a special right to know the strategic situation in which they will serve.

Mr. Secretary, I ask again, for the third time and with every expectation of a prompt and complete answer: **Does the China Ocean Shipping Company (Cosco) pose a potential global tactical or strategic threat to the U.S. Navy? Yes or no?** I expect your answer to understand the distinction between "port calls" and such activities by the PRC's maritime arm as shipping weapons of mass destruction to rogue nations and intelligence eavesdropping, not to mention giving the PRC a permanent beachhead on American soil.

Sincerely,

GERALD B. SOLOMON

—— DISTRICT OFFICES ——

GASLIGHT SQUARE
SARATOGA SPRINGS, NY 12866
518 587 9800

RENSSELAER COUNTY
518 477 2703

P.O. Box 71
Rome, NY 13522
518-838-1700

331 Fairview Avenue
Hudson, NY 12534
518-828-0181

71 Bay Street
Glens Falls, NY 12801
518-792-3031

This May 22, 1997, letter from Chairman Gerald Solomon of the House Rules Committee to Navy Secretary John Dalton asks Dalton to address whether COSCO "pose[s] a potential global tactical or strategic threat to the U.S. Navy." Dalton's first response to Solomon had been evasive.

DEPARTMENT OF THE NAVY
OFFICE OF THE SECRETARY
1000 NAVY PENTAGON
WASHINGTON, D.C. 20350-1000

3 June 1997

The Honorable Gerald B. Solomon
Chairman, Rules Committee
House of Representatives
Washington, DC   20515

Dear Mr. Chairman:

This is in response to your letters of May 22nd and June 3rd.
I do not believe that the China Ocean Shipping Company poses a
tactical or strategic threat to the U.S. Navy.

I regret that this matter has developed into a personal
issue. I take your concerns and my responsibilities very
seriously. I hope this closes this issue.

Sincerely,

John H. Dalton
Secretary of the Navy

In this June 3, 1997, letter, Navy Secretary Dalton curtly tells Chairman Solomon
that China's merchant marine does not pose even a potential threat to the U.S. Navy—
an analysis that is simply not accurate.

As military analysis, this does not pass the smell test. Every war planner in the world, if called upon to size up the military capabilities of the PRC, would count COSCO ships as great military assets. China itself sometimes refers to COSCO ships as "zhanjian," or warships, and boasts that COSCO workers are and will be "ready for battle" into the next century.[11] The only explanation for Dalton's response is that he was being advised, guided, and—ultimately—protected by the White House.

If cargo ships are not military assets, then the U.S. navy cannot target them, or even study their capabilities for war-planning purposes. In the event of war, the U.S. navy would have to figure out from square one how to cope with Chinese "merchant vessels." Dalton, as a former submarine officer, should know how the U.S. submarine force in World War II, at a cost of fifty-two submarines "still on patrol" (a traditional naval euphemism for "lost"), took on the warships of the Japanese empire—and also its cargo ships.

So how can John Dalton—a man with an outstanding education and track record of service to his country, a former submariner—get it so wrong and still survive? Actually, it's not hard to understand, if Dalton is performing a vital protective function for Bill Clinton, at Bill Clinton's behest—namely, keeping congressional inquiries away from COSCO. We are certainly not the first to suggest that Dalton has been unusually well protected by Clinton. Al Kamen, in his April 12, 1998, "In the Loop" column in the *Washington Post*, noted: "Finally, there's Secretary John H. Dalton whom Secretary William S. Cohen's folks are said to have wanted out now. But Dalton has too much juice in the White House. So he's staying probably until the end of the year." As it turns out, Dalton will leave by the end of 1998. But that he did indeed have "juice in the White House" is plain.

Ex-submariner Dalton should have known better. He has ended up like Richard Rich in the play and movie *A Man for All Seasons*. Having just sold out his former mentor, Sir Thomas

More, in order to further his own political career, Rich is confronted by a question from More: "That's a chain of office you are wearing. May I see it? The Red Dragon. What's this?" The ruthless bureaucrat who has been More's chief prosecutor and persecutor replies, "Sir Richard is appointed Attorney-General for Wales." More turns back to Rich and says, "For Wales? Why, Richard, it profits a man nothing to give his soul for the whole world.... But for *Wales!*"[12]

It is one of history's little ironies that Wales is not the only country that uses a red dragon as one of its symbols. But, John, for the navy secretary job?

COSCO AND THE LONG BEACH BASE

Is COSCO a threat to national security if given full control over one of the best harbors in this country? That question is pertinent because COSCO could very well gain full control of the Long Beach, California, port—thanks in large part to intervention from the White House itself. The administration has yet to give a satisfactory answer to this question.

The naval base in Long Beach closed in 1991, and in the ensuing years discussions centered on what to do with the port and the naval facilities.[13] Interestingly, the citizens of Long Beach had another bidder for part of the space COSCO now controls: the U.S. Marines. After a Marine reserve training center had been destroyed by an earthquake, the Marines were allowed temporary space on a jetty connected to the Long Beach Naval Station. All agreed the location was temporary, but the Marines figured they had an excellent chance of acquiring permanent space at Long Beach. But the city decided the Marines did not constitute "highest and best use" of the space. Eventually, it seems, the standards the Marine Corps did not meet were met by COSCO. Perhaps the Marines did not have the same level of White House support that COSCO did.

In November 1996 a Clinton administration official, Dorothy Robyn of the National Economic Council, placed a series of phone calls to Long Beach officials urging them to push the COSCO deal through. The key phone call occurred the day before the election, when Robyn held a conference call with eight Long Beach officials and said that the "national interest would be best served if the re-use [COSCO] plan proceeds."[14] Such high-level intervention is quite unusual, and one official said that the call made clear that leasing the port to COSCO was "the preference of the White House."[15]

BERGER DEFENDS COSCO

On June 18, 1997, when pushed on the subject of leasing the Long Beach facility to COSCO, NSC Director Sandy Berger wrote a four-page letter to Congress, which reads like a defense brief for COSCO.

Berger's first line of defense was a review by the Committee on Foreign Investment in the United States (CFIUS), an interdepartmental body chaired by the Treasury Department. This review, Berger claimed, also tapped into the CIA, FBI, ONI (where Dalton perhaps got his thumb into the pie again), U.S. Customs, Coast Guard, Drug Enforcement Administration, and Maritime Administration. The conclusion: "[T]here is a sound national security rationale for permitting Chinese companies to do business in this country."

The report supporting this conclusion is classified. There's a reason for that—a bad one. Classification of congressional briefings is a well-known device for keeping members of Congress from speaking out and legislating on matters of vital national security significance. Nothing discussed in a classified briefing can be discussed in public; the FBI enforces this by keeping a close ear on the public statements of members who have attended such briefings. Other administrations have used this dissent-stopping technique, but the Clinton crew has perfected it.

The CFIUS report claims to have "found no credible evidence that COSCO is engaged in espionage activities in the United States; arms, migrant or drug smuggling into the United States; or other illegal activity in the United States."

Note the present tense "is." Evidently, since COSCO smuggled illegal automatic weapons to Los Angeles gangs in the past, it doesn't count. Or maybe CFIUS members simply missed the Associated Press news item that read: "The chairman of one of two Chinese arms companies implicated in a scheme to smuggle 2,000 illegal Chinese-made weapons into Oakland aboard a COSCO ship had coffee in the White House in an affair associated with DNC fund raising. Officials of the weapons companies were indicted, but COSCO was not charged."[16]

Berger's spin on the Los Angeles weapons shipment is simple: "There is no indication the shipping company was aware it was delivering weapons cargo." The only way that could be true—since COSCO is not a private-sector firm but a wholly owned and controlled subsidiary of the Chinese government—would be if the weapons smuggling was planned and executed at a more senior level than COSCO itself, and COSCO was not clued in on it. But that is most unlikely: it would be foolish and probably fatal to put a state-owned ship at risk. Besides, since the question on the table is whether U.S. security is harmed by having a COSCO base in Long Beach, is it any reply to say the Los Angeles caper was the work of COSCO's bosses rather than of COSCO itself? Would COSCO be a better neighbor for being a tool rather than a conscious executive of Chinese perfidy?

Berger also claimed that COSCO is not involved in "other illegal activity in the United States." But besides arms smuggling, what about illegal campaign contributions? As noted in an Associated Press story on COSCO's "other illegal activities in the

United States," "Johnny Chung, a Chinese-American businessman from California, gave $366,000 to the Democrats that was
later returned on suspicion it illegally came from foreign sources.
Chung brought six Chinese officials to the White House last year
to watch Clinton make his weekly radio address. One of the six
was an advisor to COSCO."[17]

"FACILITATING" FOR COSCO

Why Johnny Chung? The reason for his selection by COSCO
appears to be his pattern of success in parlaying campaign contributions into photo ops that, in China, are very useful for estab-
lishing that the person depicted with the president is someone
with lots of access and, therefore, a good person to hire as a consultant. Chung had done this for himself and others.

For instance, at a 1994 White House
Christmas party Chung had some photos
taken of himself with Mrs. Clinton and
Secretary John Dalton—who would be so
accommodating to COSCO. Chung wrote
Dalton in January 1995 to tell him that the
pictures "came out really nice." Chung then
revealed that his own cousin was on Dalton's
staff: "I have already asked Dr. Wen-Chen

> In 1996 U.S. Customs
> agents seized two thou-
> sand automatic weapons
> from a COSCO ship. The
> cargo was destined for Los
> Angeles gang members.

Lin, my cousin who is a also [sic] member of your Research
Department, to personally deliver them to you." The secretary of the
navy responded with a glowing letter of appreciation. After thank-
ing Chung for the "wonderful" photos, Dalton wrote, "Please let me
know the next time you are going to be in Washington. I would love
to have you come by the office for a cup of coffee."

Lieutenant Colonel Liu, it seems, was suitably impressed with
this kind of access.

After successfully bringing Chairman Chen of Tangshan
Hamen Group, China's second largest brewmaster, to the White

THE SECRETARY OF THE NAVY
WASHINGTON, D.C. 20350-1000

January 9, 1995

Mr. Johnny Chung
Chairman and CEO
Automated Intelligent Systems Inc.
2771 Plaza Del Amo, Suite 809
Torrance, California 90503

Dear Johnny,

 Thank you very much for the pictures taken
at the White House. They are wonderful. I really
appreciate your doing that for us. I would very
much like to have three 8x10s of the picture of us
with Hillary and of the picture taken in front of
the portraits of President Carter and President
Johnson. Thank you very much for doing this for
me.

 Please let me know the next time you are going
to be in Washington. I would love to have you come
by the office for a cup of coffee.

 With best wishes.

 Sincerely,

 John H. Dalton

Navy Secretary John Dalton expresses his appreciation for photos DNC donor
Johnny Chung has sent him, and invites the donor for coffee at his office—demonstrating the "access" Chung's largesse earned him.

House—following a $40,000 donation to the DNC—Chung needed access for senior PRC officials, who expected him to do for them what he had done for Chen.

On February 27, 1995, Johnny asked DNC Finance Director Richard Sullivan to arrange for his next round of PRC guests:

- A meeting with President Clinton.
- A meeting with Vice President Gore.
- Lunch at the White House mess.
- A meeting with Commerce Secretary Ron Brown.[18]

Chung and his delegation met with then–DNC Chairman Don Fowler, who sent a note to one of the delegation members, Zheng Hongye—a senior adviser to COSCO—describing Chung as "an excellent facilitator."[19] But Chung's four-point request was still not granted—so he went directly to Hillary Rodham Clinton and was more successful. His wish list had actually expanded. He asked the first lady's office to arrange for:

- A tour of the White House.
- Lunch in the White House mess.
- A photo op with the first lady.
- An invitation for him to attend the president's radio address with his delegation.[20]

And so on March 11, 1995, Johnny Chung and his PRC friends attended President Clinton's weekly radio address. It all fell into place after Chung handed a check for $50,000 made out to the DNC to Hillary's chief of staff, Maggie Williams, following a March 9 photo op with the first lady.

Why the fixation on attending the president's radio address? In a society as accustomed to free speech as ours, a presidential radio address is just another politician making a speech. But in the PRC it is a different story. The media play a vastly different role in a police state from what they play in a democracy. The communist PRC ruling classes control ideas in their country by controlling their country's media; therefore, for them, a leader at a radio microphone represents the ultimate in power. It's also an old standby of communist tactics: Lenin's how-to books on revolution place great stress on controlling the radio towers. Chung's PRC guests would naturally view the White House radio address as ground zero in controlling the ultimate "political message" to America. In their ignorance about the role of the media in a free society, they thought they were getting something valuable for the chump change of $50,000. (Ask any businessperson who advertised during the Super Bowl how much it *really* costs to get a message out to the American people.)

Why Johnny Chung? COSCO apparently chose Chung because he had so successfully parlayed campaign contributions into access to the White House.

Following the radio address, Chung wanted the resulting photographs—a request that raised issues for the NSC. Clinton, too, wanted Chung's friends to get the photos—this was elementary donor maintenance, even if their contributions were illegal—but he did not want the photos widely circulated. NSC staffer Melanie B. Darby asked her senior colleagues for guidance on the release of the pictures. "These people are major DNC contributors," she wrote, "and if we can give them the photos, the president's office would like to do so."[21]

A candid reply came quickly from Robert L. Suettinger, NSC Asian expert. He remarked dryly on what he called "the joys of balancing foreign policy considerations against domestic politics." "I don't see any lasting damage to U.S. foreign policy from giving Johnny Chung the pictures,"[22] he wrote. "But as far as the other Chinese on the list are concerned, they all seem to be bona fide Chinese officials with the possible exception of James Y. Sun, 'young entrepreneur and self-made millionaire.' Got some doubts there. Notwithstanding that these guys will all hang the picture on the wall and feel grateful for a memory."[23] Later in the same memo Suettinger gave Johnny Chung what has since become a famous sobriquet: "hustler."

In our opinion, Suettinger, who turned the memo around in a little more than an hour, must have been ethically blind to exonerate the president so cavalierly. But then again, this is the same moral environment that encouraged Secretary Dalton to dismiss the idea of COSCO as a threat and Sandy Berger to write a defense brief for COSCO's occupation of Long Beach. Something was wrong, and the Chung caper shows it goes right into the Oval Office and the equally powerful first lady's office.

Chung, of course, got the photographs. He was demonstrably capable at arranging both access and visible evidence of access. So Lieutenant Colonel Liu and her associates picked him to channel their contributions, arrange their photo ops, and help them square the administration on issues of concern to COSCO, thus giving China the time and opportunity it needed to pursue its grandiose goal of naval expansion. They picked the right intermediary—and, from their point of view, the right administration.

CHAPTER 14
THE COMMUNISTS GO CAPITALIST

The Chinese have used the Clinton era to tap into American capital markets, as well as American elections and American technology. Their search for U.S. investment dollars may affect, badly, the millions of Americans who have become investors. On the Clinton/Gore watch, a high-ranking Chinese military officer has had meetings with senior officials of the Securities and Exchange Commission (SEC), and China has put stocks of inflated value into the American marketplace without disclosing their true ownership or their shaky economic underpinnings.

The communists are becoming capitalists, just like in Orwell's *Animal Farm*, where the pigs became like men, and the men like pigs, and in the end no one could tell the difference.

As part of a long-term economic strategy, China is devolving its state-owned corporations into smaller units, known as "red chips." These are represented as independent in order to raise capital in equity markets outside of China, especially in the United States. American investors, whose dollars go into these red chips, are, knowingly or not, indirectly funding the communist regime. Those who would shrug that off as long as the stock's value goes up should consider this: red chips often turn out to be mere shells through which Chinese insiders and their investment bankers play the "pump and dump" game—inflate a stock's value artificially, then sell at a huge profit, leaving smaller, slower investors holding the bag.[1]

Unearthing this type of scam is the paramount purpose of U.S. securities law. Though complex, this body of law has one simple underlying value: disclosure, or, to use the currently favored term, transparency. President Clinton put it well in a May 4, 1998, speech about the stock market: "The economists have a word called 'transparency' that they like to use all the time that I think is appropriate here. I think it's in the national interest for all potential investors to have as much information as possible." He is exactly right. Unfortunately, some of his friends in China have found ways to participate in American capital markets without living up to the president's ideal of transparency.

GETTING TO KNOW YOU

During the 1996 election cycle, Johnny Chung made a $10,000 contribution to Senator John Kerry's (D-MA) campaign in return for help in arranging a high-level meeting with the SEC. Senator Kerry's office reported that this was a "tour." The "tour" request was faxed from Kerry's office to the SEC and was set up for the same day. If it was a "tour," it was an unusual one, because it concentrated on one of the commission's upper office suites, and the "guides" were the director of the commission's Division of Corporation Finance and his deputy director. Most observers would characterize this as a meeting, not a tour. Chris Ullman, spokesman for the SEC, said Chung and his associates asked for information about getting foreign companies listed on U.S. stock exchanges.[2]

One member of Chung's entourage was Lieutenant Colonel Liu Chaoying—high-ranking PRC military intelligence operative, daughter of a top-ranking general, and a leading illegal DNC donor via Chung (according to testimony Chung has given to U.S. prosecutors). American investors have cause to be concerned that such a high-ranking member of the PRC political/military establishment was meeting with high-level SEC officials.

We do not yet know what Lieutenant Colonel Liu and the SEC officials talked about. But we know that, as part of their efforts to tap the U.S. investing community, the Chinese have attempted to use their own phony accounting standards instead of American standards to govern disclosure, and we know that they have enticed a number of U.S. investment banks, CPAs, and lawyers to try to carry them—shoddy disclosure practices and all—to American capital marketplaces.[3]

Meanwhile, Triad-connected Macau hotelier Ng Lapseng and arms smuggler Wang Jun were also being introduced to American financial circles during the 1996 election cycle. At a photo event in 1995, President Clinton was introduced to Ng by Ernest Green of the Lehman Brothers brokerage firm. Using Ng's nickname "Mr. Wu," Green told Clinton, "Mr. Wu, when Ron [Brown] was in Hong Kong, he had a small reception for him. He was very helpful. In fact, when you get ready to play golf, he's got a golf course in Macau." The president replied, "I'd like that."[4]

Wang Jun, whose February 6, 1996, White House visit has since been acknowledged by the administration itself as "clearly inappropriate," was also interested in the New York Stock Exchange, and was escorted there for a visit and a lunch at Lehman Brothers the day after that "clearly inappropriate" White House visit. Mr. Green may have a connection not only to Wang's Wall Street visit but to his White House visit as well: Phyllis Caudle-Green, Ernest's wife, wrote a $50,000 check to the DNC on February 6, 1996.

RED CHIPS

Red chips enable the PRC to bundle assets in a quasi-government conglomerate and raise money in world equity markets. We have isolated three typical characteristics of red chips: they are linked to the PRC central government through regional government; they have subsidiaries listed on the Hong Kong Stock Exchange; and they use their Hong Kong subsidiaries to arrange complex international debt and equity swaps.[5]

Red chips do not necessarily conform to U.S. accounting and accountability standards. For instance, on October 9, 1997, Chairman Gerald Solomon of the House Committee on Rules received a letter from a leader of the television network NET and of the Free Congress Foundation, the letter alleging insider trading by Hong Kong billionaire and PRC financial adviser Li Ka-shing, who also has ties to the Riadys and to arms dealer Wang Jun. The letter observed: "The United States must ensure that Beijing plays by the rules of an open, transparent market—the level playing field so central to democracy in this country. For instance, state-owned China Telecom is due to raise $3.3 billion in New York and Hong Kong this month. But the background of principals such as Li Ka-shing has not been disclosed to the SEC or the investing public as required under... the Federal Securities Act."

> **The Chinese have used the Clinton era to tap into American capital markets, as well as American elections and American technology.**

Chairman Solomon immediately forwarded the letter to the chairman of the SEC. In his cover letter, Solomon suggested that if the PRC is more than willing to provide weapons of mass destruction to terrorist nations, it is not likely to have qualms about waging economic war against America. Since the Chinese had been penetrating the Clinton administration for economic espionage, it was a short leap to imagine them trying to manipulate our capital markets.

Solomon's letter caused quite a ruckus in Asia. Li Ka-shing publicly characterized the letter as "complete bulls—, total nonsense and beneath comment." The market must have reasoned that Li was commenting a little too strongly on something that was supposedly "beneath comment": Li's fortunes began to take a nosedive. He was heavily invested in Hong Kong real estate, which plummeted in the wake of the "Asian flu." Li lost almost $2.5 billion overnight, according to our estimates.

Solomon, meanwhile, was not concerned about Li's colorful remarks, but he took very seriously a statement from China's communications minister, Wu Jichuan. The PRC government moved to support the value of China Telecom shares; Wu Jichuan said at a hastily called press conference in Ghenshan, just across the border from Hong Kong, that the government would ease accounting rules to boost the company's profits. "This is the first course of a banquet," he said, "and bigger courses will be served later."[6] Imagine the chairman of a Fortune Fifty company announcing he was going to manipulate generally accepted accounting standards to show more profits, and that there was more to come.

The SEC responded by determining that no Chinese accounting firms, except for three from Hong Kong that predated the Chinese takeover of the former British colony, are accredited to practice before the SEC on behalf of China.[7]

But that was not the end. On November 5, 1997, China denied it had violated disclosure rules, and requested that members of the U.S. Congress play a "less obstructive role" in Sino-American financial dealings.[8]

This attack on Congress was an unusual breach of protocol, especially from a country that takes protocol very seriously. In international diplomacy, affairs of state are handled by the executive branches of government. For China to attack Congress directly illustrates two facets of Sino-American relations in the mid-1990s: (1) the executive branch causes no worries to China as long as Bill Clinton heads it; and (2) China *is* seriously worried about moves in Congress to make sure SEC regulations are duly enforced against Chinese companies seeking American investment.[9]

A RED CHIP STORY

Beijing Enterprises Holding Ltd., listed since 1997, has been fingered as being under the control of the Beijing municipal government and being at the "pinnacle of the charts among red chips."[10] It lists its principal activities as "tourism, hotel management, brewery and fast-food operations, toll road operations."[11] But in Senate testimony, a different view of Beijing Enterprises emerged.

First off, Mr. Randolph Quon—fellow at the Potomac Foundation and former investment banker and fund manager in London, Geneva, Moscow, and Hong Kong, and adviser to the People's Bank of China—testified that Beijing Enterprises is a glaring example of a stock that avoids strict SEC registration requirements. Beijing Enterprises penetrated U.S. capital markets under two main exemptions to SEC rules. The first was Regulation S, which allows unregistered securities to arrive in America through off-shore transactions. The second is Rule 144(a), which allows private placement in the United States.

In addition to Quon's analysis, we found further evidence that Beijing Enterprises was a hollow shell. We found that a share of Beijing Enterprises started with a May 1997 initial public offering price of US$1.61, with 150 million shares in the offering, and thus a net worth of US$241.5 million dollars. The stock reached a high of US$8.41, a net worth of US$1.265 billion—only to crash back to US$1.99 and a net worth of US$298.5 million.[12] This was a classic "pump and dump" operation in which a billion dollars in apparent stock value disappeared.

A column in the *Financial Times*, one of the most respected authorities in international finance journalism, reported that Wall Street investment banking firms profited from the underwriting of red chips by keeping a sizable chunk of the initial public offering for themselves. This is what one American investment banking firm, along with the prestigious Hong Kong investment banking firm Peregrine, did in underwriting Beijing Enterprises. The

Financial Times columnist then reasoned: "So why do Chinese clients allow a structure that might encourage advisers to minimize proceeds? Presumably since the state is the owner, the issue price is not a management concern—whereas a surging share price could do wonders for future management remuneration packages."[13] In other words, state ownership allows Chinese corporations to evade realistic pricing of their initial public offerings. They are free to price them artificially low so as to attract investors and, as the *Financial Times* suggests, give young investment bankers an opportunity to show off for the brass when the stock seems to surge in value.

> **Unfortunately, some of Clinton's friends in China have found ways to participate in American capital markets while circumventing U.S. securities laws.**

This time, however, there *was* a bill for the "free lunch," and Peregrine had to pay it: it went bankrupt. Other American banks and investment firms were left holding the bag.[14] Later on, a judge in Hong Kong said the British directors of a Peregrine subsidiary had "creamed off" profits at the expense of creditors, so perhaps there was indeed a "free lunch" for some.[15]

Red chips have very shaky foundations. Independent accountants and tough-minded investment bankers should have learned whether Beijing Enterprises was anything more than some concession stands on the Great Wall. Because, in reality, it wasn't.

Among those who made money on the Beijing Enterprises disaster were the Riadys. They have two powerful allies in Beijing/Hong Kong financial circles: Shen Jueren, leader of China Resources, and Li Ka-shing of the ill-fated Beijing Enterprises. They are all connected as partners in the Riadys' Hong Kong Chinese Bank. Just before the Asian meltdown, Lippo Ltd. and China Resources Ltd. announced share placement with a Beijing Enterprises subsidiary. It appears that, in essence, Beijing Enterprises acquired a stake in a Lippo company listed in Hong

Kong. Lippo received HK$897 million in net proceeds (approximately US$122 million) from its deal with Beijing Enterprises. The money was then moved to Lippo/China Resources Limited, which had previously been identified as an associate of Chinese military intelligence. This means that Li Ka-shing, a senior player with Beijing Enterprises, is connected in a move of more than US$100 million to Mochtar Riady's empire, which in turn is connected to Chinese military intelligence.

As this book goes to press, it is estimated that red chips have lost anywhere from 60 percent to 80 percent of their value. The only example of success is China Telecom, which has risen 20 percent since it went public.[16] But if you can cook the books, as Wu Jichuan baldly announced his government would do ("first course of the banquet… more courses to come," etc.), then anything can be made to look good. Given the attention China Telecom's initial public offering received, the PRC cannot allow it to fail. Furthermore, Li Ka-shing, a principal in China Telecom, is also a principal in arms-smuggler Wang Jun's CITIC Corporation, whose business is satellites, a prime focus of China's military buildup.

China wants our investment capital as well as our technology. To get it, red chips such as Beijing Enterprises may have successfully exploited legal loopholes—or they may have violated U.S. federal and/or state law.[17] Congressman Solomon has forwarded information on Beijing Enterprises to New York County prosecutor Robert Morgenthau, who has a sterling reputation for using New York State law to prosecute international scams that attack the New York capital markets and banks. In situations in which the Chinese and their agents may have broken both federal and state law, state prosecution is a much better bet as long as federal prosecutors are answerable to Bill Clinton.

With even President Clinton buying into the buzz word "transparency," it has become a grand joke that, during his trip to China in the summer of 1998, he visited the PRC's showcase Shanghai

Stock Exchange. The exchange is a technological marvel, a trading floor with hundreds of computer stations. In fact, the president allowed himself to be photographed at a computer surrounded by red-vested traders. What wasn't pointed out—and what we learned when we visited the site—is that the red-vested trading floor operatives are essentially hired to sit at their desks, because all the action is in direct electronic trading. When we were there, we saw traders sleeping, reading newspapers, and wandering around talking to their friends. In essence, it is a virtual stock exchange—in a building owned by the notorious Wang Jun and Polytechnologies.

It seems that President Clinton's shady connections follow him even on major diplomatic missions.

CHAPTER 15
CONCLUSION

This began as a national security book. We initially had no idea of just how far President Bill Clinton and Vice President Al Gore had gone to secure their election and then to stay in office. In the course of our research we came to realize just how severe these problems were, just how many Faustian bargains Clinton and Gore had made to stay in power.

Two photographs in particular—both of which appear in this book's photo section—speak volumes about the deals this White House has cut. The first shows President Clinton and the first lady with Macau criminal syndicate figure Ng Lapseng. The seal of the DNC hangs like a full moon in the background. The second photo was taken at the Hsi Lai Buddhist Temple and shows Vice President Gore with Ted Sioeng. These photographs represent close to two million dollars in illegal donations to Bill Clinton and Al Gore. It is important when viewing these photographs to recall that Ng and Sioeng are in the business of exploiting Asian women for prostitution, and at least some of the two million dollars must be considered proceeds from those businesses.

When we began work on this book, of course, we were not aware of just how deep the corruption ran. Only when we went to Macau disguised as ordinary tourists did the depths of this depravity become apparent. The Chinese Triads' trafficking in Asian women is no different from similar operations in other parts of the world. Few of the women are volunteers; many are sold into slavery by their poverty-stricken families. A number are underage; younger ones are more valuable to their owners. Most of the money they make is stolen from them by those in control of their lives. Often they are encouraged to develop narcotics habits in order to keep them dependent.

We do not know what went through the minds of Clinton and Gore when they sat down to dinner with people like Ng and Sioeng. Did they not know—or, if knowing, not care—about the origins of the money they were soliciting? Is this part of a larger pattern of callousness that included President Clinton's guided tour of the White House for James Riady as American children died at Waco, and Defense Secretary William Perry's welcome for General Xu, the Chinese war criminal responsible for the deaths of his countrymen in the Tiananmen massacre?

Had President Clinton so easily forgotten his first executive order as president?

EXECUTIVE ORDER NUMBER 1

On January 20, 1993, Bill Clinton was inaugurated as our forty-second president. The weather was chilly and the sky was gray that day, but the mood inside the White House was warm and glowing. The Democrats, the "workingman's party," were back.

That afternoon, the new team of presidential advisers gathered in the White House's Roosevelt Room, just across the hall from the Oval Office. The advisers waited anxiously for words of guidance and wisdom from their newly inaugurated commander in chief. All felt positive about their political futures, excited about the direction the country had taken, and confident in their president.

The door opened, and Bill Clinton—the boy from Hope, *the commander in chief of the most powerful nation on the face of the earth*—entered smiling, and took his place at the head of the massive table. He began his first address to his staffers with a lecture on the value of presidential ethics and personal integrity. "We just have to be dominated by high standards and clear vision and we ought to have a good time doing it," the new president told them.[1]

President Clinton's Executive Order Number 1, "Ethics Commitments by Executive Branch Appointees," required the new Clinton-Gore appointees to make three pledges: (1) no lobbying for five years after they left the government, (2) no activity on behalf of a *foreign government*, and (3) no representation of a *foreign government* or *foreign corporation* for five years after being engaged in a trade negotiation [emphasis added].

The word "*foreign*" appears twenty-one times in the executive order, making it clear that the president was demanding loyalty to United States interests. To be absolutely clear, he told his new appointees, "The ethics rules that we have put forward will guarantee that the members of this administration will be looking out for the American people and not for themselves."

Yet how many of those present that day knew that they were there only because a foreign banker, later identified as a Communist Chinese agent, had rescued the Clinton-Gore team not once but twice in 1992? Could any of them have predicted that, within five-and-a-half years, the Clinton-Gore administration would be the subject of worldwide ridicule and a wave of congressional investigations for having maintained itself in power with a flood of tainted money? Who would have guessed that, in return for money, Bill Clinton and Al Gore would literally sit down to supper with a procession of agents for the Communist Chinese army, Chinese intelligence, the Macau criminal syndicate, and Cambodia's biggest drug trafficker? Who would have guessed that Clinton and Gore would use the power of the White House itself to lobby for a foreign power?

CAMPAIGN FINANCE

The Clinton-Gore record of campaign finance abuses is staggering:

- Chinese agents ensured victory for the Clinton-Gore team in the 1992 general election with a massive cascade of illegally laundered foreign funds into key states.
- More than one hundred potential witnesses of illegal foreign campaign contributions to the Clinton-Gore team have fled the country, taken the Fifth Amendment, or refused to be interviewed by investigative bodies.
- Chinese agents helped secure the 1992 Democratic presidential nomination for Clinton with a multimillion-dollar loan from an Arkansas bank under their influence.
- Chinese agents became the number one donors to Clinton and Gore in 1992.
- The Clinton Justice Department allowed the statute of limitations to run out so that illegal donations from Chinese agents could escape prosecution.
- Leading donors to the DNC are business associates of a major Tiananmen massacre war criminal that even the Chinese have jailed.
- Chinese agents tried to use their donations to Democratic senators to pressure Taiwan's banking authorities.
- Chinese agents gave $100,000 to convicted felon Webster Hubbell at the very moment the independent counsel's office was seeking his cooperation in its investigations of the Clintons.
- Chinese agents helped fund Dick Morris's brilliant stealth advertising campaign against the Republicans in 1995–1996.
- A Macau criminal syndicate figure who exploits women for prostitution laundered more than $1,000,000 in illegal donations to the DNC; he met Clinton on a number of occa-

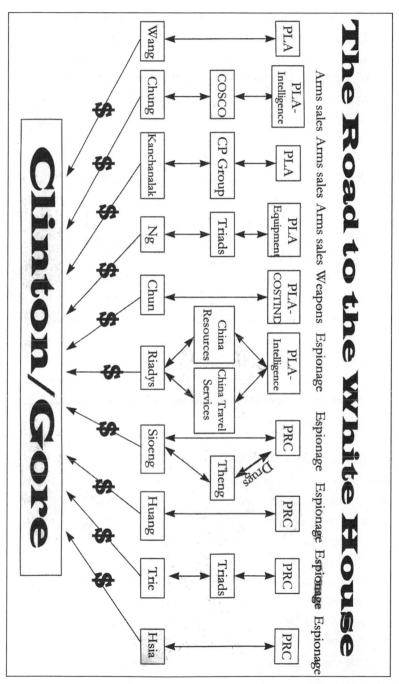

This analysis, prepared by the authors, shows the cascades of money that went into the Clinton/Gore coffers. The record of campaign-finance abuses is staggering.

sions, including on visits to the White House; and he may also have funneled more than $300,000 in illegal cash donations to the Democrats and/or hush money for Hubbell.

- A Chinese agent who is also in the business of exploiting women for prostitution donated hundreds of thousands of dollars to Bill Clinton and Al Gore, and he sat beside both the president and vice president at intimate fund-raisers.

- A Chinese agent/DNC donor with personal connections to Clinton and Gore is a business associate of Cambodia's largest narcotics trafficker.

- A Chinese agent who specializes in illegally laundering funds for the Democrats has an eight-year business relationship with Gore.

- A Chinese agent who raises funds for Gore may be assisting Chinese spies to gain entrance into the United States.

- Leaders of a Thai conglomerate that is in business with Middle Eastern terrorists and with China's biggest arms smugglers had a White House meeting with Clinton at which they were illegally solicited for campaign donations.

- A Chinese PLA spy laundered illegal campaign funds through Johnny Chung and met Clinton twice at fund-raisers.

- A Macau gambling figure and a Hong Kong billionaire in business with the PLA donated hundreds of thousands of dollars to Clinton's favorite charities.

- A Chinese gangster dumped hundreds of thousands of dollars in foreign funds on the Clinton Legal Defense Trust on the same day he delivered a letter demanding that Clinton abandon Taiwan.

- A PLA partner sat next to Clinton at a DNC fund-raiser and contributed tens of thousands of dollars in illegal campaign funds to the Democrats.

- The officers of an American defense contractor in business with China's missile builders became the number one contributors to the Clinton-Gore reelection campaign in 1995–1996.

■ After illegal campaign funds began to flow to the DNC from a PLA spy, the Clinton White House and his navy secretary helped the PLA's arms delivery boys secure the port at Long Beach, California.

The bottom line: Clinton and Gore got away with it. They got themselves elected in 1992 and reelected in 1996 on foreign money, much of it from sources hostile to the United States. Congressional committees that investigated these abuses could not bring to account a single perpetrator; only an independent counsel with the full powers to compel witnesses and documents has the ability to uncover the ugly truth that we hope this book has begun to reveal. At this writing, not one single person on the recipient side of the ledger has been charged with any crime. Some of the conduits for foreign money, such as Charlie Trie and Maria Hsia, have been indicted, but only for minor offenses. But Clinton's Executive Order Number 1 has become an obscene joke.

Who would have guessed that Bill Clinton and Al Gore would use the power of the White House itself to lobby for a foreign power?

Political corruption is like a cancer; if not defeated, it continues to replicate. All Americans, as well as our friends and allies abroad, should be concerned. When an ends-justifies-the-means political campaign manifestly succeeds, it tends to spread corrosion and cynicism throughout the system. The healthy portions of neither the Democratic Party nor the Republican Party are naturally immune.

The problem is the demonstration effect. On the Republican side some consultants are beginning to talk quietly of a "if you can't beat 'em, join 'em" political strategy. As one Republican consultant observed, Republicans have looked at their prospects for upcoming elections and asked seriously, "What can we learn from Clinton?"[2] Unless the cancer is halted promptly, this kind of thinking will surely spread. The Republicans will find themselves making the same sort of Faustian bargains for the soul of their party that Clinton and Gore did.

We are particularly concerned about the possible effects of this political corruption on the workings of the Justice Department, including the FBI. Consider what we already know: for instance, that the Clinton White House improperly held roughly one thousand secret FBI files on Republicans; that the attorney general has, as of this writing, failed to seek an independent counsel to investigate campaign finance abuses; that the attorney general allowed the statute of limitations to run out so the Riadys would not be prosecuted for 1992 offenses; and that, as Senator Arlen Specter (R-PA) suggested, the failure of the FBI to discover evidence in its own files of a Chinese intelligence operation might have been more than simple incompetence.

The corrosive influence of the Clinton-Gore actions reaches farther than we ever imagined when we began our work.

WALL STREET

One of the most quoted lines in East-West relations is Kipling's famous epitaph, "Here lies a fool who tried to hustle the east." To President Clinton and his supporters, this may ultimately be the historical legacy of his administration. However, we would like to introduce a corollary to Kipling's observation: "Here lie the fools who tried to hustle the free market."

Because accurate financial information is so difficult to acquire, especially in China, we have barely touched on the danger investors in the American capital markets face because of PRC perfidy. Nevertheless, unless the market itself, the SEC, or the district attorney in Manhattan takes action against Chinese manipulation, the U.S. capital market will continue to be penetrated by

PRC interests, and the savings of American citizens will be at risk. Companies, lawyers, and accountants in the United States are investigating loopholes and lax application of U.S. disclosure rules that have allowed the PRC to manipulate the money of American investors. If American law enforcement institutions are unprepared to detect Chinese investment fraud—just as the CIA was unprepared to detect the secret nuclear tests in India—we hope this book will inspire investors to ask more questions about the stocks they buy.

NATIONAL DEFENSE

During the 1992 campaign candidate Bill Clinton bitterly attacked George Bush's China policy. Clinton said, "In the three years since the massacre in Tiananmen square, the Bush administration has pursued an ill-advised and failed policy of constructive engagement with the aging leaders in China."[3]

But Bush's policy toward the PRC was actually pretty straightforward: *The PRC's there, and we have to deal with it, but we're not going to sugarcoat the issue.* COCOM and the full range of export controls remained in place. The U.S. military was forbidden contact with high-ranking PLA officers. Bush never went to China after Tiananmen, and PRC leader Jiang Zemin wasn't invited to the United States. And just to make certain he had the PRC's attention, Bush sold Taiwan 150 F-16 fighter planes. In diplomatic language, it would be called "correct relations" but not "warm and friendly."

Since taking office, however, Bill Clinton has assembled a record that is far, far worse than anything he decried under President Bush. The record speaks for itself:

■ *Chinese Communist Party (CCP):* After the Tiananmen massacre, the democracies of the world were careful not to give legitimacy to the CCP. But Al Gore's champagne toast with Premier Li Peng in the spring of 1997 and Bill Clinton's specific endorsement of the Jiang leadership in the summer of 1998 ended the CCP leadership's status as political and social outcasts.

- *People's Liberation Army (PLA):* The Bush policy of no contact with the bloody-handed became, under Bill Clinton, nineteen-gun salutes and Oval Office visits for the very PLA generals who had personally ordered the killing of their countrymen.

- *Proliferation:* The Clinton-Gore administration's failure to pursue known cases of Chinese arms sales to terrorist regimes has meant millions of dollars right into the overseas accounts of top CCP/PLA leaders and their families.

- *Dr. Gordon Oehler:* Ex-CIA proliferation czar Gordon Oehler has testified[4] that the Clinton administration discourages U.S. government professionals from reporting on illicit Chinese arms sales.

- *U.S. Office of Naval Intelligence (ONI):* Under new management, ONI seems not to be in the business of informing the American people about Chinese proliferation activities anymore.

- *Espionage:* If he hadn't decided that testifying truthfully might tend to incriminate him, John Huang would have been asked a number of interesting questions.

- *COSCO:* The PLA's arms delivery team has a new home in California thanks to high-level intervention from the White House and the secretary of the navy.

- *Secretary of Defense William Perry:* His efforts to give stature to PLA generals and his hope to contribute to the build-up of the PLA are inexplicable.

- *National Security Adviser Sandy Berger:* Berger was, according to Representative Nancy Pelosi, the point man for the trade office of the Chinese government.

- *COCOM:* As soon as President Clinton came to power, the administration began dismantling the export control system, paving the way for American defense production equipment to be made available to the PLA.
- *Satellites:* Under the Clinton administration the PLA launchers have learned to make their missiles more reliable; the satellites are used for forbidden purposes; and the operators are simply members of the PLA in civvies.
- *Machine tools:* The machine tools we use to make ICBMs, strategic bombers, front-line fighters, and advanced air lifters all went to China.
- *Supercomputers:* The Commerce Department doesn't even know how many supercomputers the United States has sold to the PRC, under whose control they are, or for what purpose they are being operated.
- *Military-to-military relations:* Mostly in secret, the Clinton administration is providing training in logistics and other modern war-fighting capabilities the PLA has traditionally lacked.

In their scramble to secure and maintain power, Bill Clinton and Al Gore have left a horrible legacy of corruption.

When national defense specialists gather to look over the debris of the Clinton-Gore era, we normally talk about the losses—the lost army divisions, the lost air wings, the lost carrier battle groups—from even Bush's low post–Cold War levels. Where once the United States had 15 carrier battle groups, now we struggle to keep 11. In 1990 we had 18 army divisions; now we have 10, and the 10 are lighter than their predecessors. We have exactly half (12) the number of Air Force Tactical Wings we had under Bush (24). Active duty military personnel are down by a third (700,000).[5]

But what about the more subtle damage? The sell-off of our defense industrial base? The policy changes that strengthen foes and confound our long-time friends and allies? The social shifts that make it okay to be seen with foreign intelligence agents and gangsters?

One of America's most thoughtful commentators on national defense is Wisconsin University Professor Gary Milhollin. He notes, "The danger is that we are giving away the technical edge that we've always relied upon for our security."[6] That "technical edge" includes the computer-controlled machine tools, used to make our ICBMs, that were given to a Chinese army cruise missile plant, and the American supercomputers that China's defense industrial complex has managed to acquire.

A number of our friends and allies around the world—in Europe, Israel, the Gulf States, Taiwan, Japan, South Korea—rely heavily on American military equipment. Our technical edge is their technical edge, and in many cases having that edge is far more important to them than it is to us. If we lose the technical edge in one area or two, it might not be catastrophic to us immediately. Our distance from the battlefield will protect us... for a while. For our friends and allies, if they lose their edge in air-to-air combat, for example, they may lose their country.

At his January 1997 Senate confirmation Secretary of Defense William Cohen told the Armed Services Committee, "I believe the proliferation of weapons of mass destruction presents the gravest threat that the world has ever known."[7] We agree, which is why it has been so harmful for the Clinton administration to ignore PLA arms smuggling cases. For example, at her confirmation, Secretary of State Albright conceded to a senator that PLA companies were smuggling germ warfare equipment to Iran, but that the United States had applied no sanctions to punish this illegal act. In other words, the Clinton administration let PLA arms dealers believe that it wasn't serious about stopping this kind of trade. Based on past performance, there is nothing to suggest that the PLA would not arm subnational terrorist groups in the Middle East with such WMDs, if the price was right.

In recent years—with the World Trade Center bombing in New York, the U.S. embassy bombings in the Middle East and Africa, and so forth—we have seen how America has become a target for terrorist attacks. Eventually terrorists will try to target the United States or Americans abroad with WMDs. This is what is at stake when Clinton lifts sanctions against PLA companies just to please his leading contributor.

The Clinton-Gore administration has loudly proclaimed that the United States and the PRC are in a "strategic partnership."[8] What does it mean for the U.S. to be "strategic partners" with an aggressive, communist dictatorship, one that threatens democratic states like India and Taiwan? The pictures of the president and the vice president of the United States surrounded by Communist Chinese agents made the front pages from Tokyo to Tel Aviv. The message Bill Clinton and Al Gore have sent to the world has been clear.

This message can no longer be tolerated. In their scramble to secure and maintain power, Bill Clinton and Al Gore have left a horrible legacy of corruption: making unscrupulous bargains for campaign cash; selling out our national security; losing our nation's technical edge; catering to Chinese agents, arms smugglers, and gangsters; enabling PRC intelligence to penetrate our political and defense establishments; allowing the princelings to infiltrate Wall Street; and so much more. The damage they have done is deep, but there is, we hope, a treatment for this cancer on the country.

Wall Street Journal contributing editor Mark Helprin described President Clinton as "the most corrupt, fraudulent and dishonest president we have ever known." His remedy: "One word that will do justice. One word. Impeach."[9]

We agree.

PART FOUR:
UPDATE

CHAPTER 16
WHERE ARE THEY NOW?

S ince the first edition of *Year of the Rat* was published in the fall of 1998, a wealth of new information has become available to us—guilty pleas, government documents, sworn testimony, secret memoranda, and more. Significantly, the revelations made subsequent to this book's release have confirmed what we detailed in these pages and in fact have made clear that the Clinton-Gore administration has undermined America's national security even more than we initially realized.

JOHN HUANG AND JAMES RIADY

In August 1999 John Huang pleaded guilty to relatively insignificant felony campaign finance violations involving the Democratic Party in California and is, in theory, cooperating with authorities.

James Riady, meanwhile, seems to have survived both his troubles in the United States and political events in Indonesia. In the summer of 2000 rumors surfaced that he might be indicted for money laundering, but in our opinion it is unlikely he will ever see jail time.[1] Apparently Huang is still on good terms with his old employer; he told the FBI that Riady had given him at least $20,000 since his troubles began. Riady also has been funding Huang's trips to Asia. (We don't know why the State Department didn't pull Huang's passport.)

Since 1998 Huang has been deposed under oath by Larry

Klayman, chairman of Judicial Watch; testified before the House Government Reform and Oversight Committee, chaired by Congressman Dan Burton (R-IN); and been interviewed by the FBI as part of his plea agreement. With Judicial Watch, Huang asserted his Fifth Amendment right against self-incrimination.[2] By taking the Fifth, he indicated that if he were to tell the truth about what he knows concerning the Riadys, the Clintons, and his own activities at the Commerce Department, he might expose himself to criminal penalties under the federal criminal code.

Huang's performances before Congress and the FBI were indeed troubling, but they were not without value. Most notably, there emerged previously unknown information about Huang's fund-raising connections exclusively to Al Gore:

■ *September 1993:* Huang claimed his first fund-raising for Gore was an event at the California home of a real estate tycoon. Huang used this event to introduce Gore to Mr. Shen Jueren, the chairman of China Resources, and paid for his guest, Shen, with checks from Riady-controlled shell corporations.[3] China Resources is an associate of Chinese military intelligence. Huang told the FBI he was not aware that China Resources had paid for then-Governor Clinton's trip to Hong Kong in 1985.[4]

■ *September 1993:* Gore met Shen again at a second Huang-organized event, across the street from the Sheraton Hotel in Santa Monica. Lippo employees reportedly were secretly reimbursed for their tens of thousands of dollars' worth of contributions to this event.[5]

■ *November 1995:* Huang took over the fund-raising for this event while he was an employee of the Commerce Department. Consequently, the FBI asserted that he may have been violating Hatch Act proscriptions against political fund-raising by federal employees. At least one Lippo consultant was reimbursed for the $10,000 she contributed to Gore at this event.[6]

- *November 1995:* Gore was the main draw at an event in major Democratic donor Marvin Davis's home, and Huang contributed at least $5,000.[7]

- *February 1996:* The day after the infamous million-dollar Hay-Adams evening with Clinton (see Chapter 6, "The Week That Was (II)"), Huang organized a $12,500-per-person breakfast with Gore. We believe Macau criminal syndicate figure Ng Lapseng and his associates may have attended the Gore breakfast.[8]

- *September 1996:* Huang organized an event in San Francisco at which a relative of Chinese agent Ted Sioeng contributed $20,000.[9]

The new information regarding Huang is not limited to his Gore connections. After he received immunity from prosecution, Huang confessed to illegal campaign fund-raising for Clinton and Gore in 1992 that went far wider and far deeper than was previously known. We had originally estimated that the Riady/Lippo cascade of money in the late summer and fall of 1992 amounted to about $600,000. But Huang told the FBI that the famous Riady-Clinton limousine ride set in motion the transfer of *$1 million* in illegal campaign contributions in 1992.[10] Much more money, many more conduits to disguise it. For instance, just before the 1992 election, Lippo interests put tens of thousands of dollars into CITIZENS VOTE INC. and VOTE NOW '92, two organizations associated with the Democrats.[11]

The Clinton-Gore administration has undermined America's national security even more than we initially realized.

A good deal of the Riady-Huang-Clinton-Gore money in 1992 was *cash.* Huang told the FBI that James Riady provided cash in 1992 "for Huang to travel around the country to get people to participate in [political] events."[12] Further, the FBI noted, "Huang agreed that he had numerous cash deposits in his Lippo Bank accounts from July 1992 to December 1992."[13] In January 1993

Huang received over $105,000 for "expenses related to the [Clinton-Gore] inauguration."[14] None of this was known to the American people, of course. What might the Republicans have made of it had they known before the election?

As one consequence, Riady had an even stronger claim on Clinton and Gore when they took office in 1993 than even we suspected. Huang told the FBI that, in an early effort to cash in on his "investment" in Clinton and Gore, Riady had wanted to place Huang in Clinton's National Security Council, but that was apparently too much even for the Clinton-Gore administration.[15] The Commerce Department, well out of the way of snooping reporters, was more than satisfactory.

In his FBI interview Huang also provided an interesting tidbit about Clinton friend Webster Hubbell. According to the FBI report on the interview, "When asked if Huang thought that J. Riady gave Hubbell $100,000 as [a] friendly gesture or for some other purpose, Huang replied, 'Everything has a purpose.'"

In sum, during a secret limousine ride, a foreign associate of Chinese military intelligence pledged $1 million in illegal campaign contributions to the Clinton-Gore ticket in 1992. His employee delivered on that promise, traveling around the United States with cash that has never been fully accounted for. In return for this largesse, the illegal donor could place his employee in the United States government with "Top Secret" access to American secrets about Communist China. And the foreign donor's "magician" made certain his illegal fund-raising magic was available for Al Gore.

Finally, it gave us some measure of satisfaction to watch the FBI interrogate Huang on the basis of information provided exclusively in *Year of the Rat*. For example, the bureau went after Huang about Communist Chinese Politburo member Chen Xitong, the Riadys, and their investment on Beijing's Wangfujing Street—a connection he did not deny (see Chapter 2, "Lippo and the Riadys").[16] Later, the FBI questioned him about his study of espionage before he went to Commerce (see Chapter 3, "John Huang the Magician"). This led to the following amusing report by the FBI:

> When asked by the [FBI] interviewers if it didn't seem odd that a person about to embark upon a U.S. Government career had requested documents relating to espionage, Huang replied, "I wouldn't blame you for feeling it was odd." He said, "I have no explanation."[17]

We can't top that.

CHARLIE TRIE

Like John Huang, Charlie Trie pleaded guilty to minor campaign funding offenses and is, also in theory, cooperating with the FBI. And like Huang, Trie revealed to the FBI a much larger pattern of illegal campaign contributions to the Clinton-Gore ticket in 1996, including a substantial cash element.

Trie told the FBI that he had borrowed but never repaid a loan of $200,000 from Hong Kong businessman Albert Yeung. According to Trie, "Yeung failed to obtain a visa to enter the U.S. because of [his] involvement with former Representative Stephen Solarz (D-NY), who was accused in 1993 of abusing his authority in attempting to intervene with the State Department to obtain a multi-year visa for Yeung." The FBI did not follow up on this line of questioning.

Trie was unable to explain satisfactorily to the FBI his own handwritten notes that included the words "Hughes," "Boeing," and "bribery." It's not clear if the FBI is pursuing this line of questioning.

Trie also informed the FBI that he had given First Lady Hillary Clinton a pearl necklace. The FBI did not follow up on this matter.

Despite the FBI's failure to pursue what would seem to be important matters, we have been able to solve at least one mystery thanks to what Charlie Trie told authorities. The issue in question first came to our attention in January 1997, the beginning of the Clinton-Gore administration's second term. Madeleine Albright was in the process of being confirmed as secretary of state. Senator Robert Bennett (R-UT) submitted some written questions to her, one of which asked whether Communist Chinese military companies were selling germ warfare equipment to Iran.[18]

Albright confirmed that this illicit trade was going on and indicated the administration's concern. Chapter 8 of the United States Arms Export Control Act provides a penalty for any foreign company that "knowingly and materially contributed... to the efforts by any foreign country... to use, develop, produce, stockpile, or otherwise acquire chemical or biological [germ] weapons." Considering how dangerous Chinese germ warfare equipment sales to Iran would be to the American homeland or our servicemen and women in the Persian Gulf,[19] we anticipated that the administration would immediately penalize Beijing.

It didn't happen. Beyond Albright's acknowledgment that the trade was indeed occurring, nothing. No identification of the Chinese companies selling the equipment. No description of what was being sold to Iran. No penalties for anyone.

Four months later, Senator Bennett tried again. At a public hearing in May 1997, he asked Albright about Chinese companies that were selling poison gas equipment to Iran. This time she responded by taking action, that very day naming and penalizing two Chinese government–owned companies on the mainland and one Chinese government–owned company in Hong Kong. The Beijing government complained about the penalties for weeks.

It didn't make sense. Why penalize Chinese companies for poison gas equipment sales to Iran but not for germ warfare equipment sales to Iran? Both penalties come right out of the same sentence in Chapter 8 of the Arms Export Control Act. Certainly germs in the hands of someone who hates the United States pose at least as dangerous a threat as poison gas. Anthrax is just one possible biological threat; other designer germs could be produced under some conditions. And, though it's given little consideration, almost no one in the United States is immune to smallpox.[20] So, for three years we wondered, why penalize for one action and not for the other?

Now we have an explanation.

We have learned that Charlie Trie was involved in germ warfare trade.[21] He received a commission of tens of thousands of dollars from the Chinese for brokering the sale of Swiss biological equipment to a biological institute in China. The equipment in question[22] is commonly used to produce biological weapons. The institute in question is in the same town as China's known germ warfare facility.[23]

At a March 2000 hearing by the House Government Reform and Oversight Committee, there was this exchange:

REPRESENTATIVE BOB BARR (R-GA): *So it doesn't concern you that this machinery is in the hands of the Chinese government and may be used to produce biological weapons?*
TRIE: *If they don't get it from me, they get it from someone else. They gonna get it.*[24]

Based on the evidence, this is what we believe happened: In January 1997, when Senator Bennett asked Albright the germ warfare question, the Clinton-Gore administration was between a rock and a hard place. On the one hand, classified information on the China-Iran germ warfare trade would have been well known to the American intelligence community. If Albright denied it, someone might leak to the press information on the germ warfare trade, which would jeopardize her confirmation as secretary of state. Congress doesn't like to be lied to. On the other hand, if the administration penalized the Chinese companies, it would run the risk that a public row with Beijing might lead the press to Charlie Trie. Trie struck his deal with the Chinese in late 1992, giving China's army more than four years to produce knock-off copies and sell them to the Iranians.

January 1997 should have been a happy time for Clinton and Gore as they celebrated their second inauguration. Instead they were taking a pounding in the press, with fresh revelations coming almost daily. The papers and networks were competing with stories about the Riadys, John Huang, Ted Sioeng, Chinese espionage, Chinese arms dealers in the White House, and on and on.

Most importantly, the Republicans and Democrats in Congress were negotiating over the authority and duration of the upcoming investigations by the Burton committee and by the Senate Governmental Affairs Committee, chaired by Fred Thompson (R-TN). If the connection between Trie, Chinese germ warfare, and Iran had been known at this crucial moment, it would have produced a firestorm on Capitol Hill. The Democrats would have been in no position to defend the White House or put a time limit on Senator Thompson's investigation.[25]

So the administration buried it. Albright admitted that the Chinese had made the sale so her confirmation wouldn't be in jeopardy. But there were no details, no penalties, no public shouting match with the Chinese government, and, consequently, no loose ends that would lead a good reporter to Trie.

Actually, by January 1997 Trie had fled the country, and nobody really cared about him. Clinton and Gore were the ones who had to be protected. The administration had reason to be concerned because following the trail from Charlie Trie leads to other unsavory characters, including Ng Lapseng, who made millions in illegal campaign contributions to the Democratic National Committee (DNC) and is now living safely in Macau, and Ted Sioeng, a Chinese agent who made more illegal contributions and has since fled to China. Trie even bragged to the FBI that he had been the one who came up with the idea of using the Buddhist temple in California to raise money for the Democrats. That, of course, leads to Gore and an entirely new cast of shady characters, including Maria Hsia, the longtime Gore fund-raiser and Chinese agent who in March 2000 was convicted on five felony counts related to her illegal fund-raising scheme. And we certainly can't forget about Pauline Kanchanalak, who has pleaded guilty to an illegal scheme to funnel $690,000 to the Clinton-Gore ticket in 1996.

The bottom line is that the Clinton-Gore administration was clever and dodged a very big bullet. And the Chinese army got a free pass for selling germ warfare equipment to a sworn enemy of the United States.

JOHNNY CHUNG

In March 1998 Johnny Chung pleaded guilty to bank fraud, tax evasion, and conspiracy in relation to his funneling of illegal campaign contributions to the 1996 Clinton-Gore campaign. Since then he has genuinely cooperated with investigators and with Congress. Chung testified before Congress that General Ji Shengde, the number two man in China's military intelligence apparatus, told him, "We really like your president [Clinton]," and that he gave Chung $300,000 to ensure that Clinton and Gore were successful in the 1996 election. When Chung started to get cold feet, Ji's assistant, Chinese military spy Liu Chaoying, told him that Chinese military intelligence was already using other conduits to pump illegal campaign contributions into the Clinton-Gore ticket in 1996. Chung alleged that Liu told him $500,000 had gone to Clinton fund-raiser Mark Middleton via a Singapore company.

At the request of the FBI, Chung wore a wire for furtive meetings in California with a self-professed envoy from Beijing. The envoy seemed to dangle money and a possible presidential pardon in front of Chung if he would keep his mouth shut—and harm to him and his family if he didn't. One of Beijing's highest priorities was to keep the American public from knowing of any possible connections between Liu Chaoying and Hughes and Loral, Chung was told.

THE AMERICAN CORPORATIONS

What of the American corporations that contributed to the military modernization of the Chinese People's Liberation Army (PLA)?

In June 2000 Lockheed-Martin was fined a record $13 million for sharing missile data with China.[26]

Meanwhile, the State Department killed the Hughes satellite sale to China (General Shen Rongjun's project). Hughes—or at least its insurance company—was forced to eat a loss of about a half-billion dollars for what is now space-junk. C. Michael Armstrong, chief executive officer of Hughes at the time of the satellite deal, is now chairman of AT&T.

Hong Kong's *South China Morning Post* revealed that two of the directors of the Singapore company that was to own and operate the Hughes satellite were Chinese military officers in civilian clothes and that three other directors were officials of China Resources, a longtime associate of Chinese military intelligence.[27]

As for Loral, the corporation seems not to have been bothered much by the authorities. Chairman Bernard Schwartz, for his part, has been a major donor to Hillary Clinton's 2000 campaign to become the junior senator from New York.

And in the fall of 1999 McDonnell-Douglas (which has been absorbed into Boeing) was indicted for offenses related to its selling of the Ohio machine tool plant to military end-users in China.[28] Moreover, the project for which company officials sold their souls—McDonnell-Douglas airliner production in China—was canceled by the Chinese in the spring of 2000.

THE COMMUNISTS GO CAPITALIST—REPRISE

In Chapter 14, "The Communists Go Capitalist," we noted that accurate corporate financial information is extremely difficult to acquire, especially in China.[29] Not only that, but PRC accounting standards are created "as needed," hardly the basis for prudent investments. In truth, the chapter barely touched upon the mounting danger American investors in capital markets—that is, the stock and bond markets—face because of the PRC's lack of financial transparency and disclosure.[30]

Over the past few years, however, a national security team that President Ronald Reagan originally created to lead the financial war against the Soviet Union has scored remarkable success in bringing to light the true nature of PRC business practices.[31] The goal of President Reagan's effort was, according to key National Security Council member—and primary architect of the plan—Roger W. Robinson, Jr., "to curtail subsidized Western life support to the Soviet Union."[32] It worked.

America's capital markets are vast, fair, and honest. Business enterprises worldwide are eager to enter the globally dominant U.S. capital markets, but the price is full and honest disclosure. The theory of full disclosure is simple: When you take other people's money, you are obliged to tell the whole truth—and to *keep* telling the truth—about your financial health and how you plan to use the money.

Unfortunately, the wrong sorts of PRC interests and enterprises are penetrating U.S. capital markets in an attempt to tap into the savings of American citizens without meeting the protective standards of full disclosure. Investment banks, lawyers, and accountants in the United States are helping craft China's Wall Street offerings to find loopholes or lax application of U.S. disclosure rules, letting the PLA, among other entities, create financial instruments to capture American investors' money—by the billions.

Americans across the political spectrum are horrified by the causes that this money is used to support. Human rights advocates are sickened by PLA murder in Tibet, the army's support for genocide in Sudan, and its repression of Chinese citizens. National security experts are extremely concerned about the PLA's unprecedented military modernization as well as Beijing's support for terrorist states, which are being fueled by American dollars. Labor unions are justified in objecting to cheap imports produced by PRC slave labor.[33] Environmental groups are rightly troubled over China's despoiling of sensitive ecosystems.

Americans were slow to recognize this major emerging national security threat in our capital markets. The problem was so hidden that, in 1997, Capitol Hill offices were bombarded with phone calls objecting to Republican efforts to protect American investors.[34] "You are Republicans," one typical caller objected, "why are you trying to create more government regulations?" The bill, a Market Security Act introduced in the 105th Congress, would have created a national security office in the Securities and Exchange Commission (SEC). This office would track foreign investment flowing into Wall Street and make periodic reports to Congress in order to ensure transparency and full disclosure from foreign firms in America. In truth, there were no regulations in the bill, but investment community lobbyists effectively killed the effort. In 1998 Senator Lauch Faircloth (R-NC), a sponsor of the bill, was defeated for reelection, and Congressman Gerald Solomon (R-NY), another sponsor, gave up his seat for personal health reasons.

The U.S. Market Security Act was reintroduced in the 106th Congress by Representatives Spencer Bachus (R-AL) and Dennis Kucinich (D-OH), but, as of this writing, it has simply been referred to a number of committees. Thus, barring a major event, such as a PRC attack on Taiwan, the bill will more than likely languish and die with the end of the 106th Congress.[35]

Still, things began to change in late 1999. The free markets had been pounding "red chips," and congressional oversight, combined with excellent press reporting,[36] allowed unprecedented "sunlight" to be shed on the nastiest PRC stock of all, PetroChina, a contrived subsidiary of China National Petroleum Corporation. The results were dramatic.

PetroChina is "China's flagship oil company," according to the *New York Times*.[37] China National Petroleum Corporation, China's massive state-owned energy company, is, in the words of the *Financial Times*, "an inefficient state apparatus with nearly 1m employees which is bound by no disclosure requirements."[38] In September 1999 China National and PetroChina were planning to go forward with an estimated $10 billion initial public offering (IPO) on the New York Stock Exchange and were simultaneously planning to list on the Hong Kong exchange. The money in the offering was to fund exploration and would make PetroChina the world's fourth largest publicly traded oil and gas company.[39] But raising a huge sum of money was not the only reason for the communists in Beijing to push PetroChina at the highest levels. As the *Far Eastern Economic Review* pointed out, it was hoped that PetroChina "would lay the groundwork for other capital-starved Chinese state companies to tap into the U.S. stock market."[40] It turned into a debacle.

A foreign associate of Chinese military intelligence pledged $1 million in illegal campaign contributions to the Clinton-Gore ticket in 1992.

How? A combination of savvy financial players, human rights activists, labor union executives, national security specialists, environmentalists, advocates of Tibetan freedom, and concerned congressmen led a broad-based coalition of as many as forty million Americans to try to stop the IPO.[41] Although the IPO was not entirely stopped, due to eleventh-hour privately placed bailouts, it was seriously wounded. It ultimately brought in less than $2.9 billion—far below the initial $10 billion estimate. If over a 70 percent downsizing of the offering were not enough, the firestorm that engulfed the PetroChina IPO caused two other major Chinese IPOs to be pulled from U.S. markets. Beijing thus missed out on some $15 billion in a six-month period. Moreover, the battle shed light on China National's lack of transparency and its inadequate corporate governance. And PetroChina's stock offering may have had significant material omissions that lawyers can sort out for investors who smell fraud. All in all, it was a remarkable, precedent-setting effort by nongovernmental organizations and ordinary Americans.

The battle against Communist China's invasion of Wall Street continues, but the PetroChina experience is beginning to remind insightful stock analysts of the anti-apartheid campaign against South Africa. In the words of Mark Melcher and Stephen Soukup of Prudential Securities, "There is blood on the floor already, and the prospect is that it will get increasingly sanguineous in coming years, as the much-vaunted 'globalization' trend leads American bankers ever more deeply into financing projects in nations that are considered by some to be serious security threats to the United States."[42]

But where was the Clinton-Gore administration during all this?

We now know that Lieutenant Colonel Liu Chaoying, PRC intelligence agent, was successful in offering bribes to penetrate the Clinton-Gore administration and that she also targeted the SEC.

The result? Sadly (but unsurprisingly), the Clinton-Gore team went AWOL in the fight to stop PetroChina. In fact, evidence indicates that the Clinton-Gore administration was active at the highest levels in helping the PRC every step of the way.[43] After trying to isolate Sudan with sanctions on other joint oil ventures, the administration stopped short, according to the *Christian Science Monitor*, "of imposing sanctions on China or Talisman Energy, the Canadian partner."[44] President Clinton, in a letter to Nina Shea, the director of the human rights group Freedom House, stated that he would not impose sanctions on "foreign companies' activities in Sudan."[45] Yet the administration sanctioned Greater Nile Petroleum Operating Company and Sudan's state oil company. Even *Time* magazine has pointed out the administration's "Double Standards" and National Security Adviser Sandy Berger's support to erode sanctions.[46]

As of this writing, Al Gore is asking Americans to vote for him by asking a simple question: "Are you better off today than eight years ago?" From a military or national security perspective, the answer is straightforward: *absolutely not*. And from a financial perspective, consider that, thanks to PRC fraud on Wall Street, your money may well have made its way to the leadership of Communist China, which could use it to fund the PLA or a Chinese intelligence organization, or to underwrite slavery and the murder of Christians in Sudan. As PRC fraud increasingly makes its way onto Wall Street and the pension funds of American families, Americans will discover that they are not better off than eight years ago.

CHAPTER 17
OBSTRUCTION OF JUSTICE

O n the night of December 12, 1996, President Bill Clinton
and Attorney General Janet Reno—just the two of
them—sat down for a fateful meeting in the White
House. To be fair, only they know exactly what went on. But documents and testimony that have subsequently appeared outline what must have happened: Reno sold out. In return for four more years as attorney general, she went along with a secret program to ensure that the heir apparent, Albert Gore, would be protected and that those who had benefited from the most successful foreign penetration of the American government would not be prosecuted.

To understand the importance of the December 12 meeting, we have to look back over the three months leading up to it. In mid-September 1996 the *Los Angeles Times* broke the first story on illegal campaign contributions to the Clinton-Gore reelection effort. By mid-October the press was in a feeding frenzy about John Huang, the Riadys, and the rest. Vice President Gore was seen beside the Buddhist nuns night after night as the television networks ran the Hsi Lai Temple tapes over and over. Throughout November the Republicans in Congress were bombarding Reno with demands that she appoint an independent counsel to cover campaign finance—that is, Chinagate.

At the same time, White House leaks reported that Reno would not be kept on for the second term. "She has skidded to a stop at an

unexpected career crossroads," wrote David Johnson and Todd
Purdom of the *New York Times*.[1] No one doubted the source of her
problems. She had already appointed four independent counsels, one
to investigate the Clintons themselves in the Whitewater case and
three to examine Clinton friends—Secretary of Commerce Ron
Brown, Secretary of Agriculture Mike Espy, and Secretary of Housing
and Urban Development Henry Cisneros.[2] Another independent
counsel for campaign finance would have been number five.

So, on November 29, 1996—shortly before her one-on-one meeting with President Clinton—Janet Reno for-
mally announced that she would not appoint
an independent counsel to look into campaign
fund-raising irregularities.[3]

> **In December 1996 Clinton
> and Reno struck a deal:
> four more years for Reno
> as attorney general in
> return for the most signifi-
> cant obstruction of justice
> in a generation.**

According to a December 9, 1996, memo
by FBI Director Louis Freeh that did not surface until the spring of 2000, Lee Radek, the
head of the Justice Department's Office of
Public Integrity, told two senior FBI officials in early December 1996
that he was "under a lot of pressure" and that Reno's job was on the
line.[4] Freeh added to Reno's troubles with his recommendation that
she take the campaign finance investigation away from Radek, argu-
ing that Radek's team "was not capable of conducting the thorough,
aggressive kind of investigation which was required."[5] In the memo,
Freeh also complained that Reno had not consulted with the FBI on
the matter of appointing an independent counsel; in fact, he implied
that he didn't agree with her decision and that an independent counsel would have been appropriate.

Thus, by the time of her December 12 meeting with Clinton, Reno
could bring two important gifts to the president. First, by refusing to
appoint an independent counsel, she had already placed in motion a
secret program to control and limit any true investigation of
Chinagate. Second, by rejecting three separate Republican demands
for an independent counsel, as well as Freeh's first recommendation,[6]

she had demonstrated her loyalty for the future. Clinton, for his part, knew that any replacement for Reno would face a stormy confirmation process over the independent counsel issue.[7]

So Clinton and Reno struck a deal: four more years for Reno as attorney general in return for the most significant obstruction of justice in a generation.

At the time, *Newsweek* remarked: "[Reno] keeps her job. But one more showy act of integrity and she's out."[8] There would be no more showy acts of integrity.

THE SECRET PLAN TO OBSTRUCT JUSTICE

The secret plan to obstruct justice, at the center of which sat Attorney General Janet Reno, rested on five pillars:

- Shutting down the experienced federal prosecutors in Los Angeles who were prepared to investigate Gore at the Buddhist temple.
- Appointing a relatively inexperienced prosecutor at the Justice Department as a means of restricting the investigation.
- Handcuffing the FBI's efforts to get to the bottom of Communist China's efforts to penetrate the American government.
- Resisting all efforts by Congress to force the appointment of an independent counsel, no matter what evidence turned up.
- Assisting the Clinton-Gore private witness protection service for John Huang and the like.

Shutting Down the L.A. Prosecutors

In the mid-1990s a group of tough and able federal attorneys in Los Angeles began to close in on Congressman Jay Kim, a Republican representing California's Forty-first District. In 1995 and 1996 the prosecutors nailed five foreign companies for making illegal contributions to Kim through a straw donor program. The companies were fined $1.6 million.[9] By April 1997 they had convicted Kim's campaign treasurer of concealing illegal contributions, and in August 1997 Kim and his wife pleaded guilty to accepting and concealing $230,000 in illegal campaign contributions.[10] In 1998 Kim lost the Republican primary by a wide margin.[11]

So, by October 1996 the L.A. prosecutors had convicted Kim's donors, and convicting the congressman himself was only a matter of time. They had a record of success with the exact topics on which Gore was taking heat concerning the temple—illegal foreign contributions, straw donors, conspiracy to conceal the donations. Since their former target had been a Republican, no one could accuse them of partisanship.

They wanted a shot at Gore and the temple, but the Department of Justice shut them down.

We now know that on November 1, 1996, four days before the 1996 presidential election, Lee Radek sent a secret cease-and-desist order to the Los Angeles federal prosecutors in the Gore-temple matter.[12] Radek argued that the issues they were pursuing would be handled by an independent counsel. The prosecutors complied with the order.

In retrospect, it's easy to see Justice's concern, even panic. Digging into the temple matter immediately brings to light Maria Hsia, longtime Gore fund-raiser and Chinese agent. Ted Sioeng, another Chinese agent (now fled to China), next appears. Sioeng leads to Cambodian drug lord Theng Bunma and Macau criminal syndicate figure Ng Lapseng. Ng leads to Charlie Trie, and hovering in the background is John Huang, the Riadys' man in the United States. Pulling on these strings leads to Johnny Chung, Chinese army intelligence, and Hughes and Loral. Pretty soon the Los Angeles prosecutors, had they been allowed to investigate, would have been knee-deep in millions of dollars in illegal campaign contributions, drugs and thugs, women used for forced prostitution, espionage, and threats to our national security. And Al Gore would have been at ground zero of the investigation.

L.A. PROSECUTORS

AP PHOTO/JOE MARQUETTE

AL GORE

Knee-deep in millions of dollars in illegal campaign contributions, drugs and thugs, women used for forced prostitution, espionage, threats to national security. And Al Gore would have been at ground zero of the investigation.

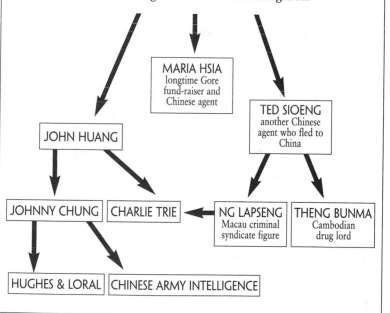

MARIA HSIA
longtime Gore
fund-raiser and
Chinese agent

TED SIOENG
another Chinese
agent who fled to
China

JOHN HUANG

JOHNNY CHUNG   **CHARLIE TRIE**

NG LAPSENG
Macau criminal
syndicate figure

THENG BUNMA
Cambodian
drug lord

HUGHES & LORAL   **CHINESE ARMY INTELLIGENCE**

Restricting the Investigation

We now also know that on the same day—November 1, 1996—that Radek sent his secret cease-and-desist order to the federal prosecutors in Los Angeles, he was also setting up an internal investigation task force *under his own control*, headed by Laura Ingersoll.[13] This is absolutely crucial, for if Radek had really felt that the Gore-temple issue was destined for an independent counsel investigation, as he told the Los Angeles prosecutors, he *never* would have set up his own task force on the matter.

Ingersoll lasted in her position for some ten months before Reno fired her. At a September 1999 public hearing, she was humiliated as Senator Fred Thompson (R-TN), chairman of the Senate Governmental Affairs Committee, read a *New York Times* account of her lack of experience. Thompson cited one case in which she had prosecuted an official for using the office copier to start a dance class.[14]

(Because Ingersoll was so inexperienced, it begs the question of why she had been appointed to head the task force in the first place. Is it possible that the Democratic administration saw her as politically reliable?)

Whether or not Ingersoll was qualified (and whether or not she had a political agenda), the Justice Department's investigation has been a bad joke. To date, Justice has produced no indictments or convictions of any recipient of the illegal campaign contributions. There has been no jail time for anyone, including the donors. The Chinese government, moreover, has not been seriously inconvenienced. In short, little effort has been made to tie up the loose ends of this conspiracy—which it surely is.

Columnist Morton Kondracke aptly summed it up:

It smells. Despite abundant evidence that Democratic fund-raisers channeled Chinese government money into the U.S. election campaign in 1996, no one is going to jail. One by one, Attorney General Reno's Justice Department has cut generous plea bargains with the money launderers and hasn't come near prosecuting any Democratic Party or White House officials.[15]

Handcuffing the FBI

Stopping the Los Angeles prosecutors in their tracks and bringing the investigation into a controlled environment at Justice was not enough; the FBI would have to be handcuffed. Although technically part of Justice, the FBI has enough independence (and friends on Capitol Hill) to be dangerous.

During the time of the Senate Governmental Affairs Committee's hearings (July–October 1997) we knew something was terribly wrong with the Justice Department's investigation and the FBI's part in it. We now know more details, specifically that in at least one area, the Charlie Trie investigation, Justice was actively blocking the FBI:

- Even though the FBI knew Trie's secretary was destroying crucial evidence, it was denied a search warrant.
- Justice forced the FBI to serve a subpoena on the secretary *before* a wiretap could be put in place. Because of the premature timing, we don't know to whom she turned when the panic set in.
- FBI field agents observed boxes being removed from the secretary's residence but were denied permission to stop the car.
- The FBI knew an important witness was going to escape the country, but the bureau was denied an arrest warrant. The next day, the witness fled to China.
- When the FBI had a witness ready to talk about $100,000 *in cash* coming in from China, a Justice Department lawyer trashed the witness before the federal grand jury.
- Even though Justice and Senator Thompson's committee were working the same territory, Justice refused to allow the FBI to share information with Thompson.

These stories, and more, were related in sworn testimony by FBI agents before Chairman Thompson in September 1999.[16] Who is alleged to have obstructed the FBI? Laura Ingersoll.

The $100,000 witness may best illustrate the problem. As I.C. Smith, former special agent in charge of the Arkansas portion of the investigation, told Chairman Thompson, a cooperating witness was ready to describe the duffel bags of money coming into the Democratic National Committee (DNC) from China via Charlie Trie. The witness, who was from Arkansas, was worried about his vulnerability; Special Agent Smith described him as "emotionally fragile." Nevertheless, Smith and his team of FBI agents brought the witness along and turned him over to Ingersoll's attorneys so he could testify before the federal grand jury.

Then the bottom fell out. According to Special Agent Smith, Ingersoll's subordinate not only was unprepared for the testimony, but he also spent most of the time discrediting his own witness before the grand jury. One member of Smith's team, Special Agent Kevin Sheridan, told Chairman Thompson that he "was embarrassed to be in the room" with Ingersoll's subordinate during the grand jury testimony. The witness was devastated by the experience.[17]

Over the summer of 1997 the FBI team became more and more outraged with Ingersoll's behavior. Special Agent Daniel Wehr told Senator Joseph Lieberman (D-CT) that Ingersoll had prohibited him from investigating the matter of whether the Democrats had solicited funds by promising access to President Clinton. "That's the way the American political system works," Ingersoll allegedly told him. Special Agent Wehr said he was "scandalized by that answer," and Senator Lieberman agreed with him.[18]

At the end of July 1997, Special Agent Smith had had enough. First he took the unusual step of going to the director, Louis Freeh, with his complaints. Freeh told Smith to put them into writing, which he did. He concluded his written comments by stating, "I am convinced the team at DOJ [Department of Justice] is, at best, simply not up to the task."[19]

By mid-September 1997 the smell from Ingersoll's operation was too much even for Reno. Ingersoll was tossed out, to be replaced by an experienced prosecutor, Charles LaBella. But her boss, Lee Radek, was untouched—he remains in charge of Justice's Public Integrity Section.

On LaBella's watch, the FBI got its search warrant and Trie's secretary admitted destroying documents, but vital time and information had been lost. Special Agent Smith thinks his memo to FBI Director Freeh did the trick in moving the investigation forward; Senator Arlen Specter (R-PA) pointed to the cascade of information that resulted after one senator in the summer of 1997 presented Freeh and CIA Director George Tenet with a series of questions about the China Connection (see Chapter 8, "A Tale of Three Cities"). Probably it was a combination. Reno couldn't handle both the FBI and Congress in revolt.

The affair closes with Chairman Thompson's admonition to Laura Ingersoll:

> You are a law enforcement officer. But not only are you are not willing to let the FBI do anything about it, you won't even tell us about it. How do you defend that?[20]

No Independent Counsel

Lee Radek froze the Los Angeles prosecutors on the grounds that their work would be taken over by an independent counsel. But since he assigned the matter to Laura Ingersoll on the same day, it seems Justice had no intention of naming an independent counsel for the Gore-temple affair or for the other Communist Chinese money issues. It was all a fraud.

In January 1997 congressional Republicans did not know of Radek's maneuvers or that Attorney General Reno had already decided to ignore Freeh's recommendation to remove Radek from the investigation. They would not learn any of this for more than three

years. They put their (misplaced) faith in Reno's reputation for independence and honesty. With all the horrors they expected to emerge
from the investigations of the Thompson committee and the House
Government Reform and Oversight Committee, chaired by
Congressman Dan Burton (R-IN), they thought it would be impossible for her to avoid naming an independent counsel.

When word leaked that, in a memo dated November 24, 1997,
Freeh had recommended that Reno appoint an independent counsel
for Chinagate, and that Charles LaBella had done the same in a
memo dated July 16, 1998,[21] the Republicans again showed faith in
the system (and again it was misplaced). This was a strategic political
error by the Republicans, but of course they didn't know that the fix
had been in as far back as November and December of 1996.

Events since 1997 have exposed the ugly truth. Attorney General
Reno has repeatedly vetoed full-scale investigations into possible
abuses by the scandal-plagued Clinton-Gore administration:

- *November 1997:* No to FBI Director Louis Freeh's recommen-
  dation of an independent counsel.
- *December 1997:* No independent counsel to investigate White
  House fund-raising calls made by Clinton and Gore.
- *December 1997:* No independent counsel on allegations that
  Energy Secretary Hazel O'Leary had solicited money from
  Chinese businessmen.
- *July 1998:* No to Justice Department investigator Charles
  LaBella's recommendation of an independent counsel.
- *November 1998:* No independent counsel to investigate Gore
  for fund-raising calls made from the White House.
- *December 1998:* No independent counsel to investigate
  Clinton's role in a possibly unlawful multimillion-dollar adver-
  tising campaign for the 1996 election.
- *January 1999:* No independent counsel to investigate a $1 million
  payment that Clinton-Gore campaign manager Peter Knight

received, possibly for helping a friend get favorable terms on a government lease.

Time after time the same dreary episode played itself out: Reno came to the Hill to defend the indefensible. Embarrassed Democrats had to support her. Republicans were reduced to rage.

In August 1998 the House Committee on Government Reform cited Reno for contempt. Chairman Dan Burton began to move for a contempt citation by the full House but was derailed when Reno collapsed in church a month later. Still, the chronology paints a clear picture of a Justice Department that blocked a full-scale investigation of Chinagate:

- *1995–1996:* The Los Angeles federal prosecutors convict illegal donors to the campaign of Congressman Jay Kim (R-CA).
- *Mid-October 1996:* Vice President Al Gore makes his TV debut in the Buddhist temple affair.
- *Mid-October 1996:* The Los Angeles prosecutors begin to investigate the Gore-temple affair for possible criminal violations.
- *November 1, 1996:* Lee Radek of the Justice Department sends a secret cease-and-desist order to the Los Angeles prosecutors on the grounds that an independent counsel would cover the investigation.
- *November 1, 1996:* Radek sets up the Laura Ingersoll group under his control to investigate Gore at the Hsi Lai Temple and other campaign finance issues.
- *November 5, 1996*: Clinton and Gore are reelected.
- *November 29, 1996:* Attorney General Janet Reno rejects Republican calls for an independent counsel to investigate campaign fund-raising abuses.
- *Early December 1996:* Radek tells FBI officials that he is "under a lot of pressure" and that Reno's job is on the line.

■ *December 9, 1996:* Freeh recommends that Radek be removed from control of the investigation.

■ *December 12, 1996:* President Clinton and Reno meet privately.

■ *December 13, 1996:* Clinton officially confirms that Reno will continue on as attorney general.

The Clinton-Gore Private Witness Protection Service

When Clinton and Gore began to get into trouble, longtime Washington observers confidently predicted that it was only a matter of time before someone in the know began to talk. It didn't happen. With the exception of Johnny Chung, not one of the major figures involved in Chinagate—or many of the other Clinton-Gore scandals, for that matter—has truly cooperated with authorities.

We believe that the answer to this puzzle lies in a kind of private witness protection service run out of the White House to take care of anyone who is a witness or a target of investigators.[22] Examples of this witness protection service occasionally show up above the waterline, such as the attempts to find a job in New York for Monica Lewinsky or the effort to give Webb Hubbell a series of paying jobs for no work.[23] But for the most part the service is deeply submerged.

Reno's Justice Department facilitates this operation. For instance, when Laura Ingersoll refused an FBI request for an arrest warrant, the person in question fled to China the next day. When the witness returned six weeks later to be questioned by the Thompson committee, "She did not tell the truth and was therefore not helpful," according to Senator Thompson.[24] Did she, with the aid of others, use the six weeks in China to prepare for her untruthful testimony? Whatever she did in China, it didn't help advance our understanding of what had occurred.

Likewise, Reno's Justice Department allowed John Huang to travel to Indonesia and other parts of Asia on Riady money before his congressional appearances,[25] and Justice has permitted Charlie Trie to travel abroad. Former Arkansas Governor Jim Guy Tucker was convicted by Ken Starr on an unrelated matter but received a light sentence on the understanding that he would cooperate on Clinton matters. Instead, he now lives in Indonesia as a business partner of the Riadys. Since he is out of the country, Arkansas has suspended its efforts to disbar him.

"THE MAGNIFICENT SEVEN"

Federal judges, of course, come to the bench as Republicans and Democrats, and they certainly don't throw away a lifetime of opinions once they put on the black robes. But for the most part they try to uphold the independence and fairness of the Third Branch of government. It is unheard of for judges to form a private clique based on which president appointed them. For the chief judge of a district court to bypass the normal rotation of case assignments in order to ensure that politically sensitive cases are heard by these judges is equally unheard of. Or at least it was until recently.

In the summer of 1999 the press discovered that in fact all this had happened. First, it became known that the chief judge of the Washington, D.C., Federal District, Norma Holloway Johnson, had used her authority to bypass the computer-controlled case assignment system. Five fund-raising cases—including the Trie, Hsia, and Kanchanalak cases—were passed out of rotation. In this same group was the case of a Florida man accused of illegal campaign contributions to Vice President Gore, as well as the Hubbell tax evasion case.

Who got the cases? District court judges in Washington, all appointed by Clinton, who had formed a clique that met privately in closed-door sessions.[26] The judges initially called themselves "The Magnificent Seven," though a later appointment increased their membership to eight.

This unusual situation probably would have continued unnoticed had not one of the Magnificent Seven, Judge Paul Friedman, put himself in the spotlight. As the judge assigned to the Maria Hsia case, he made a number of controversial rulings in her favor, but they were overturned on appeal. After the issue hit the press, the conservative group Judicial Watch filed a judicial complaint, and Chairman Howard Coble (R-NC) of the House Subcommittee on Courts weighed in by sending a letter to the chief judge.

As of this writing, Judge Johnson's judicial colleagues have quietly rescinded the rule that allowed her to bypass the normal rotation system, and a special committee of judges has been formed to consider a judicial complaint filed against her. She has hired Michael Madigan, former chief Republican counsel for the Thompson committee, as her defense attorney.[27]

THE LAW OF OBSTRUCTION OF JUSTICE[28]

As Richard Posner, chief judge of the Court of Appeals for the Seventh U.S. Circuit, notes, "'Obstruction of Justice' is an umbrella term for a variety of specific statutory crimes involving corrupting or otherwise interfering improperly with the course of justice."[29] The crimes include perjury, murdering witnesses, tampering with evidence, and the like. The U.S. criminal code contains a catchall provision that would punish anyone who "corruptly... influences, obstructs, or impedes, or endeavors to influence, obstruct, or impede, the due administration of justice...."[30] These provisions could come into play in the Chinagate case. Moreover, various statutes exist that might apply to witnesses who lie to Congress. And, given that more than one person is involved in the Communist Chinese money case, the conspiracy laws could also come into play.

At the same time that, in Judge Posner's view, President Clinton was "obstruct[ing] justice in violation of federal law" in the Monica Lewinsky matter,[31] Janet Reno and her associates were fending off the FBI, Reno's own prosecutor (Charles LaBella), the press, and the Republicans in Congress on the Chinese money issue. Perhaps Reno and the others were following a standard set by their own chief executive. When corruption starts at the top, it tends to seep down.

Since the late fall of 1996 Reno and her associates have taken a pounding in the press over their handling of the Communist Chinese money issue. For example, the *New York Post* headlined one editorial "Justice Obstructs Justice."[32] And *New York Times* columnist William Safire described Radek as the Justice official "who for years has been successfully making certain that no investigation of illegal Asian money poured into the Clinton-Gore campaign touches any of the higher-ups."[33] Interestingly, Safire's comment came *before* we knew of Radek's secret cease-and-desist order to the Los Angeles prosecutors. Clearly, public confidence in Reno's handling of this issue is in tatters.

We originally thought the administration was trying to protect President Bill Clinton. We were wrong. It seems as if it has always been about Al Gore.

As of this writing, Arlen Specter is heading a small Senate task force looking at Justice's handling of the Communist Chinese money cases, and Dan Burton's House Government Reform and Oversight Committee is investigating the case for the House. Unfortunately, Senator Specter is trying to get to the bottom of this on a shoestring, and Chairman Burton has a wide range of responsibilities that precludes him from focusing on this issue. It is our belief that the assault on the rule of law by Reno and her associates has been so severe as to demand that both the House and Senate Judiciary Committees throw the full weight of their resources into this investigation.

CONCLUSION

In any investigation, there is always the danger of what is known as "mirror-imaging"—that is, assigning your own motivations and concerns to those being investigated. We have spent our adult lives devoted to the national security of the United States, and we originally thought the administration's obstruction of justice game was designed to protect President Clinton from exposure of wrongdoing in this arena.

We were wrong. Increasingly, it seems as if it has always been about Gore and the sordid fund-raising issues.

By the time the Chinese money stories gained momentum in October 1996, Clinton and Gore were as much as reelected, given the Republicans' pathetic effort that year. The hard-eyed types in the White House were already looking down the road to a third term to keep the Clinton-Gore system in place and, above all, themselves in power. One can only imagine their horror and panic when they discovered that the Los Angeles prosecutors were poking around the Buddhist temple affair. The heir apparent had to be protected. All else—the secret plan, avoiding an independent counsel, handcuffing the FBI, the private witness protection service—flowed from this desperate need. Lee Radek's twin decisions on the same day—halting the Los Angeles prosecutors and setting up the Ingersoll task force—reveal all.

The *New York Times* editorial writers put it best when the secret Radek cease-and-desist order surfaced in the spring of 2000:

> Several extraordinary and heretofore secret documents were disclosed that suggest the lengths to which Janet Reno and her top aides went to protect Vice President Al Gore and other senior officials from a thorough, independent investigation into their fund-raising activities in the 1996 campaign.
>
> The documents are further evidence of Ms. Reno's politicized handling of the campaign fund-raising issue and of her dedication to protecting Democratic Party interests from start to finish.[34]

Attorney General Reno has indeed been a loyal servant, and no one has benefited more than Al Gore.

CHAPTER 18
PAYING THE PRICE FOR BILL AND AL

A casualty call for a U.S. service member killed in the line of duty typically starts with a telephone call to locate the next-of-kin. A man or woman of God traditionally accompanies the casualty officer, who has the sad task of telling a mother or a father, a wife or a husband, that his or her loved one has been killed in service to the country. A funeral service is conducted, "Taps" is played, and a neatly folded American flag is presented to the next-of-kin.

Tragically, since the day in 1993 when Bill Clinton and Al Gore were sworn in, hands on the Bible, as president and vice president, respectively, it has become far more likely that this scene will become a familiar one to Americans. The danger to all Americans, but especially to those in uniform, of facing an attack by a well-armed Chinese People's Liberation Army (PLA) will be the haunting legacy of the Clinton-Gore administration well into this new century.

Year of the Rat documents a case of bribery. It is a tale of money in, favors out. In exchange for Communist Chinese money flowing into Clinton-Gore coffers, the administration turned a blind eye to—or, worse, lent support to—dangerous Chinese activities. We have detailed the assaults on our national security—nuclear espionage, failure to stop Chinese arms sales to terrorist nations, and technological assistance to China's military, especially its missile programs. All of these increase the dangers to the American homeland, our friends and allies abroad, and our men and women in uniform. But since we first wrote *Year of the Rat*, we have learned of a fourth major threat to U.S. national security and world peace—the massive transfer of modern arms from Russia to China. And it happened on Al Gore's watch.

A quick visit to Vice President Gore's presidential campaign web site shows that Mr. Gore takes credit for his very close working relationship with key Russian leaders through the special Russian-American commission he cochairs. It would not be an exaggeration to say that Gore, not Clinton, has been the point man on U.S.-Russian relations since the inception of the administration. The Gore 2000 web site states definitively that, "[a]s Vice President, Gore has led important arms reduction efforts around the world."

But what Vice President Gore's web site does *not* show is the staggering increase in Russian arms sales to China since 1993. Consider just some of the many Russian military transfers to Communist China during Vice President Gore's stewardship of the U.S.-Russian relationship:

- destroyers equipped with nuclear missiles
- SU-27 fighter aircraft and SU-30 attack aircraft
- Kilo-class submarines and advanced nuclear submarine technology
- long-range cruise missile technology
- military helicopters and transports
- a wide range of air-to-air, ground-to-air, and anti-radar missiles
- space technology with direct military applications, including long-range ballistic missiles, multiple warheads, and anti-satellite technology

All of these weapons can be used against the United States military, as well as our allies.

Where did the Russians get the idea that they could sell these kinds of weapons to a country likely to use them against the United States? Well, during the Clinton-Gore administration the United States has been penetrated by the Chinese intelligence and military services at the highest levels, and the Russian leadership would have known of this from its own spying in Washington. As press reports have revealed, the Russians were able to place an electronic eavesdropping device (a "bug") inside the State Department itself. Further, highly classified documents were taken right off a desk in the secretary of state's outer office, and the spy has never been found.

Since we first wrote *Year of the Rat*, we have learned of massive transfers of modern arms from Russia to China—which happened on Al Gore's watch.

Crucially, *the United States never objected to Russian arms sales to Communist China.*[1] This would have been Gore's job: to lead the diplomatic effort to stop these arms sales. He didn't do it.

The result is a Russian-Chinese "strategic partnership" (the two nations have even agreed to conduct joint combat training) aimed at the United States.

Why has Beijing targeted its military modernization at the United States? The most immediate reason is that U.S. armed forces stand as a roadblock in the way of Communist China's control of the island nation of Taiwan. Very methodically, the PLA is putting in place the building blocks that will allow it to seize Taiwan by force, and the PLA's strategy rests on eliminating the United States as an obstruction. In the late winter of 2000 the PLA Navy took delivery of its initial Sovremenny-class destroyer from Russia. A second one will arrive in the fall, and there are ongoing negotiations for perhaps four more. These ships were designed to be "killers of aircraft carriers," as the PLA's principal newspaper declared in March 2000.[2] More ominously, the PLA's paper correctly confirmed that the SS-N-22 supersonic missiles carried onboard are nuclear capable. Each of the eight missiles the ships carry would pack a nuclear punch approximately twenty times that of the atomic bomb dropped on Hiroshima in 1945. The first batch of SS-N-22 missiles arrived in May 2000.

The U.S. military, particularly with its highly capable Los Angeles–class submarine, still has a distinct advantage over Communist China in naval forces, but nuclear-armed Sovremenny destroyers are a clear threat to American ships. But more important, we believe that, in the event of hostilities over Taiwan, Communist China would declare these ships "strategic nuclear assets" in defense of its homeland. When a "strategic nuclear asset" is threatened, the world is on the edge of a nuclear exchange. Beijing may count on this understanding among the world's nuclear powers to block the United States Navy from coming to Taiwan's aid.

If the U.S. Navy *is* ordered into harm's way around Taiwan, it will face an ominous battle situation. In the spring of 2000, a newspaper close to Russian President Vladimir Putin bragged that the SS-N-22 missiles would be targeted on American naval forces, as would other weapons sold to China, including missiles aboard Russian strike aircraft:

> We would point out that an air-naval formation comprising 956E destroyers [Sovremennys] [and] SU-27SK fighters... is fully capable of fighting as equals with the U.S. Navy aircraft carrier formation.[3]

It is unlikely that anyone aboard an American carrier battle group would survive a surprise nuclear attack under these circumstances.

Despite this significant threat to America's armed forces, Vice President Al Gore, the principal point man on U.S.-Russian relations, has made no effort to stop the destroyer sale to China. Similarly, he has made no effort to halt the nuclear missiles transfer or the attack aircraft sale.

In short, domestic corruption has not simply created a U.S.-Chinese "strategic partnership." More important, the strategic partnership has had dramatic consequences for U.S. national security and the safety of our allies abroad. As America's military might was declining, Bill Clinton and Al Gore were helping to strengthen a hostile PRC.

Many observers contend that it is too soon to predict what the legacy of the Clinton-Gore administration will be. They are right. Only in the coming years, as the families of American service members begin to receive knocks on the door from casualty officers, will Americans come to comprehend the tragic legacy of William Jefferson Clinton and Albert Gore, Jr.

NOTES

A NOTE ON SOURCES

We are of the same generation as Bill Clinton and Al Gore. Taken together, we have more than fifty years of national security service to the American people, having served at various times in the Pentagon and in United States military and civilian intelligence agencies. Over the past several years we have served as House and Senate investigators on some of the more prominent congressional inquiries of the Clinton-Gore administration.

In the winter of 1997–1998 we came to the conclusion that, from a national security perspective, the story of Communist Chinese infiltration of the American political system had not been, and was not likely to be, told correctly. The only answer was to conduct our own investigation.

Much of the information presented in this book is new. A number of previously classified documents make their first public appearances on these pages. In the course of our new investigation we went to China, Hong Kong, Macau, and Taiwan. We combed records in Hong Kong for signs of a Chinese military presence in the satellite launch business. With a young woman volunteer as a cover, we visited Macau criminal syndicate figure— and Clinton-Gore donor—Ng Lapseng's principal place of business. We got Taiwanese officials to confirm that Clinton pal Charlie Trie was a member of a Chinese criminal gang. Back home we tore open the official cover of COSCO. COSCO delivers weapons for Chinese arms smugglers, and it is about to take over the naval facility at Long Beach, California, thanks to direct, high-level intervention from the White House.

We interviewed dozens of witnesses and experts, here and abroad. Perhaps the most significant interview, which we conducted jointly, occurred in the spring of 1998, when a retired senior CIA official told us about Chinese espionage operations in the United States. Without violating his oath of secrecy, the official confirmed our own suspicions: a prime goal of the CCP is to insert someone under its direction into the highest levels of the United States government. The party wants direct access to the president and vice president. Sadly, the results of our investigation show that was achieved in this administration.

PREFACE TO THE PAPERBACK EDITION

1   Memorandum dated December 8, 1998, from FBI Director Louis
    Freeh to FBI General Counsel Larry Parkinson, relating Freeh's con-
    versation with Reno on December 4, 1998.
2   Title 18, Section 371.
3   Freeh memorandum.

CHAPTER 1

1   We do not take Beijing's June 1998 pledge to "detarget" the United States
    any more seriously than we take its arms sales promises.
2   Henceforth "Taiwan."
3   *New York Times*, April 22, 1997.
4   "Ng," the Cantonese version of his name, is pronounced "Ong" in
    English.
5   *United States* v. *Young* 568 F2d 588, 589 8th Circuit 1978. See also
    "Circumstantial evidence is not less probative than direct evidence, and, in
    some cases, is even more reliable." *United States* v. *Andrino* 501F2d 1373,
    1378 9th Circuit 1974.

CHAPTER 2

1   Analysis by Lisa Myers and Bob Windrem of MSNBC, December 18,
    1997.
2   James Riady's secretary at LippoBank California was Juwati Judistra, who
    has returned to Indonesia and refused to speak to the Senate investigating
    committee. Senate Report 105-167, "Investigation of Illegal or Improper
    Activities in Connection with 1996 Federal Election Campaigns," Senate
    Governmental Affairs Committee, chaired by Senator Fred Thompson (R-
    TN) (henceforth "Thompson Report"), Vol. 1, page 1122.
3   Through his attorney, John Huang notified the Senate Governmental
    Affairs Committee (henceforth the "Thompson committee") of his inten-
    tion to assert his Fifth Amendment rights and decline to testify.
4   Estimate from "Inside the Overseas Chinese Network" by Henny Sender
    in the *Institutional Investor*, September 1991. The figure is probably even
    higher now.
5   Associated Press (AP), May 14, 1998.
6   *Jakarta Republika* (in Indonesian), May 21, 1997.
7   Agence France Presse (AFP), January 30, 1997.
8   This comes from a Canadian media source located abroad.

9 *Washington Post*, reprinted in the *International Herald Tribune*, May 29, 1997.

10 *Washington Post*, reprinted in the *International Herald Tribune*, May 29, 1997.

11 *Asian Wall Street Journal*, March 10, 1997.

12 "Lippo Village" has been renamed "Lippo Karawaci," perhaps to give it a more Indonesian flavor. *Asiamoney*, October 1995.

13 *Business Times* (Singapore), October 19, 1993.

14 *The Economist*, August 5, 1995.

15 *International Herald Tribune*, May 28, 1997.

16 *Forbes*, July 17, 1995.

17 Reprinted in the *International Herald Tribune*, May 29, 1997.

18 As is fairly common among self-made overseas Chinese tycoons who have not had much formal education, he likes to call himself "Doctor Riady," based on an honorary degree awarded some years ago.

19 Lippo Limited annual report for 1996, at page 22.

20 November 3, 1997, letter from the CIA to a United States senator, at 13. Thompson Report at 4545.

21 *Asian Wall Street Journal*, October 17, 1996.

22 *New York Times*, October 11, 1996.

23 *Arkansas Democrat-Gazette*, April 25, 1986.

24 *The American Spectator*, September 1995.

25 Ibid.

26 *Washington Post*, reprinted in the *International Herald Tribune*, May 29, 1997.

27 *The American Spectator*, September 1995.

28 *The American Spectator*, October 1992.

29 *Business Week*, November 4, 1996.

30 See *Time*, July 21, 1997, and *Asian Wall Street Journal*, October 22, 1996.

31 *Asian Wall Street Journal*, October 17, 1996.

32 *New York Times*, February 17, 1998.

33 Ibid.

34 *Asian Wall Street Journal*, October 10, 1996.

35 *New York Times*, February 14, 1997.

36 *New York Times*, April 24, 1997.

37 *Newsweek*, May 26, 1997.

38 Cease-and-Desist Order FDIC-97-206.

39 *Los Angeles Times*, December 23, 1996.

40 Ibid.

41 Ibid.

42 *Los Angeles Times*, May 4, 1997.

43 Ibid.

44 MSNBC posting of June 8, 1998. Election statistics from *The Almanac of American Politics 1998*, by Michael Barone and Grant Ujifusa (National Journal, 1997).

45 *Los Angeles Times*, December 21, 1997.

46 Ibid.

47 *New York Times*, February 14, 1997.

48 Deposition of C. Joseph Giroir, Jr., April 26, 1997, before the Thompson committee, at 17, 19. Mochtar Riady gave $50,000 so that Arkansas's March of Dimes would name Mrs. Clinton "Arkansan of the Year." The Riadys donated $30,000 to Mark Grobmyer's nonprofit "Center for the Study of the Presidency."

49 We make no judgment as to whose door this tragedy may ultimately be laid. But the fact is that the children were alive before the FBI/ATF assault and dead at the end of it. *Dallas Morning News*, May 12, 1993.

50 This same study later became famous in the Monica Lewinsky matter.

51 This account of April 19, 1993, at the White House was extracted from a longer story by the *Washington Post* (reprinted in the *International Herald Tribune*, May 28, 1997).

52 White House WAVES records for John Huang, reprinted in the Thompson Report at 297. It was John Huang's sixth visit to the White House that week. The Riady party may have been there to press Clinton to appoint Huang to a post in the administration.

53 Thompson Report at 4911.

54 Li was premier at the time of the Tiananmen massacre. He became the leader of China's rubber-stamp National People's Congress in the spring of 1998.

55 George Black and Robin Munro, *Black Hands of Beijing* (Wiley, 1993). Munro heads the Human Rights Watch Asia office in Hong Kong and was in Beijing during the massacre.

56 Ibid at 256. For an account of flamethrowers at Tiananmen, see Timothy Brook, *Quelling the People: The Military Suppression of the Beijing Democracy Movement* (Oxford, 1992), 40.

57 Black and Munro at 256.

58 *South China Morning Post* (Hong Kong); *Business Post*, April 4, 1993.

59 Ibid.

60 *South China Morning Post*, November 9, 1994.

61 AP, November 22, 1994.

62 United Press International (UPI), December 24, 1994.

63 *Dallas Morning News*, December 25, 1996. The authors note that McDonalds heiress Mrs. Ray Kroc is a substantial contributor to the Democratic Party. We have not asked her what she thinks about this.

64 *New York Times*, March 1, 1998.

65 Thompson Report at page 4545.

66 Ibid.

67 Ibid.

68 Pronounced "gwan she" in Mandarin.

69 *Asiaweek*, November 10, 1995.

70 *Business Times* (Singapore), November 14, 1995.

71 *Asian Wall Street Journal*, July 18, 1997.

72 Thompson Report at 2507.

73 "Collectors" is intelligence community bureaucratese for "spies."

74 *Fortune*, October 31, 1994. At the time of this observation, Li Peng was premier of the PRC.

75 *Washington Post*, reprinted in the *International Herald Tribune*, May 28, 1997.

76 *New York Times*, April 24, 1997.

77 Allen Dulles, *The Craft of Intelligence* (New American Library, 1963), 24.

78 Ibid.

79 Ibid.

CHAPTER 3

1 William Colby, *Honorable Men* (Simon and Schuster, 1998), 98.

2 *Ethnic NewsWatch*, January 12, 1996.

3 "Greater China" includes China, Taiwan, Hong Kong, Macau, and overseas Chinese communities in Southeast Asia.

4 From 1972 to 1979 diplomatic relations between the U.S. and the PRC were handled by "liaison offices" in Washington and Beijing. After the U.S. granted the PRC diplomatic recognition in 1979, the liaison offices became embassies.

5 *Washington Post*, May 13, 1997.

6 Judicial Watch deposition at 118.

7 *Washington Post*, May 13, 1997.

8 Judicial Watch deposition at 103–104.

9 Ibid at 119.

10 *Washington Post*, May 13, 1997.

11 Ibid at 125.

12 Ibid at 130.

13 Thompson Report at 337.

14 *Wall Street Journal*, November 29, 1996.

15 Judicial Watch deposition at 154. Which Riady clients Huang took to the DNC in 1988 might make an interesting subject for inquiry.

16 Ibid at 132.

17 Ibid at 133.

18 *Los Angeles Times*, September 21, 1996.

19 Ibid at 166.

20 Ibid at 154.

21 Thompson Report at 4795.

22 Thompson Report at 1754.

23 *Los Angeles Times*, December 23, 1996. This is covered in some detail in Chapter 2.

24 Ibid.

25 Thompson Report at 1757.

26 Ibid at 258.

27 Ibid at 4.

28 Ibid at 259.

29 WAVES Records, Thompson Report at 297–298.

30 See, e.g. Thompson Report at 286.

31 The authors have no information on whether Huang had unreported foreign income. However, we do note that (1) as will be demonstrated, Huang and the Riadys have little respect for U.S. law, (2) the Riadys are foreign bankers, and (3) anyone who might have knowledge of this has fled the country.

32 Again, the authors have no information on whether Huang's reporting includes compensation from all sources, foreign and domestic.

33 Thompson Report at 4.

34 Ibid.

35 Ibid at 24.

36 Ibid at 54.

37 Letter of February 17, 1993, from Maeley Tom to John Emerson, deputy assistant to the president, with copies to Bruce Lindsey and David Wilhelm. Copy in Thompson Report at 307.

38 *New York Times*, October 7, 1996.

39 Interview by author [Timperlake] with Commerce security officials, June 1997.

40 Huang left the Commerce Department in early December 1995 but remained a Commerce Department employee until mid-January 1996 on a leave-without-pay status.

41 Thompson Report at 1165.

42 Ibid at 1166.

43 Huang asked the librarian for the nonprofit group, the Committee of 100, in New York. We believe she was unaware of Huang's purposes or subsequent activities.

44 As explained in Chapter 10, Chin was a long-term "plant" for Chinese intelligence who managed to worm his way into one of the CIA's operations.

45 Thompson Report at 1170.

46 Very private conversation with author [Triplett].

CHAPTER 4

1 ABC's *PrimeTime Live*, June 18, 1997.

2 Testimony of LippoBank Chairman Harold Arthur, Thompson Report at 54.

3 Thompson Report at 307.

4 Ibid at 1224.

5 See Rothkopf deposition to the Thompson committee.

6 "Why it took six months for Huang to come aboard, I don't know." Comment by Commerce Department security official. See Thompson Report at 1169, note 101.

7 *Washington Post*, December 10, 1997.

8 This is according to a chronology put together by MSNBC.

9 This is according to Treasury Department records.

10 MSNBC chronology and White House WAVES Records. See Thompson Report at 297.

11 Ibid.

12 Ibid.

13 Ibid.

14 *New York Post*, March 1, 1998.

15 *Washington Post*, December 10, 1997.

16 MSNBC chronology and White House WAVES Records.

17 Ibid.

18 *Los Angeles Times*, December 21, 1997.

19 *New York Times*, March 6, 1997.

20 *New York Times*, April 10, 1997.

21 Thompson Report at 268.

22 On June 17, 1997, the *Los Angeles Times* reported that a Commerce Department document exists that purports to be Huang's February 28, 1994, personnel form, which indicated that his start date was set for July 18, 1994. We believe that this may be an after-the-fact creation, only because Huang has sworn under oath that he didn't know he was going to get the Commerce job until late June.

23 *Washington Times*, November 27, 1996.

24 *New York Times*, April 10, 1997.

25 AP, March 5, 1997.

26 Criminal No. 98-0151, United States District Court for the District of Columbia, *United States of America v. Webster L. Hubbell, Suzanna W. Hubbell, Michael C. Schaufele, and Charles C. Owen*. This indictment was subsequently thrown out as overreaching.

27 MSNBC, May 1, 1998.

28 *Washington Post*, May 1, 1998.

29 *Washington Times*, May 1, 1998.

30 *Washington Post*, April 29, 1998.

31 The first time, of course, occurred with the Worthen loan for the New York primary in 1992, and the second time was in August 1992, with a limousine ride that resulted in a cascade of Riady money for the general election.

32 *Newsweek*, November 11, 1996.

33 Authors' private conversation with senior Democratic staff members, February 1998.

34 Press reports of Middleton's fund-raising in the 1992 election cycle are numerous. For example, see the *Arkansas Democrat-Gazette*, November 22, 1991, for a $500-per-ticket reception in Little Rock he ran called "Winner Wonderland," and a front-page story in the *Commercial Appeal* (Memphis), December 17, 1991, quoting Middleton. Columnist Mary McGrory claimed after the election that Middleton "was southern finance director and raised $66 million for the general election." *Buffalo News*, November 7, 1992.

35 ABC's *PrimeTime Live*, June 18, 1997.

36 AP, March 23, 1998.

37 *Washington Times*, November 8, 1996. Seper broke the story of Vince Foster's office files, which led to the appointment of the first independent counsel on Whitewater.

38 Judicial Watch deposition at 166.

39 Letter dated August 1, 1994, from Huang to Genevieve M. Ryan. Copy in the possession of the authors.

CHAPTER 5

1 *Washington Times*, November 18, 1996.

2 Thompson Report at 157.

3 Ibid at 124.

4 Ibid at 1207.

5 *Washington Post*, May 13, 1997.

6 Travelgate. See Thompson Report at 1410.

7 *Los Angeles Times*, April 12, 1997.

8 *Washington Post*, May 13, 1997. See also Thompson Report at 1160, note 38.

9 Private conversation with one of the authors. It is common practice for any professional, in or out of government, to try to improve his or her expertise in order to become more valuable to the organization.

10 Thompson Report at 1176.

11 Thompson Report at 113.

12 *Wall Street Journal*, October 31, 1996.

13 *Time*, November 11, 1996.

14 Patton, an Asian-American Huang may have known from campaign days, was deputy assistant secretary for the Asia-Pacific slot.

15 According to Huang's daybook entries.

16 Ibid.

17 Huang did meet with the deputy assistant secretaries who handled those regions, but apparently only at annual budget meetings. Canada or Mexico may also have come up as an afterthought in meetings devoted to other topics.

18 John Dickerson to Judicial Watch hearing.

19 Thompson Report at 43.

20 *Washington Post*, May 13, 1997.

21 Ibid.

22 Thompson Report at 162.

23 Ibid at 128.

24 Ibid at 1177.

25 *Los Angeles Times*, June 17, 1997.

26 Thompson Report at 151.

27 Ibid.

28 Ibid at 153.

29 Ibid at 155.

30 Ibid at 1180.

31 *Inside CIA's Private World*, edited by H. Bradford Westerfield (Yale, 1995), 367.

32 Triplett served in the office of the U.S. Trade Representative.

33 Thompson Report at 1180.

34 Ibid at 1324–1325.

35 This paper is in the possession of the authors.

36 *International Herald Tribune*, February 17, 1998.

37 She testified that he didn't come every week, but that's easily explainable by travel and leave time.

38 Thompson Report at 165 et seq.

39 The authors wonder about the credibility of her denial, but it was not challenged by anyone on the Thompson committee.

40 Thompson Report at 1181.

41 Ibid at 1181.

42 Ibid at 1183–1184.

43 Weaver was interviewed, but not under oath. The interview was never circulated or released by the committee, and his responses, such as we know of them, were vague. See Thompson Report at 1185.

44 So far as is known, neither was even interviewed.

45 For example, Larry Middleton, brother of Mark Middleton.

46 Thompson Report at 1184. Of his sixteen months on the job at Commerce, eleven of them were in 1995. Only January 1995 telephone records were produced.

47 Ibid at 1184–1185.

48 Ibid at 1250.

49 Huang Daybook. Thompson Report at 1390.

50 We wonder: Does the CIA have an accepted protocol for unanticipated encounters like this? What does one say—"See ya at the National Spy Club happy hour"?

51 Taxicab claims found, in Thompson Report at 1417.

52 See also *Los Angeles Times*, February 17, 1997.

53 Thompson Report at 2507.

54 Interview conducted in the Washington, D.C., area, April 7, 1998.

55 *New York Daily News*, June 10, 1997.

CHAPTER 6

1 Dick Morris, *Behind the Oval Office* (Random House, 1997), 14.

2 Ibid at 15.

3 Ibid at 33.

4 Ibid at 34.

5 Ibid at 116.

6 Ibid at 95.

7 Barone and Ujifusa at 47.

8 Morris at 139.

9 Ibid.

10 Ibid at 144.

11 Deposition of Dick Morris, pp.187–188, Thompson Report at 123.

12 Deposition of Harold Ickes, cited in Thompson Report at 59 and 60.

13 Barone and Ujifusa at 23.

14 Morris sometimes works political campaigns for Republicans and knows them well. In his book he commented that Republican strategists "liked to hold their fire until closer to election day." Morris at 153.

15 Ibid.

16 Ibid at 269.

17 Ibid at 277.

18 Ibid at 277.

19 Ibid at 149.

20 Ibid.

21 Ibid.

22 Deposition of Donald L. Fowler, pp. 290–292, in Thompson Report at 61.

23 Deposition of Bruce Lindsey, p. 1118, in Thompson Report at 1660.

24 Testimony of DNC official Richard Sullivan, Thompson Report at 148.

25 Fowler deposition at 170, in Thompson Report at 1659.

26 Deposition of Harold Ickes, pp.125–126, in Thompson Report at 1662.

27 Memorandum of interview with Marvin Rosen at page 10, in Thompson Report at 1663.

28 Thompson Report at 97.

29 White House WAVES records, Thompson Report at 299.

30 Ibid.

31 *Los Angeles Times*, December 23, 1996.

32 This issue is very controversial and took up a lot of the Thompson committee's time. Rosen's subordinate Richard Sullivan testified that the training for Huang was ordered (Sullivan testimony, Thompson Report at 109). The DNC's general counsel flatly denied that any training was ordered or took place (Joseph Sandler testimony, Thompson Report at 120). Given the overall problems with Sullivan's testimony, we believe that Sandler's statement is probably the accurate one.

33 Thompson Report at 294.

34 Telephone interview with *The American Spectator*'s executive editor, May 1998.

35 *Los Angeles Times*, December 23, 1996.

36 See Chapter 3 for a discussion of how Huang kept his security clearance after he left Commerce.

37 *Los Angeles Times*, December 23, 1996.

38 Since Huang was still at the Commerce Department at the time, he probably violated the Hatch Act, which prohibits federal employees from soliciting political contributions.

39 DNC press release of June 27, 1997.

40 Thompson Report at 37.

41 Ibid at 1700.

42 *Los Angeles Times*, September 21, 1996.

43 Thompson Report at 37.

44 *Wall Street Journal*, June 11, 1997.

45 Ibid.

46 CIA's answers to questions from a senator, November 3, 1997. Thompson Report at 4545.

47 *Los Angeles Times*, May 12, 1997; *Los Angeles Times*, May 18, 1997.

48 Thompson Report at 964.

CHAPTER 7

1 *Washington Post*, October 17, 1996.

2 See, e.g., *Washington Post*, September 3, 1997.

3 *Washington Post*, October 17, 1996.

4 "Virtually everyone at the DNC and on the Vice President's staff however, clearly understood the Hsi Lai Temple event to be a 'fund-raiser' but also repeatedly described it as such." Thompson Report at 1788.

5 Pronounced "Shaw."

6 Thompson Report at 1752.

7 Ibid.

8 Ibid at 1837.

9 Ibid at 1830.

10 *New York Times*, June 9, 1997.

11 Thompson Report at 1754.

12 See Chapter 2.

13 Thompson Report at 1755, note 31.

14 Ibid at 1758.

15 In a case like this, this term normally implies that the "unindicted coconspirator" is cooperating with authorities.

16 Indictment, Count One. We believe that the grand jury could have gone back before 1993, but the statute of limitations had probably expired.

17 Indictment, Paragraph 16.

18 Thompson Report at 1773–1774.

19 Ibid at 1765.

20 Ibid at 1759.

21 Ibid at 2506, 1768, 1769, and 2127.

22 Ibid at 1767.

23 Ibid at 2507.

24 Ibid at 4630.

25 She returned to the United States in July 1998.

26 Indictment, Paragraph 26.

27 The funds went to state Democratic parties in Ohio, Florida, California, Illinois, and Pennsylvania.

28 Thompson Report at 207.

29 *New York Daily News*, December 29, 1997.

30 The associate was Clark Wallace, a member of the U.S.-Thai Business Council, which Kanchanalak founded and controls.

31 Faxed page attachment in a Clark Wallace memo dated March 14, 1996.

32 See Thompson Report at 211–212.

33 Ibid at 212.

34 *Far Eastern Economic Review* (Hong Kong), January 23, 1997.

35 Ibid.

36 Thompson Report at 4545 et seq.

37 Ibid at 212.

38 Ibid at 213.

39 *Far Eastern Economic Review*, January 23, 1997.

40 *Wall Street Journal,* November 19, 1996; *South China Morning Post,* November 9, 1996.

41 *Wall Street Journal,* June 11, 1997.

42 *Hong Kong Standard,* November 9, 1996.

43 *South China Morning Post,* September 4, 1997.

44 *Hong Kong Standard,* July 9, 1997.

45 *Hong Kong Standard,* February 3, 1997.

46 Ibid.

47 Xinhua, June 17, 1998.

48 *Hong Kong Standard,* November 9, 1996.

CHAPTER 8

1 See Chapter 5.

2 Triads, or "tiandihui" [Heaven-Earth-Man], are secret societies that, according to some scholars, arose in China during the eighteenth century as a mutual aid brotherhood. Blood oaths were required, and members were pledged to secrecy. The main focus of the Triads over time became criminal activities, combined with mutual protection, administration of local legal activities, and revolutionary uprisings against the Ching Dynasty. The authors are concerned only with the criminal element. *The Origins of the Tiandihui* by Dian H. Murray (Palo Alto: Stanford, 1994) has an excellent history of what may ever be known about organizations whose main goal is keeping secrets.

3 *Triad Societies in Hong Kong.*

4 *Report on Asian Organized Crime,* Criminal Division, U.S. Department of Justice, February 1988, unpublished.

5 "Triads and Other Asian Organized Crime Groups," by RCMP officer Garry W.G. Clement and Canadian Immigration Control Officer Brian McAdam, 1994. This is an unpublished manuscript in the possession of the authors.

6 Ibid at 108.

7 Ibid at 39.

8 Ibid at 44.

9 Ibid at 46.

10 *Asia Times* (Hong Kong), April 25, 1997.

11 *Wall Street Journal,* February 26, 1998.

12 *Ping Kuo Pao* (Hong Kong), December 5, 1997.

13 Ibid.

14 *Die Welt*, December 5, 1995.

15 Seoul WIN in Korean, Song Ui-ho, "Organized Crime Shakes Asia: Chinese Triad and Russian Mafia's Have an Eye on Korea Now," September 1995, at 94–101.

16 Recommended reading: *Tongs, Gangs, and Triads: Chinese Crime Groups in North America*, by Peter Huston (Paladin Press, 1995).

17 Testimony of FBI Director Louis Freeh, January 28, 1998.

18 *Report on Asian Organized Crime*, February 1988. This product also notes the similarities between the Mafia and the Triads.

19 Chan claimed to have contributed the absurd amount of $20 million to Ferraro's reelection. See *Sons of the Yellow Emperor* by Lynn Pan (Kodansha International, 1994).

20 *New York Times*, October 25, 1984.

21 This is according to the Fortuna Hotel brochure, which is in the possession of the authors.

22 *Wall Street Journal*, February 26, 1998.

23 "Triads and Other Asian Organized Crime Groups" at 30.

24 Ibid.

25 Ibid at 29.

26 *Washington Post*, January 27, 1997.

27 *South China Morning Post*, October 19, 1997; *New York Times*, October 18, 1997.

28 *Wall Street Journal*, February 27, 1998.

29 Ho's university education was interrupted by World War II. He acquired an honorary doctorate from an institution supported by his business interests.

30 Dr. Ho owns casinos; he doesn't gamble in the traditional sense, but see the "Rose Garden" project, following. *Financial Times*, February 16, 1998.

31 1988 Justice report at 63. The Justice Department associates him with the Hung Mun Triad group of Hong Kong.

32 *Forbes*, November 18, 1996.

33 *South China Morning Post*, January 18, 1998.

34 *Hong Kong Standard*, June 22, 1997.

35 *Hong Kong Standard*, July 4, 1997.

36 *South China Morning Post*, July 24, 1997.

37 Ho controls the gambling monopoly that operates in the New Century Hotel.

38 1988 Justice Department Report at 63.

39 Thompson Report at 2525.

40 *New York Times*, October 18, 1997.

41 Ng operates under a number of aliases, so it is difficult to determine precisely how much contact with Clinton he had.

42 *Washington Post*, April 28, 1997.

43 Thompson Report at 970.

44 *Wall Street Journal*, February 27, 1998.

45 *Congressional Record*, September 16, 1997, beginning at page S9385.

46 The senator's questions and the unclassified answers can be found in the Thompson Report at 4545. Unfortunately, the most critical information is in the classified answers, which have never been released except to United States senators and cleared staff.

47 Thompson Report at 969. The Sioeng family also made some lesser contributions to Republican causes. See Thompson Report, beginning at 971.

48 Ibid at 964.

49 Ibid.

50 Ibid.

51 See Exhibit 12-73 at page 1108 of the Thompson Report.

52 Thompson Report at 970.

53 Ibid at 4545 et seq.

54 *Newsweek,* April 28, 1997.

55 Thompson Report at 5576.

56 See letter from her lawyer to Chairman Fred Thompson as Exhibit 12-1. Thompson Report at 982.

57 Ibid at page 4545 et seq.

58 See *Far Eastern Economic Review*, November 23, 1995.

59 *Washington Post*, July 22, 1997.

60 *Far Eastern Economic Review,* January 13, 1998.

61 *Washington Post*, February 2, 1994.

62 *Far Eastern Economic Review,* November 23, 1995.

63 Trie Indictment, Paragraph 14.

CHAPTER 9

1 *Los Angeles Times*, December 18, 1996. "Lao Ke" is "a Chinese term of familiarity."

2 Ibid.

3 Additionally credible media sources confirm the facts.

4 *Asia Times*, June 15, 1997.

5 Stephen E. Ambrose, *Eisenhower* (Simon and Schuster, 1983), 233.
  "ChiCom" was the administration's term for Chinese Communists. The
  term was used extensively by U.S. Marines during the Korean War. It was
  not intended to be friendly and was usually used in reference to weaponry.
  The term was used through the Vietnam War, often identifying weapons'
  manufacture—for example, "ChiCom grenade," etc. It will be interesting
  if combat in the Middle East keeps the terminology going—consider the
  proposition of "ChiCom ICBM."

6 Ambrose at 233. It must be noted that Eisenhower, having commanded the
  best citizen army ever fielded by America in destroying the Nazis, understood the use of force very well.

7 *Washington Times*, April 7, 1998. The original hard news source was the
  New York Times.

8 Thompson Report at 2718.

9 Ibid at 2718.

10 The 1978 border war between China and Vietnam. Though brief, this war
   led to some 100,000 casualties on both sides.

11 A border war between Russia and China in 1969.

12 Thompson Report at 2766.

13 We would liken the "Trie Report" to a clever high-school sophomore's imi-
   tation of a business consultant's brochure.

"In formulating such a gigantic policy as U.S.-Asia trades," he began, "I think
we should logically and systematically think and manage in six dimensions
such as: 1) Time, 2) Space, 3) Subject, 4) People, 5) Methods, 6) Target.

"Or," he continued at the same peak of insight:
[W]e can alternatively proceed them in terms of 5 "W"s and one
"H"—i.e.,
1) What: (methods, targets, tactics, what industries, what variables:
culture, key to successful factors)
2) Where: (which nations, which territory)
3) When: (short-term, mid-term, long-term?)
4) Who: (Who to implement? Big industries, medium? small, to achieve
our increased surplus?)
5) Which: (similar to what, Which programs to promote)
6) How: (How to implement?)

And so on, for three interminable pages.

14 Clinton went to great lengths to ensure Trie a place on this commission, even to the point of adding a seat on the already-filled commission in January 1996. The administration sought to minimize the amount of vetting that Trie underwent. In this regard, there is a significant misstatement in the minority report of the Thompson committee. The minority goes to great lengths to exonerate Trie from any suspicion that he had contacts with a foreign government: "Another relevant factor is that Trie authorized an FBI investigation of his background in December 1995, and the investigation found no problems that would prevent Trie's nomination to a Presidential commission. An individual seeking to hide contacts with a foreign government presumably would not have either subjected himself to such an investigation or emerged from it unscathed." But a letter from FBI Director Louis Freeh to Congressman Gerald Solomon says this: "The FBI did not conduct a background security investigation on Mr. Trie. FBI records do not reflect whether any other U.S. governmental agency conducted a background investigation or, in fact, whether Mr. Trie was granted a security clearance." Trie was simply awarded a clearance based on a White House–requested "Executive Agencies Name Check" by the FBI, which is a rather superficial process.

15 Thompson Report at 2535.

16 Ibid.

17 Ibid at 2719.

18 June 18, 1994, memo from David Mercer to John O'Hanlon, re: VIP requests.

19 Memorandum for Harold Ickes, from Terry McAuliffe, Laura Harrigan, Ari Swiller, February 15, 1995, re: Managing Trustee Dinners. Two VIP dinners were being arranged to identify those DNC fat cats who "will be an anchor in the 1995 and 1996 fundraising efforts." Seated with the president were Pauline Kanchanalak and Mark Jimenez.

20 August 29, 5:20 PM, government call slip to Melanne from Aiya.

21 "Triads and Other Asian Organized Crime Groups."

CHAPTER 10

1   *Wall Street Journal*, March 7, 1997.

2   Ibid.

3   Ibid. By far the best unclassified assessment of Chinese intelligence appears in *Chinese Intelligence Operations*, by Nicholas Eftimiades (Naval

Institute Press, 1994). At the time of writing Mr. Eftimiades was a senior analyst with the United States Defense Intelligence Agency (DIA), America's premier military intelligence organization. This chapter represents the short course on the subject and draws heavily from Mr. Eftimiades's work.

4 See, e.g., *Washington Post*, February 11, 1997; Thompson Report.

5 Congressional resolutions urging that the visa be granted passed the House unanimously and the Senate by all but a single vote.

6 *Washington Times*, October 13, 1987.

7 *Los Angeles Times*, November 20, 1988.

8 Ibid. Los Alamos and Livermore are federal laboratories that conduct research into nuclear weapons.

9 Ibid.

10 The following is based on FBI File NF-200-NF-27223, classified "Secret," portions declassified.

11 Richard Baum, *Burying Mao* (Princeton Paperbacks, 1994), 276. Dr. Baum is professor of Political Science at UCLA.

12 *Los Angeles Times*, February 27, 1992.

13 Ibid.

14 *Asia Times*, April 25, 1997.

15 *Cheng Ming* (Hong Kong), September 1, 1996. For a more complete account see Eftimiades. See also the account by former GRU Colonel Stanislav Lunev in *Insight*, November 17, 1997.

16 Interview with retired American intelligence officer, Washington, D.C., area, April 1998.

17 *Cheng Ming* (Hong Kong), December 1, 1994.

18 Senate Report 105-10, "Country Reports on Human Rights Practices for 1996," Committee on Foreign Relations, United States Senate, January 1997, at 616.

19 *Moskovskiye Novosti* (Moscow), June 2, 1996.

20 Kyodo News Service, June 4, 1990.

21 Reuters, March 10, 1995.

22 Eftimiades at 38–43.

23 Interview with retired American intelligence officer, Washington, D.C., area, April 1998.

24 *Los Angeles Times*, November 20, 1988.

25 Ibid.

26 *Los Angeles Times*, November 2, 1997.

27 *Yi Chou Kan* (Hong Kong), January 27, 1995.

28 Interview with a Canadian journalist who covers security matters in Asia, April 1998.

29 *Tung Hsiang* (Hong Kong), May 15, 1997.

30 See discussion of COSCO in Chapter 13.

31 *Cheng Ming* (Hong Kong), March 1, 1997.

32 *Yi Chou Kan.*

33 Eftimiades at 80.

34 Interview with the Honorable Martin Lee, Hong Kong, April 1998. See also *South China Morning Post*, December 1, 1994.

35 China Travel Service brochure.

36 *Washington Times*, December 10, 1993.

37 *New York Times*, January 23, 1994.

38 Reuters, March 25, 1998.

39 *Baltimore Sun*, November 15, 1997.

40 Reuters, May 17, 1996.

41 *Nucleonics Week*, January 4, 1996.

42 *Izvestiya* (Moscow), February 21, 1996.

43 Roger Faligot and Remi Kauffer, *The Chinese Secret Service* (Headline Books, 1989), 425.

44 *New York Times*, November 22, 1990.

45 "Meeting the Espionage Challenge: A Review of United States Counterintelligence and Security Programs," Report of the Select Committee on Intelligence, United States Senate, 1986, at 15.

46 This account of the Chin case is derived from Eftimiades at 32 et seq.

47 Ibid at 32.

48 Ibid at 60.

49 "Strengthen Intelligence Work in a New International Environment to Serve the Cause of Socialist Construction," speech by Defense Minister Chi Haotian recounted in *Cheng Ming* (Hong Kong), January 1, 1997.

CHAPTER 11

1 Winston Churchill, *The Gathering Storm* (Cassell & Co. Ltd., 1948), 299, 310.

2 *Merriam Webster's Collegiate Dictionary* (Merriam, 1996), 56.

3 *Jerusalem Post*, May 29, 1998.

4 Statement on the occasion of the U.S.-North Korean Nuclear Agreement, October 14, 1994, *Public Papers of the Presidents*.

5 Nuclear, chemical, and biological weapons, as well as the materials and technology to produce them.

6 *The Selected Works of Deng Xiaoping* (Foreign Languages Press, 1984), 317.

7 A list of these companies can be found in "China's Defense-Industrial Trading Organizations," U.S. Defense Intelligence Agency document PC-1921-57-95 (unclassified).

8 *Lien Ho Pao* (Hong Kong), September 16, 1994.

9 At the time, her father was the head of the Chinese Navy.

10 Some parts of her career appear in the 1996 Annual Report of CASIL. Other parts are based on an interview with an administration official who wishes to remain anonymous.

11 James A. Baker III, *The Politics of Diplomacy* (Putnam, 1995).

12 This description of family money is based on an interview with a Chinese arms dealer in Hong Kong some years ago.

13 *The Weekly Standard,* November 6, 1995.

14 Ibid.

15 At one point in early 1998, the *Washington Times*'s Bill Gertz was averaging one highly classified administration document on China every ten days.

16 *Washington Times,* June 12, 1996.

17 *Washington Times,* June 13, 1996.

18 "The Acquisition of Technology Relating to Weapons of Mass Destruction and Advanced Conventional Munitions," report by the CIA to Congress, June 1997, at 5.

19 *Washington Times,* October 21, 1997.

20 "Worldwide Maritime Challenges 1997," published by ONI, Washington, D.C., March 1997, at 22.

21 *Washington Times,* September 8, 1997.

22 See also "China's Record of Proliferation Misbehavior," an Issue Brief dated September 4, 1997, from the Nuclear Control Institute, Washington D.C.

23 Letter of August 27, 1993, from Admiral William O. Studeman, acting director of the CIA, to Senator John Glenn (D-OH), chairman, Senate Committee on Governmental Affairs, printed in Senate hearing 103-208 at 185.

24 Answer by Secretary of State Madeleine Albright to question submitted for the record by a senator, January 8, 1997. See also the *Deseret News,* January 24, 1997.

25 *Washington Post*, March 26, 1996.

26 In the issue of June 19–25, 1995, *Defense News* quoted a classified CIA report entitled "China-Iran Missile Technology Cooperation: A Timeline Approach."

27 *Ha'aretz* (Tel Aviv), May 29, 1998.

28 *New York Times*, January 31, 1996.

29 *Ha'aretz* (Tel Aviv), May 26, 1995.

30 *Washington Times*, July 23, 1996.

31 *Washington Times*, July 23, 1996.

32 Reported by German Intelligence in *Der Spiegel*, April 14, 1996.

33 *Washington Times*, June 16, 1998.

34 *Wall Street Journal*, March 15, 1994.

35 *Washington Times*, February 5, 1996.

36 Answers by Assistant Secretary of State Winston Lord to questions submitted by a senator, August 6, 1996.

37 COSCO was caught transporting two hundred boxes of rocket fuel to a Pakistani missile research center. *Far Eastern Economic Review*, October 3, 1996.

38 *Washington Post*, August 25, 1996.

39 The *Stark* was struck by two Iraqi-fired, French-made *Exocet* missiles. The C-802 is a Chinese copy of the *Exocet* but with longer range.

40 AP, June 17, 1997.

41 China National Precision Machinery Import Export Corp. This brochure is in the hands of the authors.

42 50 U.S.C. 1701.

43 *Congressional Record*, April 8, 1992, at 55076.

44 Answer to a question from Representative Chris Smith (R-NJ), hearing (Review of the Clinton Administration Nonproliferation Policy) before the House International Relations Committee, June 19, 1996. Printed in the hearing record at page 8.

45 For a more thorough discussion of how the Clinton administration dismantled the American export control system, see also "The Peking Pentagon" by Kenneth Timmerman in the April 1996 issue of *The American Spectator*; "Sell Them Anything" by Matthew Rees in the September 8, 1997, issue of *The Weekly Standard*; and "Clinton administration failed to monitor China's use of missile-technology exports" by Murray Wass, *Salon*, May 29, 1998.

46 *Proliferation Watch*, the Senate Committee on Governmental Affairs, July–August 1993 issue.

47 *The Weekly Standard*, September 8, 1997.

48 Ibid.

49 *Salon*, May 29, 1998.

50 COCOM, sometimes known as the "Coordinating Committee," was composed of NATO (minus Iceland) plus Australia and Japan. It was originally set up in the late 1940s to control war material exports to communist countries.

51 *New York Times*, October 2, 1995.

52 *The Weekly Standard*, September 8, 1997.

53 *Who's Who in China, Current Leaders* (Foreign Languages Press, 1994), 102.

54 COSTIND also has intelligence functions. See Chapter 10.

55 See, for example, *Wen Wei Po* (Hong Kong), March 6, 1996.

56 In 1995 Perry announced that he had visited China eight times, "twice in an official capacity." We believe one of those official visits was in the Carter years, and one was his October 1994 visit as secretary of defense. He may be counting his 1988 visit as head of the Defense Science Board to be unofficial. That leaves five visits unaccounted for. See *The American Spectator*, April 1996.

57 Private conversations with administration officials who wish to remain anonymous. Spring 1993.

58 This letter is in the authors' possession.

59 Some democratic countries, such as Switzerland, cooperated with COCOM even though they were not members of the organization. (The Department of Defense reply is in the authors' possession.)

60 *The American Spectator*, April 1996.

61 *Far Eastern Economic* Review, January 11, 1996; January 18, 1996; and February 1, 1996.

62 *China Trade Report* (Hong Kong), September 1994.

63 Telephone interview, 1995.

64 Interview with Defense Department official, 1995.

65 Copy is in the possession of the authors.

66 See *Wall Street Journal*, May 22, 1996.

67 *Boston Globe*, June 4, 1989.

68 Colleges identified by Amnesty International in "People's Republic of China: Preliminary Findings on Killings of Unarmed Civilians, Arbitrary Arrests and Summary Executions since June 3, 1989."

69 Michael Fathers and Andre Higgins, *Tiananmen: The Rape of Peking* (Doubleday, 1989), 112.

70 An internal PLA count (*Eastern Express* [Hong Kong], June 11, 1996) was 3,700 killed at Tiananmen, but we believe this did not count those carried away by relatives for private cremations. To be related to a counterrevolutionary in China is to lose all social benefits.

71 Interview with an administration official, spring 1998.

72 The Clinton administration knows that the American public would not approve of its military exchanges with the PLA if the people knew about them. Therefore, it makes every effort to keep them under wraps. The above account is based on a number of conversations and interviews with administration officials and others.

73 Xinhua, January 12, 1998.

74 The documents in question include memoranda of discussions between the two leaders, contingency press guidance, and a decision paper on whether the taxpayers should fund Xu's Hawaiian holiday.

75 Statement by an American army general, in the author's [Triplett] presence, June 1995.

76 Timothy Brook, *Quelling the People* (Oxford University Press, 1992), 161.

77 *Washington Times*, May 30, 1998.

78 *Washington Post*, April 17, 1998.

CHAPTER 12

1 *Aviation Week*, August 5, 1996.

2 *Aviation Week*, April 20, 1998.

3 *Aviation Week,* September 1, 1997.

4 Ibid.

5 Mao announced the establishment of the PRC on October 1, 1949.

6 Announcement by Xuan Jiajun, vice president of the Chinese Academy of Space Technology, *China Daily*, March 21, 1998.

7 *Paris Air and Cosmos/Aviation International*, June 20, 1997.

8 Announcement by Xuan.

9 Also known as Tsien Hsuen-shen.

10 See *Thread of the Silkworm* by Iris Chang (Basic Books, 1995), at 236.

11 Ibid, picture caption between pages 204 and 205.

12 *China Today: Defense Science and Technology Vol. 1* (National Defense Industry Press, Beijing), 272. According to the United States Air Force, at least thirteen Chinese intercontinental ballistic missiles target the United States. We do not consider the Clinton-Jiang "detargeting" agreement to be meaningful.

13 *The Military Balance 1997/98*, (The International Institute for Strategic Studies, 1997), at 170.

14 *China Today* at 400.

15 *Jane's Intelligence Review*, November 1991.

16 At present they must retrieve the satellite film and do not have the capability to make real-time observations from space.

17 *Chinese Views of Future Warfare*, ed. Dr. Michael Pillsbury (U.S. National Defense University, 1997), 263.

18 Ibid at 308.

19 ONI-1430S-001-94-SAO [portions declassified].

20 Ibid at xiii.

21 Ibid at 19.

22 Ibid at xiii.

23 *Liberation Army Daily*, December 25, 1995.

24 See *Liberation Army Daily*, February 14, 1996.

25 *Hong Kong Sing Tao Jih Pao*, June 23, 1998.

26 Prepared statement of Dr. William Graham, May 21, 1998.

27 Ibid.

28 *New York Times*, January 24, 1996.

29 Mr. Sokolski was Secretary of Defense Richard Cheney's deputy for non-proliferation in the Bush administration and has written extensively on this subject. See, in particular, his "US Satellites to China" in *Jane's International Defense Review*, April 1994.

30 Ibid.

31 *Nuclear Weapons Databook Vol. 5* (Westview Press, 1994), at 385.

32 This letter is in the possession of the authors.

33 The Warsaw Pact was the Soviet answer to NATO and went out of business with the demise of the Soviet Union.

34 General He is a longtime official of the PRC's First Academy, which is responsible for missile and space launch research and development.

35 For example, on September 15, 1992, Candidate-for-President Bill Clinton said, "Despite China's behavior, the Bush administration has approved the sale of six space satellites for China." Press release from Little Rock.

36 Speech before American aerospace workers at Goddard Space Flight Center, Maryland.

37 Jerusalem Channel 2 Television Network, February 16, 1996.

38 *Hong Kong Standard*, March 26, 1996.

39 *Aviation Week*, February 26, 1996.

40 Reuters, May 22, 1998.

41 COSTIND had successful launches in May and July 1998, for example.

42 *Washington Post*, May 25, 1998.

43 MSNBC, May 21, 1998.

44 *New York Times*, May 24, 1998.

45 MSNBC, May 21, 1998.

46 *New York Times*, July 18, 1998.

47 Our account is based on Jeff Gerth's reporting in the *New York Times* of June 13, 1998, and June 18, 1998, and on AP reporting of July 2, 1998.

48 A good look at American spy satellites is provided in the September 1, 1997, issue of *Aviation Week*. The discussion of antennas is particularly useful.

49 *Washington Post*, June 24, 1998.

50 *Washington Post*, June 25, 1995.

51 *Aviation Week*, June 1, 1998.

52 AFP, November 15, 1995.

53 This account is based on pages 466–478 of *Critical Mass* by William E. Burrows and Robert Windrem (Simon and Schuster, 1994).

54 *Aerospace China*, June 1996.

55 *Aviation Week*, November 11, 1996.

56 *Jane's Intelligence Review*, August 1997.

57 In January 1994 Clinton partially lifted the ban on satellite launches by transferring the export licenses for some satellites from State to the ever-friendly Commerce Department. One of those so transferred belonged to Hughes. *New York Times*, April 13, 1998.

58 *Washington Post*, January 26, 1997.

59 *New York Times*, July 18, 1998.

60 Ibid.

61 Triplett.

62 Answer to question from Representative Chris Smith (R-NJ), hearing ["Review of the Clinton Administration Nonproliferation Policy"] before the House International Relations Committee, June 19, 1996. Printed in the hearing record at page 8.

63 Mr. Armstrong sent a "bitter" letter to Clinton complaining about anti-proliferation sanctions affecting his business. *Washington Post*, June 25, 1998.

64 *Far Eastern Economic Review*, April 30, 1998.

CHAPTER 13

1 Jeff Gerth covered this in the *New York Times*, May 15, 1998.

2 *New York Times*, May 16, 1998.

3 *Washington Post*, May 24, 1998.

4 *Far Eastern Economic Review*, July 18, 1991. The *Review* attributes its facts to intelligence sources.

5 *Far Eastern Economic Review*, October 3, 1996.

6 One of the authors, having fired numerous automatic weapons as a Marine second lieutenant, can attest to the fact that automatic weapons should not be allowed in the hands of drug gangs; the police would most certainly be outgunned.

7 Congressman Duncan Hunter (R-CA), who chairs a key National Security subcommittee, discovered COSCO's Iran connections. *Washington Times*, October 1, 1997. Pakistan is one thing, Iran is another. Iran is an openly anti-American power attempting to develop nuclear capability.

8 Ibid.

9 *New York Times*, July 21, 1994.

10 Ibid.

11 *Guoij Shangbao* (Beijing), April 27, 1997.

12 Robert Bolt, *A Man For All Seasons*.

13 *Christian Science Monitor*, March 28, 1997.

14 *New York Times*, May 9, 1997.

15 Ibid.

16 AP, March 9, 1997.

17 Ibid.

18 Thompson Report at 786.

19 Ibid at 787.

20 Ibid at 787.

21 Melanie B. Darby, April 7, 1995, memo to Roseanne M. Hill, Stanley O. Roth, and Robert L. Suettinger. 10:12 AM.

22 Suettinger memo to Darby, April 7, 1995, 11:24 AM.

23 Ibid.

CHAPTER 14

1 U.S. securities law gives Americans extensive rights to full disclosure about the companies they invest in. There are a few loopholes for foreign companies, however, that the Chinese have exploited. Concerned investors may want to contact their brokers or their lawyers after reading this chapter.

2 *Los Angeles Times*, December 2, 1996.

3 Audited financial information—critical to the "full disclosure" values of U.S. securities law—depends for its reliability on fixed, nonmanipulable accounting standards. In the U.S., accounting standards are superintended by the Financial Accounting Standards Bureau (FASB), which is an arm of the American Institute of Certified Public Accountants. All U.S. firms use the standards set by FASB for disclosing their information to the investing public. The desire of Chinese firms to use other standards puts into doubt the reliability of their financial information—assuming they give out any.

4 This exchange is from a White House tape belatedly turned over to Senator Fred Thompson. See Thompson Report.

5 Ibid at 46.

6 Bloomberg (Hong Kong), October 16, 1997.

7 "Foreign Accountants Qualified to Practice before the Commission as of 9/10/97, Hong Kong: Gen Litang, Stephens Moore, and Rowland Moores." SEC Document.

8 Dow Jones & Co. (Beijing), November 6, 1997.

9 But Congress is moving to do just that, with a bill sponsored by Congressman Solomon and Senator Lauch Faircloth (R-NC) to create a national security office in the SEC, to ensure that no foreign government could manipulate the American stock market and harm American shareholders.

10 Charles de Trenck, *Red Chips* (Asia 2000 Limited, 1998), 58.

11 Ibid at 58.

12 IPO, high and low prices are from a *New York Times* story on red chips' decline, and a financial report from Hong Kong.

13 *Financial Times*, August 16, 1997

14 A preliminary injunction in United States Bankruptcy Court, Southern District of New York, filed by liquidators of Peregrine trying to hold off creditors includes Morgan Stanley; Merrill Lynch; J.P. Morgan Securities; the Goldman Sachs Group; Chase; Citicorp/Citibank; and others.

15 *Financial Times* (London), March 2, 1998.

16 *New York Times*, April 29, 1998.

17 Although we have focused on the equities markets, the Chinese may be fiddling with bonds, too. The Dow Jones News Service reported on July 15, 1998, that China's "most recent debt offering was not sold principally to investors as believed but bought primarily by banks and financial institutions working on behalf of the Chinese government... in order to achieve

the low yields the Chinese government wanted for what has become its benchmark 30-year bond.... This move is considered highly unorthodox even by the standards of the Chinese government."

CHAPTER 15

1 White House press release, January 21, 1993.
2 *Washington Post*, August 9, 1998.
3 Clinton press statement from Little Rock, U.S. Newswire, September 15, 1992.
4 *Washington Times* and *Washington Post*, June 12, 1998, reporting Dr. Oehler's testimony before the Senate Foreign Relations Committee.
5 *The Military Balance 1997/98*, 13.
6 Interview, June 7, 1998.
7 Answer to a question from Senator Edward Kennedy, January 22, 1997.
8 First proclaimed during the October 1997 visit of Jiang Zemin to Washington and confirmed by the Clinton return visit in June 1998.
9 *Wall Street Journal*, October 10, 1997.

CHAPTER 16

1 See, for example, a Fox News report from July 7, 2000.
2 Huang took the Fifth before Judicial Watch over a thousand times. We speculate that Huang may have been concerned about the reaction of Judge Royce Lamberth if he lied in his deposition.
3 FBI interviews with John Huang DOJ-H000041.
4 Ibid, DOJ-H000290.
5 Ibid, DOJ-H000049.
6 Ibid, DOJ-H000169.
7 Ibid, DOJ-H000073.
8 Ibid, DOJ-H000155.
9 Ibid, DOJ-H000163.
10 Ibid, DOJ-H000042.
11 Ibid, DOJ-H000039. This is only an example; others are scattered throughout the FBI's interrogation of Huang.
12 Ibid, DOJ-H000060.
13 Ibid, DOJ-H000062.
14 It must have been a great party! Ibid.
15 Ibid.
16 Ibid, DOJ-H000295.
17 Ibid.

18 Question submitted for the record, Senate Foreign Relations Committee, January 8, 1997.

19 The CIA believes that Iran may wish to put germ warfare warheads on its new missiles. Testimony of CIA Director John Deutch before the Senate Select Committee on Intelligence, Senate Hearing 104-510, 82.

20 Believing the threat from smallpox was over, the United States stopped immunizing children and adults two decades ago. Even those who had previously been immunized would have little or no protection at this stage.

21 This information comes from a number of FBI interviews with Charlie Trie in the summer and fall of 1999.

22 A 500-liter fermenting machine which can be used for the cultivation of micro-organisms, viruses, or toxins.

23 Under the terms of the 1972 Biological Weapons Convention, each nation that had a germ warfare facility had to identify the facility.

24 Paul Sperry, WorldNetDaily.com, March 2, 2000.

25 By exercising party solidarity, the Democrats were able to limit Thompson to calendar year 1997. Since he had to do investigations first and report afterward, as a practical matter he was limited to three or four months of public hearings.

26 Reuters, June 14, 2000.

27 *South China Morning Post*, March 10, 1999.

28 AFP, October 20, 1999.

29 We were not surprised to read in the June 20, 2000, edition of the *Financial Times* this comment from Joe Zhang, head of China research at UBS Warburg: "The era of the red chips was over in 1997." One wonders how much U.S. pension fund investment capital disappeared into the private bank accounts of communists in Beijing.

30 "The poor quality of accounting in China has undermined the credibility of the stock market and made it more difficult for banks to judge the creditworthiness of prospective clients." This statement in the *Financial Times* was quoted by John Berlau in an *Investor's Business Daily* story, "Are 'Red Chips' a Trojan Horse?" (January 4, 2000). *Investor's Business Daily* and especially John Berlau are excellent at keeping the investment community informed about the PRC's financial activities. The same article pointed out that a recent audit of

one hundred Chinese firms indicated that eighty-one had falsified their accounts.

31 As the story goes, at a dinner party shortly before Ronald Reagan's first inauguration, the president-elect asked each of his advisers to state, in five minutes or less, what Reagan's agenda as president should include. William Casey, a man who was one of the leaders in defeating Nazi Germany, took the opportunity to state that the Soviet Union was evil and deserved to be destroyed, and that there should be no more accommodation to the Soviets' interests. The Western financial markets could be an instrument for cutting off the economic props that had kept communism alive for so long, he said. During dessert, Reagan looked up at the assembled group and said, "I'll take Casey's option."

It is interesting to note that this story may well represent the perfect solution to the challenge America is facing today with the PRC. The man who subsequently had primary responsibility for executing President Reagan's and CIA Director Casey's plan to wage economic battles against the Soviet Union was Roger W. Robinson, Jr., the National Security Council's senior director of international economic affairs. Reagan termed him the "architect of a security-minded and cohesive East-West economic policy." Robinson is now chairman of the William J. Casey Institute of the Center for Security Policy.

32 Interview with Ed Timperlake, June 14, 2000.

33 "The Securities and Exchange Commission collects little information helpful in monitoring PRC commercial activities in the United States. This lack of information is due only in part to the fact that many PRC front companies are privately held and ultimately—if indirectly— wholly owned by the PRC and CCP itself. Increasingly, the PRC is using U.S. capital markets both as a source of central government funding for military and commercial development and as a means of cloaking U.S. technology acquisition efforts by its front companies with a patina of regularity and respectability." Report of the House Select Committee on U.S. National Security and Military/Commercial Concerns with the People's Republic of China ("Cox Report"), Vol. 1, page 57.

34 One of the authors [Timperlake] took many such calls at the House Committee on Rules. Many of the calls came from former senior congressional staffers who had gone through the famous revolving door

to become lobbyists. These lobbyists were successful in campaigning against the bill.

35   This is not to belittle their effort. Eventually something will pass. The stakes are too high to continue to ignore the largest PRC financial "pump and dump" operation in history. Republican lobbyists who knew better and distorted the debate should be ashamed of themselves.

36   Throughout the battle to tell the American people the truth about Bill Clinton and Al Gore, Paul M. Rodriguez and his investigative team at *Insight* magazine have been days, weeks, months, even years ahead of breaking stories. Tim Maier and J. Michael Waller have been exceptionally diligent in getting it right and getting it first.

37   *New York Times*, April 8, 2000.

38   *Financial Times*, June 20, 2000.

39   *Washington Post*, January 27, 2000.

40   *Far Eastern Economic Review*, April 6, 2000.

41   Congressman Frank R. Wolf (R-VA) was especially convincing, for at a critical moment he wrote a letter to SEC Chairman Arthur Levitt and to Chairman Richard Grasso of the New York Stock Exchange. It was a powerful, elegant plea to delay the IPO. Interview with Roger Robinson by Ed Timperlake.

42   "PetroChina Dustup: The Start of Something Big," Mark L. Melcher, Stephen R. Soukup, *Global Equity Research, Potomac Perspective*, Prudential Securities, March 22, 2000.

43   Early in the PetroChina effort Secretary of State Madeleine Albright was speaking out on human rights violations in Sudan. Two different sources told the authors that at the same time National Security Adviser Sandy Berger was getting tremendous pressure from PRC leaders to help Beijing. Albright became strangely silent.

44   *Christian Science Monitor*, March 3, 2000. The author, Jane Lampman, also pointed out that "China's involvement goes deeper than oil wells. Some 10,000 Chinese work in the oil region, where some of the most heavy-handed tactics of the government have been carried out."

45   President Clinton, February 18, 2000, letter to Ms. Nina Shea, director for religious freedom, Freedom House.

46   *Time*, February 28, 2000.

CHAPTER 17

1   *New York Times*, November 14, 1996. Some commentators pointed
    to George Stephanopoulos as the source of the White House attacks
    on Reno. See comment by Michael Barone on *Hardball with Chris
    Matthews*, CNBC, December 13, 1996.

2   She also enraged the White House by allowing Whitewater Independent
    Counsel Kenneth Starr to investigate the truthfulness of White House
    Counsel (and close Hillary Clinton ally) Bernard Nussbaum. Ibid.

3   *Washington Post*, November 30, 1996.

4   Radek denies the comment, but there are two witnesses.

5   Memo from FBI Director Freeh titled "Democratic National Campaign
    Matter" and dated 12/9/96. Released June 2000 by the House
    Government Reform and Oversight Committee.

6   On November 24, 1997, Freeh recommended to Reno that an inde-
    pendent counsel be appointed. This aroused much public controversy,
    but it was not until spring 2000 that we learned that as early as
    December 1996 he had implied his support for an independent coun-
    sel investigation.

7   See *Baltimore Sun*, December 1, 1996.

8   *Newsweek*, December 23, 1996.

9   Barone and Ujifusa at 246.

10 Ibid, 284.

11 Ibid.

12 *Washington Times*, May 20, 2000.

13 Radek told the Senate Governmental Affairs Committee on
    September 22, 1999, that the Ingersoll task force had started up in
    "December 1996," which might imply after the December 12 Reno-
    Clinton meeting. But Ingersoll immediately contradicted him, insist-
    ing, "Mr. Radek approached me and assigned me to the matter on
    November 1, 1996"—the same day the cease-and-desist order went
    out to Los Angeles (of which the committee was ignorant in
    September 1999). See Senate Hearing 106-318 at 65.

14 Ibid, 68. The *New York Times* article was published on September
    17, 1997.

15 *Roll Call*, August 2, 1999.

16 See Senate Hearing 106-318.

17 Ibid, 60.

18 Ibid, 41.

19 Ibid, 109.

20 Ibid, 91.

21 The LaBella memo was co-authored by James DeSarno, assistant director of the FBI.

22 Richard A. Posner, chief judge of the Seventh Circuit, calls it a kind of "underground railroad" (*An Affair of State* [Harvard, 1999], 69).

23 "The timing, sources, and extent of the payments [to Hubbell, including those from Revlon] make the belief that they were hush money reasonable." *United States* v. *Hubbell*, 167 F.3rd 552, 563 (D.C. Cir. 1999) (per curiam), quoted by Posner, 26n.

24 Senate Hearing 106-318 at 87.

25 Testimony of John Huang before the House Government Reform and Oversight Committee, December 1999.

26 *Washington Times*, August 5, 1999.

27 We believe Madigan deserves a large share of the blame for the failure of the Thompson committee in 1997.

28 This section draws heavily on the excellent description of obstruction of justice found in Judge Posner's account of the Clinton-Lewinsky affair. Judge Posner has very definite views on the issue of Clinton's guilt: "We shall see that the charge of perjury is solid, that the President in several instances obstructed justice in a legal sense, and he has never admitted lying about his relationship with Lewinsky."

29 Ibid, 37.

30 18 U.S.C. 1503, quoted in Posner, 38n.

31 Ibid, 54.

32 *New York Post*, September 27, 1999.

33 *New York Times*, February 10, 2000.

34 *New York Times*, March 11, 2000.

CHAPTER 18

1 In the spring of 2000, Senator Robert Bennett (R-UT) sent a series of written questions to Secretary of State Madeleine Albright asking if the administration had made any effort to stop Russian arms sales to China. Her answers were incomplete, and she did not provide any evidence of an administration effort to stop these arms sales. In short, she ran for cover.

2 *Jiefangjun Bao*, in Chinese, March 22, 2000.

3 *Moscow Nazavisimaya Gazeta*, March 15, 2000.

INDEX

Aberdeen Proving Grounds, 131
Acheson, Dean, 116
Adams, James Ring, 66
advertising, 62–64
AGFA, 131
Albright, Madeleine, 236, 238
Aldrich, Gary, 30
Almanac of American Politics, 63
American Security Bank, 24
Ang-Du International, 99, 101
appeasement, policy of,
    135–158
APT, 169
arms dealers, 3, 167–169, 263
Arms Export Control Act, 236
Armstrong, Michael, 177–178,
    240
Asia, business practice, 17
Asia-Pacific Mobile Telecom-
    munications Company, 175
Asia-Pacific Telecommunica-
    tions Company. *See* APT

Bachus, Spencer, 242
Baker, James, 138, 167
Bank of China, 24
Bank of Trade, 11

bank regulators, federal, 11
banks, Taiwan, 12
Barone, Michael, 63
Barr, Bob, 237
Bayh, Evan, 48
Beijing, 14–18
Beijing Enterprises Holding
    Ltd., 210–212
Bennett, Robert, 236–237
Bentsen, Lloyd, 131
Berger, Samuel R., 182–184
Berger, Sandy, 190, 244;
    COSCO and, 197–199
Berry, Paul, 11
Bethlehem Steel, 24
Boeing, 150, 240
Bradbury, Curt, 34
Branch Davidian, 13
British East India Company, 20
Brown, Ron, 3, 30, 32, 33, 80,
    97, 173, 248
Burton, Dan, 97, 232, 238, 256,
    257
Burns, Nicholas, 139
Bush, George, 12, 150, 151,
    170, 223
Business Leaders Reception, 36

California investments, 11
campaign policies, 62–63, 74,
    81, 218–220
Cardozo, Michael, 111, 117
Carter administration, 53, 144,
    154, 163–164
cash transfers, 10
CASIL, 137
CATIC, 150
CCP, 2, 14–15, 19, 46, 71
cease-and-desist orders, 250,
    261, 262
Century Plaza Hotel, 69, 74
CFIUS, 197–198
Challenger, 167
Chamberlain, Neville, 135, 143,
    156
Chan, Eddie, 92
character, 1, 217
chemical warfare, 236–237
Chen Xitong, 14–15, 15–16,
    234–235
Chi Haotian, 152
ChiCom, 109
Chin, Larry Wu-tai, 31,
    132–133
China: agents, 18; business
    groups, 80; Carter and,
    163–164; China Resources
    and, 17; Clinton and, 190;
    congress of, 15; corruption,
    14; defense, 3, 77, 123, 139,
    153, 161–163, 175, 178,
    181, 188, 223–224; demon-
    strations, 177; DNC, 72;
    economy, 18, 50, 52, 205;
    embassy, 4; Gore and,

264–265; government, 51,
    128; Indonesian relations, 8;
    influence in U.S., 124; intelli-
    gence, 16–18, 20, 51, 59, 73,
    125–134, 137, 176, 232; Iran
    and, 141, 173, 236–237;
    missiles, 171–172; Russian
    relations, x, 131, 264–265;
    policies, 133; satellites, 175;
    smuggling, 137, 178, 198;
    society, 24; Taiwan and,
    112–116
China Aerospace Industrial
    Holdings Ltd. *See* CASIL
China Construction Bank,
    101–102
China National Aero-
    Technology Import and
    Export Corporation. *See*
    CATIC
China National Petroleum
    Corporation, 242–244
China National Precision
    Machinery Import-Export
    Corporation, 142
China Ocean Shipping Com-
    pany. *See* COSCO
China Orient Satellite Telecom-
    munications. *See* COSAT
China Resources, Hong Kong,
    17–18, 19, 73, 212
China Telecom, 212
China Travel Service, 18, 130,
    134
Chinachem group, 82
Chinagate, 68, 248, 257–258,
    260

Chinese Communist Party. *See* CCP

Chinese Liaison Office, 24

Chinese Views of Future Warfare, 162

Christopher, Warren, 174, 182

Chun Hua Yeh, 123, 128

Chung, Johnny, 83, 187, 188, 199–202, 215, 239–240, 250–251, 258

CIA, 16, 35, 43, 49–50, 51, 75, 139; Huang and, 57; investigations, 18; Lippo and, 52

Cisneros, Henry, 248

CITIZENS VOTE INC., 233

Cleland, Max, 45

Clinton, Bill: as Arkansas attorney general, 9; bust of, 13; campaigning, 62–64, 88, 139, 218–222; character of, 1, 217; China connection, 71, 100, 114, 232; domestic affairs, 13; foreign policy, 217, 223–224; fund-raising, 7, 101, 218–221; governor, 26; legacy of, 1, 245, 263–267; national defense, 224–225; obstruction of justice, 260; ratings, 61; Reno and, ix, 247–249; scandals, 35

Clinton administration: Arkansas affairs, 35; China and, 2, 138–139, 114, 155; commerce administration, 25; disasters, 35; elections, 174, 215; financing, 12; incompetence, 3; knowledge of, 35, 47; PLA and, 152; security clearances, 31

Clinton, Hillary: 10, 19, 64, 240; Chung and, 201; fraud and perjury, 39–40; Huang and, 33, 41; Trie and, 117, 235

Coble, Howard, 260

Cochran, Thad, 164

COCOM, 143, 146

Cohen, Bill, 142

Colby, William, 23

Cold War, 148, 225

Collins, Susan, 56, 65

Columbus transfer of information, 147–150

commentary, political, 62

Commission on Science, Technology, and Industry for National Defense. *See* COSTIND

Committee on Foreign Investment in the United States. *See* CFIUS

communist ideology, 127, 137, 210–213

Congressional Research Service, 83

Conrad, Kent, 34

Contract with America, 61

COSAT, 178–179

COSCO, 134, 188–203; Clinton and, 190, 195; U.S. navy and, 192–194, 203

COSTIND, 123, 128, 137, 144, 162, 163, 166–167, 171, 174, 178

courage, 1
cover-up, 3, 10, 56
CP Group business, 80
Craft of Intelligence, 19

Daimler-Benz Aerospace, 179
Daley, Bill, 31
Dalton, John H., 190–196, 199
Darby, Melanie, 202
Daschle, Tom, 34
Davis, Marvin, 233
death, coincidental, 32
DeFrank, Thomas, 138–139
democracy, 2
Democratic control, White
  House, 34
Democratic National Com-
  mittee. *See* DNC
Democratic Senatorial Cam-
  paign Committee, 11, 78
Deng Xiaoping, 14, 51, 137,
  178
Department of Commerce, 4,
  41, 46; Huang and, 27–28,
  30, 38, 40, 232, 234
Department of Justice, x, 250,
  252, 258
Department of State, 265
Department of the Treasury, 54
Ding Henggao, 144
DNC, 26, 41; Asia connection,
  11, 48; campaigning, 7, 63;
  Chung and, 199; contribu-
  tions, 13; fund-raising, 7, 12,
  26, 69–70, 71, 73–76, 80,
  100, 123, 173–174, 199–201,
  218–219; Huang and, 59, 65;

returned money, 68, 123;
  security clearance and, 31;
  telephones, 4; Trie connection, 97, 238, 254; Victory
  Fund, 27
Dole, Bob, 61, 63
drugs/narcotics, 3, 77, 81,
  88–92, 102–103, 215–216,
  218
Dukakis, Michael, 73
Dulles, Allen, 20
Durbin, Dick, 43

East Timor, 54
economics, 20, 50
education, Chinese, 24
Eftimiades, Nicholas, 123, 132
Eisenhower, Dwight, 109
election, 1992, 34
Elizabeth I, 143
Entergy-Lippo, 37, 41
Er Bu, 51, 128, 130
Espy, Mike, 248
Estes, Howell, 159
Europe, threat to, 2
evidence, circumstantial, 4

Faircloth, Lauch, 242
Farley, Michael, 17
Faust, 2
FBI investigations, 78, 100, 222,
  232–235, 239–240, 253–255
Federal Deposit Insurance Cor-
  poration, 11
Federal Securities Act, 208
Ferraro, Geraldine, 92
Fifth Amendment, 3, 7, 27, 41,

58, 76, 82, 99, 101, 102,
    111, 218, 232
First National Bank of Louisville,
    24
FOB, 13, 34, 45, 58
Fok, Henry, 94–95
Forbidden City, 15
foreign policy, U.S., 2, 78
Fortuna Hotel, 93–94
Foster, Vince, 35
Fowler, Don, 64–65, 81, 201
Frankenstein, John, 147
Freedom House, 244
Freedom of Information Act,
    154–155
Freeh, Louis, ix, 92, 100, 248,
    254, 258
Friedman, Paul, 259–260
Friend of Bill. See FOB
Fu Lin Restaurant, 108
Fuggers of Germany, 20
fund-raising. See Clinton, Bill;
    DNC; Gore, Al; Huang, John

Gaffney, Frank, 110
Gandhi, Yogesh K., 69
Garten, Jeffrey, 58
Geer, James, 125, 129
Georgia, 12
germ warfare, 236–237
German military, 179
Gerth, Jeff, 161
Gertz, Bill, 139, 189
Gilman, Ben, 83
Gingrich, Newt, 63
Giroir, Joe, 10, 13, 34, 38, 64,
    67

glass ceiling, 71
Global USA, 11
Godfrey, Harry, 125
Gore, Al, ix, 20, 23, 27, 71,
    141, 147–150, 232–233,
    245, 257; protection of, x,
    247, 250–251, 261–262,
    263–267
Graham, William, 164
Greater Nile Petroleum Operat-
    ing Company, 244
Green, Ernest, 207
Grobmyer, Mark, 11, 13, 38
Gulf allies, 2
Gulf War, 140, 143, 179

Haley, Maria, 37
Hatch Act, 232
Hay-Adams Hotel, 68, 74, 233
health care plan, 78
He Kerang, General, 169, 175
Helms, Jesse, 168
high-tech exports, 81
Hill, Nolanda, 33, 39, 41
Hip Hing Holdings, 27, 29, 31, 66
Hitler, Adolf, 135
Ho, Stanley, 94, 95, 99
Hon, Yip, 94, 96
Hong Kong China, Ltd., 37, 38
Hong Kong economy, 97
House Government Reform and
    Oversight Committee, 97,
    232, 237, 256, 257, 261
House Rules Committee, 30
Hsi Lai Buddhist Temple, 27,
    68, 69, 71–76, 101, 215,
    247, 257

Hsia, Maria, 12, 27, 69, 71,
    72–76, 239, 250–251,
    259–260
Huang, John: 3, 12, 13, 48,
    134, 250–251; access, 20, 31,
    32, 54; Arkansas, 24, 35;
    campaign money, 64, 231;
    Clinton and, 13, 25, 26;
    cover-up, 58; Department of
    Commerce, 47; deposition,
    26; DNC, 31, 65–70; FBI,
    232–235; fund-raising, x,
    26–27, 68, 78; Gore and,
    232–233; history of, 23–24;
    Hsia and, 75; national secu-
    rity, 43, 49–50; Riadys and,
    7, 258; spy, 23
Hua-Mei, 146
Hubbell, Webster, 10, 20, 35,
    36, 40, 46, 48, 60, 87, 218,
    234, 258
human rights, 2, 79
Hun Sen, 103
Hughes Electronics, 77,
    175–178, 184; China and,
    171, 177, 240, 250–251

ICBM, 131, 164, 166, 168
Ickes, Harold, 32, 62, 64
IEP, 44
IMET, 54
immigration, Asian, 72–75
Immigration and Naturalization
    Service, 72
independent counsel, 255–258
Inderfurth, Karl F., 156
India, 2, 176

Indonesia Commercial Strategy
    meeting, 54
Indonesian government, 8, 17,
    54
Indonesian Central Bank, 17
information, 53–54, 143–145,
    147, 160, 177
Ingersoll, Laura, 253–255, 257,
    258, 262
Intercontinental Ballistic
    Missiles. See ICBM
International Economic Policy.
    See IEP
International Trade Administra-
    tion. See ITA
Investigative Group, Inc., 118
investigative task force, 252
investment strategies, 20
Iran, 80, 142, 184, 190, 236
Iran-Iraq Arms Non-
    Proliferation Act, 142
Iranian Revolutionary Guard
    Navy, 158
Israel, 2
ITA, 44, 58
Italian commerce, 20

Jacoby, Lowell E., 140–141
Jakarta, 8, 28, 54
Japan, 2, 176
Jefferson Hotel, 69
Ji Shengde, General, 239
Jiang Zemin, 128, 140, 223
job assistance, 10
Johnson, Judge Norma
    Holloway, 259–260
Jones, Paula, 67

Judicial Watch, 26, 27, 41, 44, 173, 232, 260
Judistra, Juwati, 44
justice, obstruction of, 247–262

Kanchanalak, Pauline, 69, 71, 77–79, 239
Kelly, Michael, 39
Kennedy, Edward, 74, 78
Kennedy, Patrick, 74
Kerry, John, 206
KGB, 128
Khmer Rouge, 103
Kim, Jay, 249–250, 257
Kissinger, Henry, 133
Klayman, Larry, 232
Knight, Peter, 256–257
Kondracke, Morton, 252–253
Korean War, 95, 116–117
Kucinich, Dennis, 242

LaBella, Charles, 255, 256, 260
Lake, Anthony, 113
Lamberth, Judge Royce C., 78
LANDSAT, 162
Lavine, Susan, 98
Lee Teng-hui, 112, 124
Lee, John K. H., 69
Lee, Dr. Peter, 131
Legend Air, 45
Lenzner, Terry, 118
Lewinsky, Monica, 68, 258, 260
Lewis, Maureen, 111, 146
Li Ka-shing, 15, 208, 211–212
Li Peng, Premier, 14, 19, 129
Lieberman, Joseph, 29, 52, 254
Lin, Wen-Chen, 199

Lindsey, Bruce, 29, 34, 39–40, 46, 64
Lippo, 130; China, 16, 37; CIA, 57; Huang, 28, 232, 233; information, 50; Insurance Group, 38; loans, 16; national security, 43; securities, 52; Tower, 15; Village, 8, 17
Lippo Bank, 8, 17, 19, 25, 34, 54–55
Lippogate, 68
Lippo Karawaci. *See* Lippo Village
LippoLand, 17
Little Rock, Arkansas, 57, 67
Liu Chaoying, Lieutenant Colonel, 83–84, 137, 142, 187, 188, 199, 206–207, 239–240, 244
Liu Huaqing, General, 154, 174
Long Beach Naval Station, 196
Lockheed-Martin, 178, 240
Loral Space Systems, 77, 170–174, 177, 240, 250–251
Los Angeles prosecutors, 249–251, 262
lying, 71–72

Macau, 87–88, 92–99, 129
Madigan, Michael, 260
Magaziner, Ira, 78
Magnificent Seven, 259–260
MAMCO, 150
Mao Tse-Tung, 109
Market Access and Compliance. *See* IEP

Market Security Act, 242
McCarthy, Leo, 27
McDonalds, China, 16
McCain, John, 142
McDonnell-Douglas, 147–150,
    240
media, role of, 202
Meissner, Charles, 3, 32, 44, 46,
    48, 53, 58
Melcher, Mark, 244
Messerschmitt-Boelkow-Bloem,
    179
MEM DISSEM, 50
Middleton, Mark, 11, 36–40,
    82, 87, 98, 110–111, 239
Milhollin, Gary, 144
military, U.S.: airplanes, 148;
    counterintelligence, 132;
    information, 40, 51,
    131–132, 133, 167–169,
    175; Mercury program, 161;
    missile sanctions, 181; navy,
    196; satellite, 184; strategy,
    153; trade, 78; Trade Repre-
    sentative, 53, 54; visa pro-
    cess, 76; weapons, 142
Miller, G. William, 111
Ministry of State Security. See
    MSS
missile, Taiwan, 109; threat,
    Chinese, 124–125, 264–265
Mitchell, Martha, 71
Morris, Dick, 61, 62, 64, 218
Morrison, Micah, 99
most favored nation, PRC, 81
Motorola, 176
MSS, 51, 127, 129, 133

NAFTA, 48
Nannygate, 35
National Bank of Georgia, 9
national intelligence, Asia, 48
national security, 2, 3, 47, 49,
    172, 197, 231, 261, 263
National Security Council
    (NSC), 54, 234, 241
Ng Lapseng, 36–40, 87, 93, 96,
    97–98, 102, 207, 108, 215,
    233, 238, 250–251
Nickerson, Colin, 151
Nie Li, 146
Nixon, Pat, 71
Nixon, Richard, 133
nondisclosure of funding, 12
Norinco, 77, 80, 81
nuclear power, 2, 50, 51, 107,
    131, 141
Nussbaum, Bernard, 35
Nye, Joe, 83

Oakland, California, 190
Oehler, Dr. Gordon, 139–140
Office of Naval Intelligence
    (ONI), 140, 162
Ohio, 13
O'Leary, Hazel, 256
Outlaw, Dailin, 108
Owens, Wayne, 78

Pacific Leadership Council, 27
Pakistan, 156, 189
Panetta, Leon, 64
Patton, Nancy Linn, 47–48, 58
Pelosi, Nancy, 127, 182
pension funds, Arkansas, 10

People's Armed Police, 177
People's Liberation Army. *See* PLA
People's Republic of China. *See* PRC
Peregrine, 210–211
perjury, Huang, 28
Perry, Dr. William, 109, 144–147, 150, 153
PetroChina, 242–244
Philippines, 2; military, 176
Phnom Penh, 88, 103–104
PLA, 2, 15, 71, 76, 83, 127, 137, 141, 145, 149, 154, 157, 184, 220, 240, 241, 263, 265; Clinton and, 136; defense, 79, 107, 110, 161; Taiwan and, 109, 177
poison gas equipment, 236–237
Poly Group, 94, 137, 178–179, 190
Pomfret, John, 94
Posner, Richard, 260
Pratt & Whitney, 131
PRC, ix, 2, 15, 51, 124, 132, 153, 157, 184, 266; immigration, 76; Huang and, 59; stock exchange and, 207–208, 240–245; Taiwan and, 107, 109, 264–265
Presidential Legal Defense Trust, 110–111, 117–118
pricing agreement, information sales, 167
prostitution, 88–92, 93, 102, 215–216, 218
Putin, Vladimir, 266

Qian Xuesen, 161–162
Quon, Randolph, 210

Radek, Lee, 248, 250–252, 255, 257–258, 261–262
radio, 202
Reagan administration, 53, 241
Reno, Janet, ix, 247–249, 252, 255–257, 260, 262
Report on Asian Organized Crime, 92
Republican campaigning, 63, 221
Republicans: incompetency of, 4; Ohio, 13; regulations, 242
Riady, James and Mochtar, 7, 9–21, 130; access, 13; American business, 28; Arkansas and, 24–25, 69; Beijing, 15; campaign aid, 10, 27, 34, 64, 233; Chinese intelligence agency, 18; Clinton and, 13, 19, 26, 67; Communist connection, 17; DNC, 29, 66; Hong Kong, 211; Huang and, 24–25, 54, 231, 233, 258; Indonesia and, 21; information, 54; Los Angeles connection, 11; money laundering, 231; U.S. intelligence and, 20, 43
Rose Garden, 96–97
Rose Law Firm, 34, 38
Rosen, Marvin, 65
Ross, Brian, 33, 39, 41
Royal Canadian Mounted Police, 88–90

Rothkopf, David, 36, 46, 53
Rothschilds, 20
Rubin, Jamie, 175
Rubin, Robert, 14, 37
Russia, 128, 148, 178, 241,
    264–265

safe house, 55
Safire, William, 56, 261
San Jose Holdings, 29
satellites, 160
Schmidt, Susan, 39
Schwartz, Bernard, 172, 177,
    240
SEC, 205, 208–210, 222, 242
Secret Service records, 28
secrets, keeping, 38–39
Securities and Exchange Com-
    mission. *See* SEC
security clearance, 29–30, 31
security secrets, 29
Seguin Savings Association, 191
Senate Banking Committee, 35
Senate Governmental Affairs
    Committee. *See* Thompson
    committee
Senate Intelligence Committee,
    18, 59, 132
Seper, Jerry, 41
Sharif, Prime Minister, 156
Shea, Nina, 244
Shen Juejen, 232
Shen Rongjun, General,
    174–176, 240
Sherburne, Jane, 38
Sheridan, Kevin, 254
SIGINT, 176

Simon, Paul, 34
Singapore, 176
Sioeng, Ted, 68, 69, 75, 99,
    100–103, 215, 233, 238,
    250–251
Smith, I. C., 254, 255
society, Chinese, 24
Sokolski, Henry, 166
Solarz, Stephen, 235
Solomon, Gerald, 30, 43, 191,
    208–209, 212, 242
Soukup, Stephen, 244
space control, U.S., 159–161
space launch vehicles, 164
space warfare, 159–185
Specter, Arlen, 100, 255, 261
Spence, Floyd, 147
spy, 23
Starr, Kenneth, 38, 259
state finances, 10
Stephens, Inc., 9, 15, 19, 50, 52,
    55–57, 58
Stephens, Jackson, 9, 10, 57
Stewart, Janice, 53
stock exchange, 53, 76,
    205–209, 212–213,
    222–223, 243–245
Sudan, 244
Suettinger, Robert L., 113,
    202–203
Suharto, President, 8, 55
Sun, James Y., 202–203
Sun Yee On triad, 82

Taiwan, 2, 265; elections, 109;
    independence, 112–115;
    Lippo Bank, 12; military, 24,

176; policy toward, 153, 266; Strait Crisis, 112; U.S. relations, 12, 112–116
Talisman Energy, 244
Tenet, George, 100, 255
Teresa, Mother, 104
terrorism, 227
Theng Bunma, 103–104, 250–251
Thompson committee, 26, 31, 49, 53, 56, 75, 80, 94, 101, 102, 112, 114, 117, 238, 253, 256
Thompson, Fred, 31, 49, 56, 124, 252, 255, 258
Thomason, Harry, 45
Tiananmen sanctions, 170
Tiananmen Square Massacre, 14–15, 83, 125, 129, 130, 152, 223
Tiananmen waivers, 174
Tibet, 2
Tom, Maeley, 29, 34, 66
Torricelli, Robert, 29
Toy Center Holdings, 29
Trade Policy Coordinating Committee, 54
trade relations, 48
trading, insider, 52–53
Treasury Department, 4
Triad, 95, 96, 97, 119, 128, 215; Chinese espionage and, 134; Four Seas, 107; political loyalties, 91, 88–94
Trie, Charlie, x, 36–40, 68, 87, 98, 107–119, 235–239, 250–251, 253, 258

Troopergate, 67
Truman, Harry, 127
Tucker, Jim Guy, 258–259
Twining, Charles, 104

Union Planters Bank of Memphis, 24–25
United Front Works Department, China, 51, 128
United Nations inspections, 179
Unlimited Access, 30
U.S. Capitol basement, 1

Vietnam, 2, 50
VOTE NOW '92, 233

Waco, Texas, 13
Wallerstein, Dr. Mitchell, 130–131
Wang Jun, 76, 77, 94, 137, 190, 207, 212
Wang, Nina, 69, 71, 82, 99
Wangfujing Street, 15–16, 234–235
Warner, John, 191
Warsaw Pact, 168
Watergate, 71, 117
weapons, 77; sales, U.S. to China, 145; smuggling, 190
Weapons of Mass Destruction. *See* WMD
Weaver, Vernon, 56, 57
Wehr, Daniel, 254
White House: access, 13, 78; coffee, 79–80; defense team, 40; Huang and, 28
Whitewater, 11, 38, 40, 171, 248

Wilhelm, David, 66

Willard Hotel, 55

Williams, Maggie, 201

Wisner, Frank, 145

witness protection service, 249,
    258–259

witnesses, 3, 76

WMD, 136, 139, 140, 143,
    157, 226

women, role of, 71

Woodward, Bob, 124

World Jewish Restitution
    Organization, 95

Worthen Bank, 9–10, 25, 34,
    36, 46

Wu, Bin, 125–127, 134

Xinhua News Agency, 73, 153

Xu Huizi, General, 154

Yeung, Albert, 235

ABOUT THE AUTHORS

EDWARD TIMPERLAKE, a Naval Academy graduate with an MBA from Cornell University, has served as a Marine Corps fighter pilot, as a professional staffer in Congress, and in the Defense Department. He now serves on the board of the Vietnam Children's Fund, a pro bono effort to rebuild elementary schools in Vietnam. Timperlake lives near Washington, D.C.

WILLIAM C. TRIPLETT II is the former chief Republican counsel to the Senate Foreign Relations Committee. He has more than thirty years of experience working on China and national security. He lives with his family near Annapolis, Maryland.

In addition to *Year of the Rat*, Timperlake and Triplett have written *Red Dragon Rising: Communist China's Military Threat to America* (Regnery, 1999; ISBN 0-89526-258-4), which, according to nationally syndicated columnist Cal Thomas, "documents in chilling detail the way the Beijing regime is becoming a military threat to the United States."